Leaving Certificate His...
Europe and the Wider Worl...

Dictatorship and De... ...cy 1920–1945

Seán Delap

FOLENS

Editor
Margaret Burns

Design/Layout/Cover
Melanie Gradtke
Set in Caslon 11 pt

© 2004 Seán Delap

ISBN 1-84131-538-9

Produced in Ireland by Folens Publishers, Hibernian Industrial Estate,
Greenhills Road, Tallaght, Dublin 24.

 **Acknowledgements**

The author and Publisher would like to thank the following for permission to reproduce photographs, cartoons, posters and drawings:

AA.VV., Cento Anni a Roma 1870–1970 Fratelli Palombi Editori, Roma, Aerospace Publishing, AKG Images, Associated Press, Bibliothèque nationale de France, Bildarchiv Heinz Bergschicker (Berlin), Bildarchive Preußischer Kulturbesitz, Bundesarchiv (Koblenz), Camera Press Ireland Ltd, Daily Mail, David King Collection, Eric Salomon, courtesy of MAGNUM, Hulton Deutsch, Hulton|Archive – Getty Images, The Illustrated London News Picture Library, Imperial War Museum, Keystone Press Agency (Paris), Lenin Museum, Mary Evans Picture Library, Peter Brookes and The Times © NI Syndication, London, Novosti Press Agency, Popperfoto, Punch Cartoon Library, Robert Doisneau/Rapho, Robert Hunt Library, Roger-Viollet (Paris), Süddeutscher Verlag GmbH, The Estate of David Lowe and The London Evening Standard, The Glasgow Herald, The Kobal Collection Ltd, The Mansell Collection, Ullstein bild, Warder Collection, Writers and Publishing Incorporated.

Contents

Politics and Administration

Society and Economy

Culture/Religion/Science

Introduction

This textbook covers *Dictatorship and Democracy, 1920–1945,* which is Option 3 in the Field of Study, **History of Europe and the Wider World, 1815–1992** in the new Leaving Certificate History Syllabus.

The book is laid out in a user-friendly way. **Key Personalities, Key Concepts** and **Case Studies** are all highlighted within the text.

Key Personality boxes are intended to identify people a student should encounter as a matter of course in their study of the topic, but are also to assist the Ordinary Level students in finding a pathway through the elements. In the case of some major personalities, such as Lenin and Hitler, their 'Key Personality' boxes should be considered a doorway to further information within the relevant chapters.

Key Concepts are 'gateway' concepts that will help a student to find a 'way in' to engagement with the main issues of the topic. These are especially important for Higher Level students as they explore the topics in more depth.

In addition, the first reference to a Key Personality* or Key Concept[+] is flagged using the symbols shown in this sentence.

As far as possible the information in the book has been divided into the various perspectives as outlined in the new Leaving Certificate History Syllabus: Politics and Administration; Society and Economy; Culture, Religion and Science.

The language in the text is suited to mixed-ability classes. Difficult historical terms are explained where appropriate in text boxes in the margin of the page. Bracketed explanations of difficult words are also given within original documents. Some important terms are also highlighted in bold.

Questions at the end of each chapter are clearly marked for either Ordinary or Higher Level students, taking into account the different requirements for each level. In line with the syllabus requirements, many of the Ordinary Level questions are stimulus driven and the Higher Level questions are essay-based and involve contextualisation of subject matter.

The use of documents in the study of history is an important part of the new Leaving Certificate Syllabus. To achieve this, the book combines the text with a collection of documents, cartoons and pictures. This enables students to take on the role of the historian by allowing them to examine closely the historical material associated with the listed elements of the course.

Dedication

To Imelda, Aoife and Seán and
In memory of my father

Working with Evidence

Introduction

When we study history we seek to find out about the past. We must not only look at *what happened*, but also attempt to explain *why* and try to understand *the results*. To do this it is necessary to find historical evidence, which gives us an overall picture.

Historical evidence can be divided into two main categories: Primary Sources and Secondary Sources.

Primary Sources

A primary (first) source provides first-hand evidence. This type of source is written or made at the time the event took place. Primary sources may include original photographs, films, letters, diaries and transcripts of interviews. They would also include books written by those who witnessed the events unfold.

Secondary Sources

A secondary (second-hand) source provides evidence from someone who did not live during the time or did not witness the events happening. Secondary sources include textbooks and history books.

It is important to note that just because a source is primary, this does not mean it is any more reliable or useful than a secondary source. All sources of historical evidence must be analysed to determine their reliability. It is important therefore to check sources for bias, propaganda, selectivity, balance and objectivity.

Bias:
Giving preference to a particular viewpoint.

Propaganda:
Organised spreading of information which may or may not be true.

Selectivity:
Telling only part of the story.

Balance:
Giving equal information on the various interpretations of a person's actions, or an

Objectivity:
Presenting the information in a way which does not give favour to one particular viewpoint.

It is important to remember that even sources that are clearly biased can be valuable to the historian. A speech by a dictator like Hitler regarding the Jews would contain clear examples of bias and information that could easily be shown to be wrong. However, the source may be valuable to the historian as an example of Nazi anti-Jewish propaganda.

When a student is faced with a piece of historical evidence, there are certain questions that he or she should ask while looking at that source.

Written Sources

With a written source you should:

1. Identify 1) who wrote the source, and 2) when it was written. Try to find out as much about the author as you can. Many books will include a short biography on the author.

2. Ask yourself why the author wrote the document, book, etc. Did the author have a special interest in the subject in the written source? Is the author a member of a political party, a cultural movement, an army, etc.?

3. Find out where the document comes from: a book, official records, private records, newspaper accounts, transcripts from interviews, etc. Identify whether the document is a primary or secondary source.

4. Once you have identified the author and the date, you must now study the content of the written source. Ask yourself if the content is factual or opinionated. Does the source give a straightforward account of what happened, or is it based on the opinion of the author? Written sources will usually contain a mixture of opinion and fact.

5. Ask yourself if the source has been written for a particular audience. For instance, a public speech may be written to stir up a particular response from the audience. It may not contain the true views of its author, and may therefore be unreliable.

Visual Sources
Cartoons

Political cartoons are a common and popular source of historical evidence. Analysing cartoons can be quite a difficult task as cartoons are not usually concerned with presenting a balanced view.

1. Firstly you must place the cartoon in its historical context. What period does it belong to: 1916 Rising, War of Independence, World War I, etc.? To find this out you will need to consult other sources, like a history book, to familiarise yourself with the historical background to which the cartoon belongs.

2. Similar to written sources, it is important to determine where the cartoon comes from. Find out which publication it came from. Try to discover if the newspaper or magazine from which the cartoon came is controlled or influenced by a particular political party or organisation.

3. Study the characters in the cartoon. Are they presented in a realistic manner, or are their features exaggerated? Does the cartoonist attempt to show the subjects in a good, bad or humorous way? Do you consider the cartoon to be biased in any way?

4. Look at the background in the cartoon. Are there any symbols or signs that might give you more information on the purpose of the cartoon?

5. Most cartoons will include a caption. Read the caption. Ask yourself if you consider the caption to be a fair comment on the situation?

▲
A cartoon by Peter Brookes published in the Times of London in 2004 commentating on George W. Bush and his war record. He has used the poster below, from 1915, as his inspiration.

Posters

As with all other sources, it is important to find out who or what organisation issued the poster. Posters will usually advertise a message from a political viewpoint and can therefore often be considered examples of propaganda. However, posters are still important pieces of historical evidence. The message contained in the poster will give the historian a good idea of the political viewpoint at that time. Use the same set of guidelines for analysing posters as you would use for cartoons.

Photographs and Films

Although original photographs and films are usually very valuable historical sources, the camera occasionally does lie. Photographs can be doctored (changed). This was a common practice during Joseph Stalin's leadership of the Soviet Union from 1927–53, where those who were considered disloyal to Stalin were airbrushed (removed) from the photograph.

The angle of the photograph can also influence the scene by blocking out a vital piece of evidence. For instance, a wide-angled photograph of a politician giving a public speech may show a small attendance at the meeting, while a

▲
A World War I poster published in 1915.

▲
The second photograph has been doctored. Can you name two differences?

short-angled shot may only show the front row of the audience, which could give a very different view. Ask yourself the following questions:

1. Who took the photograph and what was the occasion?

2. Is the photo posed or natural?

3. Is the photo intended to show the event or the people in it in a good, neutral or bad way?

In the case of documentary films it is important to establish the independence or otherwise of the producers of the film.

Tables and Graphs

It is important when dealing with tables and graphs that you check the information contained in them very carefully. Check that the information is not selective. For instance, if you were studying a chart showing unemployment figures in a particular country, the average unemployment rate could be presented in different ways depending on the number of years included in the table or chart. When using charts or graphs as historical sources, it is not good enough simply to describe the information contained in them. You must use the information to compare the different figures, and identify trends that show change.

Conclusion

Don't expect sources of evidence to give all the answers to your questions. Different historians who have read and looked at the same sources can still come to different conclusions. They can do this by placing different emphasis on the various aspects of the same factual information. Historians can sometimes revise or change their views on a historical personality or event as new evidence comes to light. It is important when studying history that you consult a number of different sources to support or confirm the information before you come to a conclusion. You must also be aware that your conclusion, like those of all historians, can never be permanent.

Dictatorship and Democracy 1920–45

Introduction

The political upheavals that resulted from World War I had far-reaching consequences for the stability of Europe. The once-powerful empires of Austria-Hungary, Germany and Tsarist Russia had all crumbled under the strain of war and were replaced by a series of smaller, fragile states. Prior to World War I the tendency was towards liberalism in government, but this was replaced in the inter-war period (1919–39) by an increasing number of dictatorships. In Italy, Germany, Spain and Portugal, as well as many Eastern European countries, dictators overthrew weak democratic governments that were unable to deal with difficult political and economic problems.

Despite the difficulties of the inter-war period, democracy continued to flourish in Britain, Holland, Belgium, Switzerland, Denmark, Norway and Sweden, where democratic structures of government had been firmly established before World War I.

Key Concept: Democracy

Democracy is a system of government in which all individuals have a right to choose their rulers by voting for them in elections. Free and fair elections, as well as the right to freedom of speech and association, are all guaranteed under the democratic system of government.

Key Concept: Dictatorship

The key characteristic of a dictatorship is that a single individual or party controls the state. Freedom of speech is not allowed and opposition parties are banned. Although elections may take place in a dictatorship, they are usually neither free nor fair. The dictator controls all aspects of state affairs.

European Dictatorships Which Came to Power During the Inter-war Period

Country	Dictator	Country	Dictator
Soviet Union	*Stalin 1927–53*	Yugoslavia	*King Alexander 1929–39*
Italy	*Mussolini 1922–45*	Romania	*King Carol II 1938–45*
Germany	*Hitler 1933–45*	Bulgaria	*King Boris III 1934–45*
Spain	*Franco 1939–72*	Albania	*King Zog I 1928–38*
Portugal	*Salazar 1932–68*	Greece	*General Metaxas 1936–40*
Austria	*Dollfuss 1933–34*	Estonia	*Konstantin Päts 1934–40*
Hungary	*Admiral Horthy 1920–45*	Latvia	*Karlis Ulmanis 1934–39*
Poland	*Marshal Pilsudski 1926–35*	Lithuania	*Antanas Smentona 1934–39*

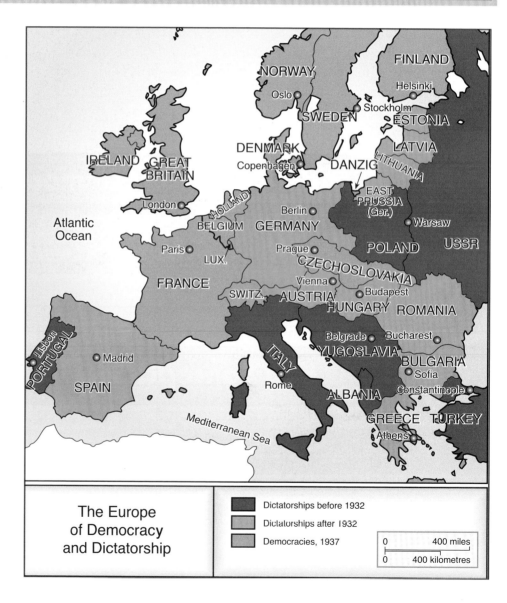

The Europe of Democracy and Dictatorship

Dictatorships before 1932

Dictatorships after 1932

Democracies, 1937

0   400 miles
0   400 kilometres

1 The Origins and Growth of Fascism in Italy

Key Concept: Fascism

Fascism came about in Europe during the inter-war period (1919–39). It developed as a result of poor economic and social conditions, which were common to many European countries in the period following World War I. The first Fascist state was established in Italy.

In its narrowest interpretation, Fascism refers to the movement that Mussolini* (p. 5) headed in Italy from 1922 onwards. In a broader sense it refers to those political parties in many European countries which, despite certain differences, followed a similar ideology (belief) to Mussolini and Hitler* (p. 20).

Fascist regimes placed a strong emphasis on nationalism and the absolute power of the state. People were encouraged to work hard, not for themselves, but for the good of the state. All Fascist states were lead by a charismatic (popular) dictator backed by a single party. Opposition parties, trade unions and free elections were banned. Fascist leaders were opposed to democracy, liberalism and communism+ (p. 48), and were often anti-Semitic+ (against Jews) (p. 180). Their regimes were built up through a mixture of propaganda+ (p. 33) and terror.

In economic terms, Fascists often followed the principles of economic nationalism. Economies were protected by placing taxes on imports and great efforts were made to make the country self-sufficient *(an autarky)*. In

The Fascist dictators Benito Mussolini and Adolf Hitler.

Nationalism:
Loyalty and pride towards a nation.

Self-sufficiency or autarky:
The ability to supply one's own needs. In the case of a country, it usually means having raw materials for industry as well as foodstuffs, and so not depending on another country.

* = Key personality   += Key concept

contrast to communism, Fascism is not in principle opposed to ownership of private property or a business, as long as these contribute to the welfare of the state.

For Fascism the State is an absolute before which individuals and groups are relative. Individuals and groups are 'thinkable' in so far as they are within the State…

The Fascist State organises the nation, but it leaves sufficient scope to individuals; it has limited useless or harmful liberties (freedoms) *and has preserved those that are essential. It cannot be the individual who decides in this matter, but only the State.*

If every age has its own doctrine (belief), *it is apparent from a thousand signs that the doctrine of the present age is Fascism.*

From **The Doctrine of Fascism**, by Benito Mussolini, 1932.

Reasons for the Rise of Fascism in Europe

- Economic factors played a major role in the rise of dictatorships in Europe in the inter-war period. Major economic and social instability weakened European political life. Uncontrollable inflation[+] (p. 131) in Europe wiped out the value of savings, and high unemployment figures convinced many, especially among the middle classes, that their present form of government was failing them. By 1920, prices were three times higher in Britain than before the war, five times higher in Germany, 14,000 times higher in Austria and an incredible 23,000 times higher in Hungary.

- Dissatisfaction with the terms of the peace treaties following World War I was also a contributing factor in the rise of Fascism. This is particularly true in relation to Germany and Italy. Germany's harsh treatment at Versailles (1919) was blamed on the unfortunate politicians, who had little option but to accept the humiliating terms of the Treaty. Italy's failure to secure all that was promised in the Treaty of London (1915) also caused great resentment (p. 7). The peace treaties did not create states that satisfied all nationalities. The creation of the vast state of Poland, for instance, caused friction over its border with some of its neighbours, including Lithuania, Czechoslovakia, Russia, and especially Germany.

- Following the rise of communism in Russia in 1917, a wave of fear swept across Europe that the Russian Revolution would spread. The outbreak of communist revolts in Berlin, Vienna and Budapest in 1919 added to this fear. Fascism, rather than democracy, was seen by many as a more effective barrier against communism.

Inflation:

An increase in the price of goods and services in a country and a fall in the value of money.

- Fascism prospered in countries where democracy was not well established. This is especially true in relation to Eastern Europe, with the emergence of successor states, which grew from the old Empires of Germany, Austria-Hungary and Russia, following the Peace Treaty in 1919. The new nation states of Austria, Hungary, Poland, Yugoslavia, Czechoslovakia and the Baltic States all introduced a democratic system of government following their independence in 1919. Weak multi-party governments were elected in most of the new democracies. These governments rarely lasted a full term in office. With the exception of Czechoslovakia, every Eastern European state had established an authoritarian (one leader, one party) or semi-Fascist regime by 1936.

- Fascism enjoyed its broadest support among the middle classes, particularly in rural areas. Following the war, the middle classes felt trapped between the unionised workers on the one hand, and a powerful moneyed class on the other. They believed that their best interests were no longer served by the democratic system and increasingly looked for an alternative type of government.

It was from such conditions that Italian Fascism emerged in 1922, and Nazism in Germany in 1933.

Fascism in Italy

The first Fascist dictatorship was established in Italy. World War I created major economic and social problems for Italy, which caused tensions that the weak Italian political system was unable to manage. There was, therefore, an opportunity for someone like Mussolini to fill the political vacuum.

 ## Key Personality: Mussolini

Benito Mussolini was born in the Italian region of Romagna in 1883, the son of a socialist blacksmith. The Romagna area had a reputation for agrarian (relating to land) violence. Mussolini's father and grandfather were both jailed for their left-wing (socialist) beliefs.

Early Political Career

Like his father, Mussolini joined the Italian Socialist Party. He lived in Switzerland for a number of years to avoid being drafted for military service. There, he wrote articles for the leftist press. He returned to Italy in 1905 and became a substitute teacher. After a brief period, he left the teaching profession to concentrate on journalism, becoming the editor of the weekly newspaper *Lotta di*

Classe (The Class Struggle). He became well known within the Socialist Party when he sided with the extremists during a bitter debate at the Party's annual conference in 1912 between constitutional socialists, who wanted to bring about change through the democratic system, and revolutionaries, who sought to overthrow the Government by force. In the same year he became the editor of the socialist newspaper *Avanti* (Forward), which quickly turned him into a recognised journalist.

When World War I broke out in August 1914, he at first wrote about the importance of peace. However, later that year he made a complete U-turn and, in his editorials, called for Italy's intervention on the side of the Allies (Britain, France and Russia). He wrote with the same passion he had displayed earlier in the cause of peace. He believed that if Italy failed to get involved in the war it would play no part in the re-shaping of Europe in any peace agreement that might follow. As a result of these views, he was forced to resign from the party in 1914. In 1915 he founded his own newspaper *Il Popolo d'Italia* (The People of Italy), the front page of which carried two slogans: 'The man who has iron has bread' and 'Bayonets turn ideas into revolution'.

Mussolini as a young socialist.

Mussolini and The War

Mussolini was conscripted into the Italian Army in September 1915. His record as a soldier during the period 1915–17 was largely unimpressive, although he himself liked to tell stories of 'going over the top' to attack the Austrians, and of picking up enemy grenades and throwing them back. Like Hitler he was promoted to the rank of corporal, but unlike Hitler he never received medals for bravery. His army career ended in February 1917 when he was injured during a training exercise.

Following his time in the Army, Mussolini returned to his job as a journalist. The disorders of post-war Italy presented Mussolini with an opportunity to take control. Italy faced huge problems. Mussolini, through his editorials in *Il Popolo d'Italia* became one of the government's chief critics.

Post-war Problems

1. Resentment with the Treaty of Versailles

Italy entered World War I in 1915 under the terms of the Treaty of London. According to this treaty Italy was promised parts of Dalmatia along with other territories. President Wilson of America rejected these claims at the Versailles Conference in 1919, claiming that Dalmatia rightly belonged to the newly-created Yugoslavian state. Resentment in Italy increased when the Italian Government officially dropped its claim to Dalmatia under the terms of the Treaty of Rapallo in 1920. Italian nationalists were furious and in 1920 the Italian poet, Gabriele D'Annunzio, accompanied by a group of black-shirted ex-soldiers, temporarily occupied the Yugoslavian port of Fiume.

> **Dalmatia:**
> Dalmatia was in Croatia, which was part of the Austro-Hungarian Empire up to 1919 and became part of Yugoslavia after the Versailles Treaty.

2. Social and Economic Problems

World War I exposed the weaknesses of the Italian economy. During the years 1914–18 prices rose by 250%. Savings were wiped out and wages could not keep up with inflation. This in turn led to a wave of strikes by industrial and agricultural workers.

Over 50% of the Italian working population were engaged in agriculture. Some 90% of farmers owned holdings of less than three acres; not nearly enough land from which to make a living. During the war the Government promised to implement a land distribution programme, thus raising the expectations of Italian peasants. When the plan was not put in place after the war, a wave of unrest spread across rural Italy. A strike by farm labourers in the Po Valley in 1920 left the harvest rotting in the fields, much to the annoyance of wealthy landowners.

The war also increased unrest amongst the industrial working class. A fall in the value of the Italian currency helped the export of industrial goods and increased the wealth of the factory owners, while workers' wages struggled to keep up with inflation. In 1920 over 500,000 striking workers demanding better pay occupied the steel factories in Milan.

3. The Failure of Democracy

The electoral system of **proportional representation** (PR) was introduced in Italy for the first time in 1919. This system led to the appearance of many small parties, which in turn led to weak coalition governments. Between the years 1919 and 1922 there were five different governments, none lasting long enough to begin to tackle Italy's growing economic problems.

> **Proportional representation:**
> A system of voting in which each political party is represented at parliament in proportion to the number of people who vote for them in an election.

The Rise of Fascism

The term 'Fascism' derives from the word *fasces*, which refers to a bundle of rods tied around an axe. This was a symbol of authority in Ancient Rome. However, in 1919 the term was used to describe various Italian gangs that were anti-communist. In 1919 Mussolini founded a *fascio* in Milan. Mussolini's Fascist Party members wore a uniform, that gave them the name 'Blackshirts'. In the general election of that year, the Fascist Party failed to win any seats and could manage only 2% of the vote in Milan. The Socialists gained 40 times more votes than the Fascists. Mussolini considered leaving politics and becoming a busker. His old newspaper, *Avanti*, delighted with Mussolini's failure, sarcastically wrote his political obituary (death notice) in its editorial. It stated that 'a body in a state of putrefaction (rotting) has been found today in Milan. It seems to be that of Benito Mussolini.'

Mussolini in the back of a car leaving the royal palace following his appointment as Prime Minister in 1922.

Demobilise:

To disband troops at the end of a war.

Between 1919 and 1921 social and economic conditions continued to get worse. Demobilised soldiers were unable to find work. The fortunes of the Fascist Party began to improve slowly. In the general election of 1921, Fascists won 35 seats. Although this was a respectable result, it still left them well short of an overall majority. Once more Mussolini considered his options. He briefly thought about dropping his strong opposition to socialism, but was persuaded not to do so by other leading Fascists.

As social unrest continued, the numbers in the Fascist squads were increasing as the unemployed, students, peasants and anyone who wanted change joined up. Even the Catholic Church began to support Mussolini; in return he promised to end the long dispute between Church and State that had been going on since the unification of Italy in 1870 (p. 188).

The *agrari* (large landowners), industrialists and banks, fearful of social unrest and the spread of communism, began to finance the Fascist Party.

The great breakthrough for the Fascists came in 1922 when Mussolini and his Fascist squads succeeded in breaking a national strike, which had been called by the Socialists. The Fascists set about restoring order and managed to seize control of the streets in Milan, Genoa and Turin. In Milan the Fascists attacked the offices of Mussolini's former newspaper, *Avanti*, and drove the Socialists out of the town hall.

The March on Rome, October 1922

Success brought many converts and Fascism became a mass movement. Over 2,300 Fascist squads were established throughout Italy. By October 1922,

Mussolini's advisors were urging him to stage a
coup d'état (take power by force) by marching on
Rome from different parts of Italy. On 24 October
Mussolini challenged the Government to either
solve Italy's problems or leave it to the Fascists to
do so. On 30 October about 30,000 Fascists began
to march on Rome. Mussolini, fearing arrest,
remained close to the border in the North of Italy.
The Liberal Prime Minister, Luigi Facta, asked the
King to order the Army to move against the
Fascists, but the King refused. Instead he invited
Mussolini to talks in Rome, during which he
offered him a position as a Government Minister.
Mussolini refused this offer declaring that he
would 'not enter by the tradesman's entrance'.
Fearing trouble, the King gave in and invited

▲
Mussolini (third from the left) during the March on Rome in 1922.

Mussolini to become the Prime Minister of Italy. Mussolini left Rome and re-
entered with his Fascist bands in a triumphant parade, thus giving rise to the
myth of the 'March on Rome'. Mussolini did not, as the myth goes, force his
way to power; rather, he was invited by the King to become Prime Minister.

Mussolini's First Government, 1922–24

There were only three Fascist ministers in Mussolini's first government.
However, all decisions had to receive Mussolini's approval. Mussolini used this
period, 1922–24, to strengthen his power.

In 1923 he turned his Fascist squads into a legal Fascist Militia for National
Security **(MVSN).** Later on in that year, he introduced a new electoral law *The
Acerbo.* This law allowed for the party with the largest vote to take two-thirds
of the seats in parliament. The law was popular as it would end the terrible
political instability that Italy had suffered since the introduction of proportional
representation after World War I.

During the election campaign of 1924 (the first under the new system) the
Fascists used violence and threats to influence the vote. It was therefore no
surprise when the Fascist Party emerged with 65% of the national vote,
allowing them to control parliament.

The Aventine Secession, 1924

The Socialist leader Giacomo Matteotti demanded an inquiry into the conduct
of the election. He published a pamphlet entitled **'The Fascists Exposed'** in
which he detailed the abuses that had taken place during the campaign. These
included attacks on opposition newspapers, large-scale impersonation (voting
under a false name) and the threatening of voters. Within a week of starting

The murder of Giacomo Matteotti (second from right) in 1924 almost led to the collapse of Fascism in Italy. Matteotti was a socialist leader and the author of a pamphlet entitled 'The Fascists Exposed'.

this campaign, Matteotti was kidnapped by Blackshirts in broad daylight and brutally murdered. The public held Mussolini responsible and demanded his resignation. Almost overnight Mussolini's popularity fell. He later admitted that if the opposition had attempted a *coup*, he would easily have been overthrown.

A number of factors saved Mussolini. Firstly, the opposition parties withdrew from parliament in protest. This event became known as the *Aventine Secession* (its name refers to an incident in Ancient Rome when the ordinary people, or *plebes*, refused to come down from the Aventine hills outside Rome until the rich Romans treated them better). The *Aventine Secession* gave Mussolini a lifeline as it took away the opposition's only legal method of forcing Mussolini to resign. Another factor which saved Mussolini, was the King's refusal to intervene. It seems that he feared for his own position, as he had during the March on Rome in 1922.

Steps Towards Dictatorship

Following the Matteotti incident, Mussolini decided that the time had come to take firmer control over Italian politics.

In 1925 he gave a speech in which, for the first time, he accepted full responsibility for the excesses of the Fascists:

I declare that I and I alone assume the political, moral and historical responsibility for all that has happened. If Fascism has been a criminal association, if all the acts of violence have been the result of historical, political and moral climate, the responsibility for this is mine.

In December 1925 Mussolini removed the King's right to appoint or dismiss government ministers. From January 1926 onwards all decrees (laws) signed by Mussolini (now referred as *Il Duce – the leader*) automatically became law. Strict censorship was applied to the press. So many legal obstacles were placed in the way of privately-owned newspapers that many closed down. Writers and scholars who failed to promote Fascist values were forced into exile.

Administration of the Fascist State

Law and Order

Law and order was not enforced in Italy with the same degree of violence and persecution as was the case in Nazi Germany (p. 30). In 1926 a special police force, the **OVRA** (*Opera Volontaria Repressione Anti-Fascists* or Volunteer Organisation for the Repression of Anti-Fascism), was established to seek out and deal with opponents of the state. Penal (prison) settlements were set up in the Lipari Islands, north of Sicily, for political prisoners. **Confino,** or banishment, to remote villages was used for lesser offences.

Mussolini dealt with the Sicilian Mafia and the *Neapolitan Camorra* (organised crime families) more effectively than any other government in the twentieth century. The power of organised crime bosses was greatly reduced when the Fascists abolished elections and ended the jury system in courts. For years the Mafia had flourished in Southern Italy by corrupting local politicians and by threatening witnesses and juries. Over 2,000 Mafia suspects were imprisoned during the period 1926–39.

The Corporate State

Mussolini claimed that through the establishment of the 'Corporate State' he had developed an alternative to both communism and capitalism. Although private enterprise was encouraged, the Fascist Government could also intervene in economic matters as it saw fit. Separate corporations (councils) were established to manage the various areas of the economy. There were corporations for steel, agriculture, teachers and so on. Employers and workers were equally represented on these corporations. Three members of the Fascist Party acted as arbitrators (go-betweens).

Members of each corporation were encouraged to put the interests of the state before their own. The corporations settled disputes about pay and working conditions. For that reason, trade unions and strikes were banned. In 1938 Parliament was officially abolished and replaced by the Assembly of 22 Corporations.

Propaganda

Propaganda is information, often exaggerated or false, which is spread by political parties in order to influence public opinion. Similar to Hitler (p. 20), Mussolini established a Ministry of Propaganda. He placed it under the control of Achille Starace, the secretary of the Fascist Party. Opposition newspapers were banned and strict censorship was imposed. Mussolini was presented to the public as the perfect example of the spirit of Fascism. He was often portrayed as a great sportsman. His office light would be kept on throughout the night giving the impression that he was working tirelessly for Italy.

Mussolini showing his athletic prowess.
Describe how this picture could be seen as an example of propaganda in Fascist Italy.

Education was strictly controlled. All schoolteachers had to be Fascist Party members. Textbooks were rewritten to suit Fascist beliefs. History was reconstructed, exaggerating the role of Mussolini and Italy in World War I. Even children's storybooks contained cartoons of Mussolini saving the world from all sorts of evil.

Youth Movements

The Fascist Party also controlled children's leisure time. A youth organisation was founded in 1926 to co-ordinate their activities. From the ages of eight to fourteen, boys joined an organisation called the *Balilla* (named after an Italian hero), where they were trained both physically and morally. The organisation had a creed (a type of prayer), which read as follows:

I believe in the genius of Mussolini, in our Holy Father Fascism, in the communion of martyrs, in the conversion of Italians and in the resurrection of the Empire.

Young men train in the Balilla Fascist children's units, in Italy in 1939.

On reaching the age of fourteen, children advanced to the *Avanguardisti,* where a greater emphasis was placed on military-type exercises. At eighteen many members of the youth organisations joined the ranks of the Fascist Party. Membership of the party was necessary for anyone who wished to be employed in the state administration.

Economic Policy of the Fascist State
Public Works

A public works programme tackled unemployment. The malaria-ridden **Pontine Marshes,** on the outskirts of Rome, were drained and the land was reclaimed. Hydroelectric stations were built and *autostrade* (motorways) connected large Italian cities with the coastline. Mussolini ordered that the *autostrade* follow a straight line were possible, and that slow lanes be built to prevent traffic hold ups. Much of the Italian railway network was electrified and Mussolini boasted that the trains now ran on time. The number of unemployed people was reduced in the short-term during the construction of such projects.

Autarky and the Battle for Grain

Mussolini believed that Italy should be self-sufficient *(an autarky)* in the production of essential food. Accordingly he introduced a 'Battle for Grain'. Farmers were given grants to grow wheat instead of fruit and olives. Although there was a huge increase in grain production, the policy led to hardship in southern Italy, where the land and climate were better suited to the cultivation of citrus fruits and olive groves.

The Battle for the Lire

In 1925 Mussolini fixed the then Italian currency, the lire, at the artificially high rate of 90 lire to the pound sterling. He borrowed large amounts of money from America to do this. These loans were recalled in 1929 after the Wall Street Crash (p. 135), which led to a dramatic fall in the value of the lire. In an effort to force its value back up again, Mussolini halved wages, which caused a huge fall in living standards and a rise in unemployment.

Italy's economic difficulties were added to by Mussolini's insistence on increased military spending. By the mid 1930s, over a third of national income was being spent on military expansion. The gap between the industrial north and the poorer agricultural south continued to widen during Mussolini's reign.

▲ Mussolini standing on a tractor that had been ploughing land reclaimed from the Pontine Marshes.

The Battle for Births

In 1927 Mussolini declared that the Italian population should, by 1950, have risen from 40 million to 60 million. He argued that only in this way could Italians defend themselves against 90 million Germans and 200 million Slavs (an Eastern European race).

The taxing of bachelors encouraged marriage. Private firms and the civil service were ordered to discriminate in favour of employing family men. Despite Mussolini's best efforts, the Italian birth rate continued to decline.

> **Note!**
>
> *Church-state relations in Italy will be dealt with in Chapter 14.*

Foreign Policy

Mussolini's foreign policy objective was to gain territory and status for Italy. He stressed that Italy was not a satisfied state but 'a nation hungry for land'. He believed that Italy not only needed a strong army and navy, but also 'an air force that would blot out the sun'. However, Italy's foreign policy objectives were limited somewhat by the country's lack of industrial resources (such as coal and oil). Nonetheless, it did not prevent Mussolini from using propaganda to convince many European powers of Italy's strength.

Relations with Nazi Germany, 1933–35

At first Mussolini felt threatened by the rise of Hitler. In 1933 Hitler's plan to unite all German-speaking peoples in Europe posed a threat to parts of Northern Italy (which had previously been part of the Austro-Hungarian Empire), where over 200,000 German speakers lived.

When Austrian Nazis murdered their Prime Minister, Engelbert Dollfuss (an Austrian nationalist who was against a union with Germany) in 1934, Mussolini sent 40,000 troops to the border to prevent a *coup d'état* there. Hitler was unprepared for war at this stage and decided to back off. In 1934 Hitler visited Italy in an effort to improve relations. Mussolini was unimpressed by his visitor, referring to him later as a 'silly little clown' and a 'talkative monk'.

In 1935, Italy, Britain and France met in Stresa in Northern Italy to express their alarm at Hitler's rearmament plans (p. 88). They established what became known as the **'Stresa Front'** and drew up a joint resolution condemning Hitler's actions.

The Abyssinian (Ethiopian) War, 1935–36

The Abyssinian War proved to be a turning point in the direction of Mussolini's foreign policy. His days as a peaceful diplomat were now over and Italy began to drift slowly towards an alliance with Nazi Germany.

Mussolini wished to establish a new **Roman Empire.** He once boasted that he would turn the Mediterranean into an Italian lake. He therefore saw the conquest of Abyssinia as a step towards gaining control of North Africa. It would also serve as an act of revenge for Italy's humiliating defeat there in 1896. It was also no coincidence that the invasion in 1935 coincided with a slowdown in the Italian economy. Foreign victories abroad would take attention away from growing economic problems at home.

How and why was Mussolini able to achieve power in Italy?

There were many factors which influenced Mussolini's grasp of power in Italy. These factors included; the major instability of the European economy, the dissatisfaction with the peace treaties following world war 1, fears of the Russian revolution spreading across Europe and the support of fascism by middle class society. World War 1 created major economic and social problems for Italy, which caused tension that the weak Italian political system wasn't capable of managing, therefore, there was a place for someone like Mussolini to grasp power.

yooouree ny. Honey bunch, Sugar plum,
pumpy-umpy-umpkin, you're my sweetie pie.
You're my honey cake, gum drop, shnuckum
schnuckem, you've the apple of my eye.

and I love you so and I want you to
know that I'll always be right here,
and I love to sing sweet songs to you,

Because you,

are,

so,

dear.

B. you've been accepted to Hogwarts.

PS. This owl will explode in 4 seconds.

'...or Harry! cry

yes, big 5,

Harry did you put your name in the Goblet of fyeece!!

March on Rome.
murder of Matteoti ~ COMMUNISTS.
Ruled by degree.
post war versailles.
fear of communism.
A corpo law.
Inflation + economy.
Failure of democracy xD xD xD
Secret police
propaganda.

⚔ Totalitarianism ~ King + Church ~ Church
not totally totalitarianism.
corporate state ~ control.

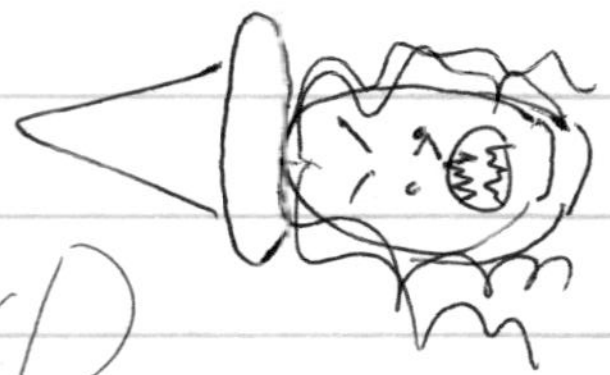

xD xD xD xD xD xD xD xD xD xD xD xD xD
xD xD xD xD xD xD xD xD
xD xD xD xDD xD xD
xD xDDD xD) xD
xD xDDD) xD
xD xD xD
xD xD
xD

Casimhe the sand witch

youre my honey bunch
sugar plum
pumpy-umpy-umpkin
youre my sweetie pie
youre my cuppy cake
gumdrop
youre the
apple of my eye
and ...

Mussolini realised that Britain and France would be unwilling to intervene, as they were preoccupied with Hitler's plan to rearm Germany. The British Foreign Secretary, Anthony Eden, visited Rome and pleaded with Mussolini not to invade. His pleas fell on deaf ears and Italy invaded in October 1935. Heavy bombers and poisonous gas were used against the Abyssinian tribesmen. This outraged international opinion and pressure mounted on the western democracies to take action.

The Abyssinian leader Emperor, Haile Selassie, appealed to the League of Nations for help. The League of Nations was an organisation that had been set up in Geneva in 1920 to help solve international disputes in a peaceful way. The League declared Italy to be the aggressor, but failed to agree on a plan of action. At first, Britain and France suggested dividing Abyssinia between Italy and Abyssinia, but when public opinion reacted unfavourably to this, they decided that economic sanctions (a ban on the trade of certain goods) should be applied. However, the sanctions did not include essentials such as coal, iron or oil and had little or no effect on Italy. The Italian population reacted bitterly to the idea of sanctions. Although the sanctions were limited, Italy began to rely more and more on Germany for trade agreements.

By May 1936 the conquest was complete and Italy once more became an empire, much to the delight of the Italians.

The Rome-Berlin Axis, 1936

Relations between Italy and Germany further improved when they helped Franco's right-wing forces in the **Spanish Civil War** in 1936. Mussolini hoped that Franco's victory in Spain would help to increase his influence over the Mediterranean region. He also felt that a foreign victory abroad would increase his status at home and divert attention from domestic problems. In fact, Mussolini's involvement in the war had the opposite effect. Italian soldiers found the going tough and their tactics and weapons were shown to be outdated. This had the effect of drawing Mussolini closer to Hitler as he now became increasingly dependent on the Nazi regime for strength.

How does the cartoonist see the Rome-Berlin Axis and the relationship between Mussolini and Hitler?

In November 1936 Mussolini's son-in-law and Foreign Minister Count Ciano signed the first of a number of treaties with Hitler. The 'Rome-Berlin Axis' stated that European power revolved around an axis connecting Rome with Berlin. This statement flattered Mussolini.

In September 1937, Italy, Germany and Japan signed the 'Anti-Communist Pact', which aimed at the destruction of the USSR and an end to the spread of communism.

The Pact of Steel, 1939

Italy and Germany eventually signed a military agreement in May 1939. The 'Pact of Steel' committed each party to aid the other in any future war. Mussolini was led to believe that a war was not likely to occur for at least another three years.

In August 1939, the German Foreign Minister, Joachim von Ribbentrop, informed Italy that war was not far off. Mussolini was shocked, as Italy was unprepared for war. He announced to Hitler that he could not participate in a war unless the Germans supplied Italy with vital war materials. The list was so long that it could not possibly be met, thus allowing Italy to avoid the war. The list requested seven million tons of oil, six million tons of coal, two million tons of steel, a million tons of timber, 17,000 military vehicles and 150 anti-aircraft guns. Hitler accepted that it was impossible for him to meet with Italian demands and asked only for Mussolini's political support.

▲
Mussolini, Hitler and Count Ciano discuss strategy at a conference in October 1940. Describe the mood of the meeting from your reading of the photograph.

Italy Enters the War, 1940

Following Hitler's successful invasion of Belgium, the Netherlands and France in 1940, Mussolini changed his mind and decided to join the war alongside Hitler (p. 106). The war went badly from the start, with Italian forces suffering major defeats in Greece and North Africa. Mussolini's involvement in the war would eventually lead to his overthrow and death in 1945 (p. 113).

Assessment

Mussolini's regime was based on a mixture of bluff, propaganda and bravado (boasting). His successes were in reality very few. His regime was built on the myth of Italian strength and superiority. When he failed to achieve his aims at home, he sought to divert attention from his failures through an aggressive and expansionist foreign policy, which led to the collapse of Italian Fascism in 1943.

Although Mussolini did have some short-term economic successes, and managed to make peace with the Catholic Church (p. 188–89), the benefits of such measures were greatly exaggerated by the use of propaganda. Despite all the publicity surrounding land reclamation, only about one-tenth of the programme had been completed by 1939.

An Historian's View

Mussolini was neither born great nor had greatness thrust on him, but had to fight his way out of obscurity by his own ambition and talents. So well did he succeed that he ruled Italy as a dictator for over 20 years and attracted more popular admiration than anyone else had received in the whole course of Italian history. At a peak of success he then fell an easy victim to the flattery that he invited or ordered from his cronies, and was beguiled (tempted) *into playing for the yet higher stakes of world dominion. But he lacked the necessary resources, whether the material resources of a rich country, or the requisite* (necessary) *personal qualities of mind and character. By the time of his death in 1945 he left to his successors an Italy destroyed by military defeat and civil war; he was, by his own admission, the most hated person in the country; and having once been praised to excess, was now being blamed for doing more harm to Italy than anyone had ever done before.*

From **Mussolini** by Denis Mack Smith, 1987.

Ordinary Level

Study the cartoon and answer these questions.

1. Why were Britain and France unwilling to fight against Italy over the Abyssinian dispute in 1935?

2. According to the cartoon, is Mussolini paying any attention to their warnings?

3. What effect did Mussolini's invasion of Abyssinia have on the future direction of Italian foreign policy?

Write a paragraph on one of the following:

1. Law and order in Fascist Italy.

2. Mussolini's economic policies.

3. Mussolini's foreign policy.

THE AWFUL WARNING.

FRANCE AND ENGLAND (together ?).

"WE DON'T WANT YOU TO FIGHT, BUT, BY JINGO, IF YOU DO, WE SHALL PROBABLY ISSUE A JOINT MEMORANDUM SUGGESTING A MILD DISAPPROVAL OF YOU."

Higher Level

1. Account for the rise of Fascism in Italy.

2. Evaluate the performance of Benito Mussolini as leader of Italy, in both internal and external affairs.

3. 'It has been said that Mussolini's rule brought significant benefits to Italy.' Discuss.

Study the document below, which is an extract from Mussolini's proclamation of 26 October, 1922, ordering the Fascists to March on Rome:

'Fascisti! Italians!'

The Army, the reserve and safeguard of the nation, must not take part in this struggle. Fascism … does not march against the police, but against a political class both cowardly and imbecile (stupid), which in four long years has not been able to give a government to the nation. Those who form the productive class must know that Fascism wants to impose nothing more than order and discipline upon the nation and to help to raise the strength which will renew progress and prosperity (wealth). The people who work in the fields and in the factories, those who work on the railroads or in offices, have nothing to fear from the Fascist Government. Their just rights will be protected. We will even be generous with unarmed adversaries (enemies). Fascism draws its sword to cut the multiple Knots which tie and burden Italian life. We call God and the spirit of our five thousand dead to witness that only one impulse sends us on, that only one passion burns within us – the impulse and the passion to contribute to the safety and greatness of our country.

Fascisti of all Italy! Stretch forth like Romans your spirits and your fibres! We must win! We will. Long live Italy! Long live Fascism!

1. How does Mussolini justify the Fascist takeover of power?

2. According to this proclamation, why do the Italians have nothing to fear from a Fascist takeover?

3. What promises does Mussolini give which might appeal to large sections of the Italian population?

4. It is claimed in the proclamation that the Italian political system has failed to give a government to the nation during the years 1918–22. Using your knowledge of Italian history, how accurate do you consider this statement to be? (Higher Level only)

The Origins and Growth of the Nazi Party in Germany

Key Personality: Adolf Hitler

Adolf Hitler was born in the Austrian border town of Brannau in 1889 to middle-class parents. His father was a customs officer who hoped that his son would follow him into the civil service. However, following his father's death, Hitler left school at the age of 16, without graduating.

In September 1907 he moved to Vienna, where he failed to gain entrance to the Fine Arts Academy due to his lack of qualifications. He supported himself by selling picture postcards of Vienna scenes, which he painted.

It was during his stay in Vienna that Hitler began to develop his political and racial theories. In the magazine *Ostara*, which was published by Lanz von Liebenfels, Hitler read about 'blond blue-eyed heroes' and about the importance of 'racial hygiene'. From the writings of the German Nationalist Georg von Schonerer, he absorbed the message that all German-speaking peoples should be united in

▲ Adolf Hitler (1889–1945), the Nazi leader.

one country. It was probably at this time that Hitler also became familiar with the works of the anti-Semitic writer, Houston Stewart Chamberlain.

In May 1913 Hitler moved to Munich in Bavaria in order to avoid military service in Austria. The Munich police forced him to return to Vienna. However, on his return to Austria he was declared medically unfit to serve in the Army and was allowed back to Munich. When World War I broke out in August 1914, Hitler volunteered to serve in the German Army. He fought on the Western Front, where he was promoted to the rank of corporal. Hitler participated in the Ludendorff Offensive of April 1918, for which he was awarded the Iron Cross, First Class, for bravery.

When the war came to an end in November 1918, Hitler was in hospital recovering from a gas attack. He was disgusted when Germany surrendered.

Following the war, Hitler was employed by the Army intelligence wing to investigate the activities of a small right-wing party, the DAP (*Deutsche Arbeiterpartei* or German Workers' Party).

The Origins of the Nazi Party, 1919

The German Workers' Party had its origins in post-war Bavaria. Anton Drexler formed it in Munich in 1919 as a radical right-wing party. Hitler initially joined the party as a Government spy, but was soon converted to the Party's beliefs. By 1923 Hitler had become the undisputed leader of the Party. He changed the Party's name to the National Socialist German Workers' Party (Nazi Party – the word 'Nazi' is a short form of the German *Nationalsozialismus*). They adopted the hooked cross or swastika as their symbol.

His fiery speeches, blaming the Jews, democracy and the communists for Germany's ills, struck a cord with the general population. A defence band, the **SA** (*Sturmabteilung* – German for 'Assault Division' and sometimes translated 'stormtroopers'), was created under the leadership of Ernst Röhm. This brown-shirted movement broke up left-wing meetings and attacked anti-Nazis and Communists.

▲
The swastika, the Nazi Party symbol.

The Weimar Republic, 1919–33

In 1918 a provisional Government was set up in Germany following the defeat of the German armies on the battlefields of World War I. In November 1918, this Government agreed to an armistice (truce) and the withdrawal of the German armies. The *Kaiser* was then forced to abdicate. The period of German history from 1919 to 1933 is known as the Weimar Republic. It was named after the city of Weimar, where a national assembly sat to make a new constitution for the defeated country. What emerged was a presidential democracy or republic. Many Germans saw the Weimar Republic as the result of defeat and not victory, and this fact affected its survival.

From the very beginning the Weimar Republic faced a range of problems, including several rebellions, economic problems, and deep divisions between different groups in society. The political parties loyal to the Weimar Republic were too weak and disunited to act as acceptable alternatives to extremists, such as those in the Nazi Party, who were determined to see its destruction.

> **Abdication:**
> The act by which a king or queen gives up the throne.

Democracy in Trouble

During the first four years of its existence, the Weimar Republic faced major political and economic crises. In 1919 the **'Spartacists'**, led by Rosa Luxemburg and Karl Liebknecht, attempted to overthrow the Government and set up a socialist republic in Germany.

The following year there was an attempt at a right-wing *coup* in Berlin. It was led by a former civil servant, Wolfgang Kapp, and became known as the **Kapp *Putsch*** (attempted violent overthrow of a government). This episode proved the Army to be unreliable in stopping revolution, as military leaders either joined the *Putsch* or refused to fire on old comrades.

German soldiers occupying Government Headquarters in Berlin during the **Kapp Putsch** in 1920.

Although both of these attempts ended in failure, extremists waited in the wings for an opportunity to strike again.

The Myth of Dolchstoss (Stab in the Back)

The German Army encouraged the myth that the Weimar politicians had stabbed the Army in the back. The Army leader, Paul von Hindenburg, referred to the politicians who had signed the armistice in November 1918 as the **'November criminals'**. He claimed that the Army had not been defeated, but had been betrayed by the politicians who had accepted the peace. Hatred towards these politicians, who had also signed the Treaty of Versailles, quickly spread. In 1921 Matthias Erzberger, a signatory of the armistice, was assassinated. Walther Rathenau, the German Foreign Minister, was shot in 1922 outside the *Reichstag* (German Parliament) in Berlin after he expressed the view that the terms of the Treaty of Versailles would have to be accepted.

The Economic Collapse

The question of **reparations** (compensation) for damage caused during World War I proved to be the greatest threat to German democracy in the early days of the Weimar Republic. In 1921 the Reparations Commission, set up under the Treaty of Versailles, finally fixed Germany's debt at £6,600 million (c. €8,400 million) which was to be repaid in annual instalments of £100 million. Germany protested that they could not meet such demands. When Germany failed to pay its instalment in January 1923, the French Premier, Raymond Poincaré, ordered French troops to occupy the industrial Ruhr region in Germany to extract payments by removing iron, steel and coal (p. 84). The Germans resorted to passive resistance by going on strike and refusing to co-operate with the French. The French reacted with mass arrests and over 147,000 German workers were evicted from the Ruhr.

The shutdown of the industrial activities in the Ruhr region had a devastating effect on the value of the German mark. The state bank *(Reichsbank)* began to print paper money to pay the workers on strike. This caused uncontrolled inflation. Prices increased and the German currency became worthless (p. 150).

The great inflation of 1923 caused deep resentment in Germany, especially among the German middle classes, who saw their savings and pensions wiped out. Adolf Hitler and his Nazi Party sought to make use of this deep anger and

Passive resistance:
A non-violent refusal to co-operate.

Inflation:
An increase in prices and fall in the value of money.

loss of confidence in democracy. Hitler promised work for the unemployed and stability for the middle classes. In 1923 he attempted to seize power in what became known as the **Munich Putsch.**

The Munich Putsch

When the French marched into the Ruhr in 1923, Hitler claimed that the reparations should not be paid and that the French must be driven out of the Ruhr. He attempted to seize power by force after a meeting at a Beer Hall in Munich on 08 November, 1923. With the support of a conservative politician, **Ludendorff,** an ex-army general and war hero, he proclaimed himself President of Germany. He planned to march on Berlin, just as Mussolini had marched on Rome a year earlier (p. 8). However, Hitler's plans came unstuck when one of his commanders lost his nerve and informed the Government of his plans.

French troops occupying the Ruhr area in 1923. Their arrival was met by a campaign of passive resistance by the German population.

The attempted *coup* was easily put down and Hitler was arrested. He used his trial as a propaganda exercise for the Nazi Party. His light prison sentence of five years reduced to nine months demonstrates that the judiciary were sympathetic to his cause. Hitler learned a valuable lesson from his failure. He now realised that power would not be achieved by force, but instead by taking advantage of the weaknesses of democracy and the Weimar Constitution. He also knew that he would need the support of industrialists to finance the Nazi Party, and the respect of the Army, because it could prevent his rise to power.

When I resume active work it will be necessary to pursue a new policy. Instead of working to achieve power by armed conspiracy (plan) we shall have to hold our noses and enter the Reichstag against the Catholic and Marxist deputies. If outvoting them takes longer than outshooting them, at least the results will be guaranteed by their own constitution! Sooner or later we shall have a majority and after that we shall have Germany.
Hitler speaking to a friend visiting him in Landsberg Prison, 1924.

Key Concept: Herrenvolk

The *Herrenvolk* (**'Master Race'**) was an idea that the Nazis developed from various European writers. They believed that the Germans and other northern European people (Aryan) were members of a superior race. In Hitler's view, the Aryans had given the world its highest form of culture and were destined to rule over 'lesser people'.

While in prison, Hitler wrote his autobiography, ***Mein Kampf*** (My Struggle). His ideas about the 'master race', his hatred of the Jews and his plans for a greater Germany are expressed clearly in this book. He planned to build a strong Aryan state. He concluded that there was a Jewish conspiracy to spoil the purity of Germans by cross-breeding with inferior races. He also wished to unite all German-speaking people under one leader. Expansion should not be in Africa or Asia, as had been the case before 1914, but eastwards, by enslaving the 'lesser' Slav people. This expansion of Germany eastwards within Europe became known as *Lebensraum*⁺ (p. 81) or 'living space'.

▲
Gustav Stresemann (1878–1929), the 'good German'.

The Stresemann Period 1923–29

The years 1923–29 are often referred to as the golden years of the Weimar Republic. Germany entered a period of relative prosperity and managed to break away from its political isolation. This was largely due to the skills of Gustav Stresemann. Stresemann became the Chancellor of Germany for a few months in 1923, but he continued on as Foreign Minister in successive coalition governments until his death in 1929.

Stresemann wished to portray himself as the 'good German' anxious to fulfil the terms of the Treaty of Versailles. In this manner, he hoped that France and Britain would not become alarmed if Germany proposed a revision of the treaty.

Economic Recovery

Stresemann's first step in this direction came in 1923 when he urged the workers in the Ruhr to end their policy of passive resistance. In April 1924 the American banker Charles G. Dawes established a more moderate schedule for German reparations. In the same year, the USA made the first of a series of loans to help the German Government restore the value of the mark. Five years of economic growth followed.

In 1929 an international board, led by the American banker Owen D. Young, recommended a further review of reparations. The Young Plan reduced the sum by about three-quarters and allowed for instalment payments until 1988.

Nazi Support Drops

In 1924 the Nazi Party had 24 seats in the *Reichstag*. However, this number had reduced to 12 by 1928 as a direct result of the more prosperous 'Stresemann years'. In the 1928 general election, the Nazi Party secured only 2.6% of the popular vote. Support for the Party at that time was mainly confined to small rural towns in the northwest of Germany.

The Collapse of German Democracy

The onset of the Great Depression[+] (p. 136) following the Wall Street Crash in America in 1929 ruined Germany's economic revival. American loans were recalled and the demand for German exports slumped. Unemployment rose sharply from 1.3 million in 1929 to 6 million by 1932. This led to the resignation of Chancellor Hermann Müller. Müller's departure marks the beginning of the end of parliamentary democracy in the Weimar Republic.

Since 1919 no single party had held a majority in the *Reichstag*. However, up to 1930, three of the largest pro-republican parties, the Catholic Centre Party, the Social Democratic Party and the People's Party co-operated to form coalition governments. The alliance between these parties fell apart when Heinrich Brüning, the leader of the Catholic Centre Party, became Chancellor in 1930. He attempted to stabilise the economy by introducing severe cutbacks on public spending. The Social Democrats rejected these reforms, forcing Brüning to rely on emergency power as allowed for under **Article 48** of the Constitution. Emergency laws allowed him to reduce public spending by cutting wages, lowering prices and slashing unemployment benefit.

Brüning's emergency measures might have worked if they had been given a chance. However, he lacked the political skill required to sell such harsh measures to an angry public.

The unpopularity of these policies resulted in an increase in support for extremist parties from both the left and the right wings. The elections from 1930 onwards saw a rapid increase in votes for both the Communist Party and the Nazi Party.

Left-wing:
A political term used to describe supporters of socialist and communist parties.

Right-wing:
A political term used to describe those who support conservative parties. Fascism is considered to be on the extreme right of political activity.

	May 1928	September 1930	July 1932	November 1932	March 1933
Communists	54	77	89	100	81
Nazis	12	107	230	196	288

Hitler promised that he would stop the 'Red Tide' (Communists were known as 'reds' due to the colour of their flag). Leading German industrialists, such as

Fritz Thyssen and Emil Kirdorf, fearing a Communist takeover, donated large sums of money to the Nazi Party.

Presidential Election, 1932

In 1932 Hitler decided to test the mood of the people by entering the presidential contest against the sitting President and war hero, Paul von Hindenburg. Although Hindenburg won the election with a comfortable majority, Hitler managed to secure a very respectable 13 million votes.

The 'Cabinet of Barons', 1932

Within a few weeks of the presidential election, Brüning, now nicknamed the **'Hunger Chancellor'**, was forced to resign. The President, Hindenburg, appointed a 'stop-gap' administration led by Franz von Papen, an ex-leader of the Catholic Centre Party, on 01 June, 1932. Papen's cabinet included many non-party aristocrats and received very little support from the general public, which dubbed it 'The Cabinet of Barons'. When Papen failed to receive support for his policies in the *Reichstag*, he dissolved the parliament and held a general election in July 1932. The election result proved disastrous for Papen. The small right-wing Nationalist Party that he now supported won only 44 seats, while the Nazis fell short of an overall majority with 230 seats (37% of the vote).

By now German politics was slipping out of control. Germany was drifting towards a civil war. In 1931 the local police in Prussia, an area in East Germany, recorded more than 300 political murders. From mid-June to mid-July 1932 there were 461 cases of political rioting. The riots had even spread to the *Reichstag*. On 25 May, 1932, the Nazis and the Communists fought a pitched battle in the parliament.

The political unrest continued throughout the autumn of 1932. Fresh elections were held in November. Surprisingly, the support for the Nazi Party dropped and they won only 196 seats.

▲ Adolf Hitler and President Paul von Hindenburg. The President invited Hitler to form a government on 30 January, 1933.

Hitler Becomes Chancellor, 1933

From December 1932 to January 1933 an Army General, Kurt von Schleicher, was Chancellor. Papen, who was annoyed by his own removal, now turned to Hitler. In early January 1933 they reached an agreement whereby Hitler would become Chancellor and Papen Vice-Chancellor. Papen used his personal ties with the aged Hindenburg to persuade him to dismiss Schleicher and appoint Hitler in his place. The President eventually gave way and Hitler became the Chancellor of Germany on 30 January, 1933. Papen convinced Hindenburg that he could control Hitler and the Nazis claiming, 'We have hired him. Within two months we will have pushed Hitler so far into the corner that he'll squeak.' Josef Goebbels*, a leading member of the Nazi Party, had a different interpretation of the situation, declaring, 'We have arrived at our goal. The German revolution begins.'

Goebbels was right. By mid-1934 every trace of German democracy had been erased by the Nazis.

? Questions

Ordinary Level

Study the cartoon and answer the questions below. The cartoon, which was published by the *Daily Mail* in Britain in January 1923, is commentating on the French occupation of the Ruhr.

Exclusive picture from the 'Valley of the Tomb of the Kings'

1. What are the French taking from the Ruhr Valley?

2. Who are being represented as 'Coal Kings' in the cartoon?

3. What is the reaction of the 'Coal Kings' to the French occupation of the Ruhr?

4. Why did the French consider it necessary to occupy the Ruhr in January 1923?

5. What effect did the occupation in the Ruhr have on the rise of Hitler and the Nazi Party?

Write a paragraph on one of the following:

1. Hitler's early political life.

2. Hitler's rise to power.

3. *Herrenvolk* ('Master Race')

Higher Level

1. Describe the circumstances that brought about the rise of Hitler and the Nazi Party in Germany during the period 1923–33.

3 The Nazi State

The Establishment of a Dictatorship, January–March 1933

When Hitler became Chancellor of Germany in January 1933, he led a 12-man cabinet that contained only two other Nazis, Herman Goering, Minister of the Interior for Prussia, and Wilhelm Frick, Minister of the Interior for Germany. Hitler's immediate aim was to secure power for the Nazi Party alone. As soon as he was in power he called a fresh election for 05 March, 1933.

Steps Towards a Dictatorship

1. Control of The Police

Herman Goering enrolled thousands of Nazis into the Police Force. In February 1933 this Nazi-dominated Police Force directed a campaign of violence and intimidation against opposition parties.

2. The Reichstag Fire, 27 February, 1933

The excuse for an all-out assault on the Communist Party was provided on 27 February, 1933. A Dutch Communist, Marius van der Lubbe, set fire to the *Reichstag* in Berlin. Hitler used this as a reason to attack the Communists, claiming that it was a signal for a Communist revolution. Over 4,000 Communists and Socialists were arrested, making it difficult for them to contest the forthcoming election.

3. Election, 05 March, 1933

Under a cloud of threats and terror the Nazis gained an extra 92 seats in parliament. Although the Communist vote dropped by over a million, the Nazis failed to gain an overall majority and had to rely on the support of Papen and the small Nationalist Party. This gave the Nazi Party a slim majority of 52%.

4. The Enabling Act, 23 March, 1933

Once in power, the Nazis set upon a full-scale policy of bullying and creating fear. Hitler wanted the *Reichstag* to transfer full power to him for a period of four

▲
The German parliament, the **Reichstag**, in flames 27 February, 1933.

years so that he could re-establish stability in Germany. He needed a two-thirds majority to do this. When the *Reichstag* met in a Berlin Opera House on 23 March, 1933, Hitler filled its public galleries with yelling Nazi supporters. Most left-wing politicians stayed away. The Socialist Democratic Party was the only party brave enough to oppose Hitler. All the other parties voted for the Enabling Act (23 March, 1933), which effectively ended the Weimar Republic by allowing Hitler to rule by decree (without parliament) for a period of four years.

Key Concept: Totalitarianism

Totalitarianism is a political system in which there is only one political party, and this party controls everything. No opposition or rival viewpoints are tolerated. Mussolini, Hitler and Stalin established such governments in the inter-war period.

Hitler used the power given to him by the Enabling Act to set up a totalitarian regime in Germany. The state would regulate every aspect of a citizen's life. The state was all important and the individual served the state. This is the opposite of a democracy, where the state serves the people.

Gleichschaltung (Co-ordination)

Ein Reich, Ein Volk, Ein Führer ('One Empire, One People, One Leader')

After 1933 Hitler followed a policy of *Gleichschaltung* (co-ordination), which brought as many aspects of life as possible under the control of the Nazi Party. From 1933 onwards, Nazi Germany became known officially as **The Third Reich** (Empire). The First *Reich* had been the Holy Roman Empire, from 960 until its overthrow by Napoleon in 1806. The Second *Reich* had been established by Bismarck in 1871, and lasted until the end of World War I in 1918. On coming to power in 1933, Hitler predicted that the Third *Reich* would last for a thousand years!

▲ Herman Goering (left), commander-in-chief of the **Luftwaffe** (Air Force) and Heinrich Himmler, Chief of the SS.

The chief preoccupation (concern) of the new regime has been to press forward with the greatest energy the creation of uniformity throughout every department of German life; this is called 'Gleichschaltung' a term taken from the electrical industry.

The federal states have almost ceased to exist as separate national entities; officialdom has been purged (cleaned out) of Jews and Marxists. The same method has been applied to the municipalities, provincial districts, social organisations; all professions, trades, sports and education. A legal basis for this cleansing operation has been created by the passage of a number of laws.

From a letter by John Rumbold, British Ambassador in Berlin, to Sir John Simon, 26 April, 1933.

Centralisation of Government

In May 1933 trade unions were banned and were later replaced by the Nazi **Labour Front,** under the leadership of Dr Robert Ley. In 1934 he produced a law regulating national labour and appointed 'Trustees of Labour' to look after workers' rights.

In January 1934 Germany ceased to be a federal state when the *Länder*, or regional assemblies, were abolished. The legal profession was purged of non-Nazis and new Nazi People Courts were established. The state police came under Nazi control as Heinrich Himmler, the SS leader (see below), became the new Chief of Police.

Police State

In order to control the German people, the Nazis established special police agencies to deal with those who spoke against the regime. Two terror organisations, the **SS** (*Schutzstaffel* or Protective Squad) and the *Gestapo* (*Geheime Staatspolizei* or Secret State Police), were used to track down and silence opponents of the Nazi regime.

The SS was founded in 1925 to provide Hitler with personal bodyguards. Under the leadership of Heinrich Himmler it developed into an elite organisation boasting a membership of 240,000 by 1939. In 1933 Himmler formed a unit of the SS, the **'Order of the Death's Head',** which supervised 18 concentration camps where political prisoners were imprisoned. The first concentration camp was opened at a former munitions factory at Dachau, Bavaria, in March 1933.

Himmler also took charge of the dreaded *Gestapo* from 1934 onwards. The *Gestapo* penetrated every aspect of private and public life in order to seek out resistance to the Nazi regime. The SS and the *Gestapo* were subject only to the commands of Hitler and were placed beyond the reach of civil law.

The Night of the Long Knives, 29 June, 1934

By 1934 Hitler had become increasingly worried about the strength of Ernst Röhm's defence band, the SA. When Hitler failed to implement a programme of social reform, tensions began to mount between Hitler and the SA leader. The SA believed in a **'Second Revolution',** which would bring radical social changes. Hitler was unwilling to do this, as it would be opposed by the industrialists who had financed the rise of the Nazis, and by the officer class of the German Army. High-ranking officers were worried that the SA had plans to take control of the German Army leadership. In addition, Hitler could not tolerate the existence of a private army that gave most of its allegiance to Röhm.

Hitler cleverly struck a deal with the Army: the SS and the German Army would eliminate Röhm and the SA, and in return the Army would not oppose Hitler's plans to end the office of President following Hindenberg's death. On 30 June, 1934, during what became known as 'The Night of the Long Knives', Röhm and other SA leaders were dragged from their beds and murdered. Some 400 members of the SA were killed. The following day Hitler called a press conference and explained to the German people that the SA had been planning a Communist takeover. The German public, who were willing to give up the niceties of democratic freedom for the sake of an improved economic situation, largely accepted this.

▲
Ernst Röhm (left), leader of the SA, with Franz von Papen. The SA's call for a 'Second Revolution' caused friction with Hitler. Röhm and other leaders were murdered in June 1934.

The Army

With the death of President Hindenberg in 1934, the last remaining threat to Hitler was removed. As agreed with the Army, no new President was elected. Hitler simply merged the posts of Chancellor and President into a new title, *Der Führer* (Leader). This effectively gave Hitler control of the Army, as the President had been the Commander in Chief. From then on, every soldier in the German Army took an oath of unconditional obedience to Hitler.

Education

The Nazi curriculum placed considerable emphasis on three main subjects: History, Biology and Physical Training. History was rewritten to fit in with Nazi ideology. Lessons concentrated on the origins of the Nazi Party and on the history of the Aryan Race. Biology classes stressed the importance of racial

Aryan:
A term used by the Nazis to refer to non-Jewish, blond-haired, blue-eyed white people. The Nazis considered such people to be 'pure German'.

purity. Physical training was seen as an important step in the rebuilding of the *Herrenvolk* ('Master Race'). Religious instruction was gradually phased out and from 1935 onwards attendance at school prayers became optional. All teachers had to attend training courses, which were organised by the Nazi Party. By 1936 some 32% of all teachers were members of the Party.

Teachers are directed to instruct their pupils in the nature, causes and effects of all racial problems, to bring home to them the importance of race, to awaken pride in their membership of the German race and the will to co-operate in the racial purification of the German stock.

Order from the Reich Minister of Education, Dr Rust, January 1935.

The Nazi education system was extremely sexist. Female enrolment in universities was limited to 10% of the total number of entrants. It also became more difficult for girls to enter higher education as many girls' schools placed an emphasis on subjects such as cooking and sewing, rather than on science and technology. All of this fitted in with Hitler's attitude to women: *Kinder, Kirche und Küche* (Children, Church and Kitchen).

Elite schools, known as NAPOLA (National Political Educational Establishment), or Adolf Hitler Schools, were established to produce highly-educated future Party members.

▲
Hitler Youth demonstrating their skills of semaphore.

Youth Movements

The Battle for the mind starts in the cradle.

Hitler.

Hitler believed that Germans should have large families so that they could outnumber the 'inferior' races of Eastern Europe. The future of the Third Reich, which Hitler predicted would last for 1,000 years, depended on the youth. The **'Hitler Youth'** was formed in 1926. Two years later a similar organisation, the *Bund Deutscher Mädel* (League of German Maidens) was established for girls. Younger boys and girls between the ages of 10 and 14 could join the *Jungvolk* and *Jungmädel*. Boys entering the *Jungfolk* had to undergo an initiation test in which they were expected to run 12 metres in 12 seconds. They also had to partake in a two-day hike and demonstrate their skills of semaphore (arm or flag signalling) and arms drills. When they advanced to full membership of the Hitler Youth, it became an occasion of great pride as they were presented with the Hitler Youth dagger, inscribed with the motto **'Blood and Honour'**.

Similar to the education system, Nazi youth movements were sexist. While boys involved themselves in military exercises, girls were taught the skills of domestic duties.

By the end of 1934, the Hitler Youth boasted a membership of 3.5 million. Although the Hitler Youth had originally attracted working-class children, it gradually became dominated and led by the sons of middle-class and wealthy Germans. During the war the Hitler Youth demonstrated its loyalty to Hitler by fighting to the bitter end in the defence of Berlin in April 1945 (p. 118).

Key Concept: Propaganda

Propaganda is information, often exaggerated or false, which is given out for a particular purpose, usually to spread a particular doctrine or belief. During the inter-war years, 1919–39, it came to mean information which is spread by political parties in order to influence the public. Hitler's rise to power was much aided by the clever use of propaganda by a master of the art, Josef Goebbels.

Hitler claimed in *Mein Kampf* that support for the Nazi Party could be won over and strengthened by the clever use of propaganda.

All effective propaganda must be confined to a few bare necessities and then expressed in a few simple phrases. Only by constantly repeating will you succeed in imprinting an idea onto the memory of a crowd.

From **Mein Kampf** by Adolf Hitler, 1924.

Key Personality: Josef Goebbels

Josef Goebbels was the chief propagandist of the Nazi Party. He became an admirer of Hitler during the Munich *Putsch* in 1923 and was appointed leader of the Nazi Party in Berlin in 1926. He founded his own newspaper, ***Der Angriff*** (The Attack) in 1927, in which he voiced his Nazi opinions and hatred of the Jews. It was Goebbels who introduced the term **'Heil Hitler'** (long live Hitler) as the regular form of greeting party members.

When Hitler became Chancellor in 1933 Goebbels entered cabinet as head of a newly-formed **Reich Ministry of Information and Propaganda.** Seven departments were created to control every aspect of cultural life; The Reich Chambers of Fine Arts, Music, Theatre, Literature, The Press, Radio and Films.

Goebbels' importance lessened somewhat when Hitler's power became secure from 1934 onwards. However, his importance increased again towards the end of the war when Germans had to be convinced of the need to continue fighting. He stayed loyal to Hitler

Josef Goebbels (1897–1945), chief propagandist of the Nazi Party.

until the very end. On the day after Hitler's suicide (01 May), Goebbels poisoned his entire family and shot himself.

Aspects of Nazi Propaganda

1. Case Study: The Nuremberg Rallies

Source A

Mass assemblies are necessary because they have a strengthening and encouraging effect on most people. A man, who enters such a meeting in doubt and hesitation, leaves it inwardly fortified (strengthened). *He has become a member of a community.*

From **Mein Kampf** by Adolf Hitler, 1924.

The Origins of the Nuremberg Rallies

The first Nuremberg Rallies took place in January and August 1923 and attracted 20,000 spectators. At first they were held in conjunction with other right-wing groups such as the Battle League. From 1926 onwards they became a yearly Nazi custom known as *Parteitage* or Party Days. They were generally held in September to coincide with the annual Nazi Party Congress. For those who could not attend the rallies, annual magazines, which included the main speeches, were published from 1934 onwards.

The annual September Party rallies at Nuremberg were used very effectively to spread Nazi propaganda. Hitler would deliver up to 20 speeches and attend army manoeuvres during the week-long festival. The **'Blood Flag',** which the Führer had carried during the failed Munich *Putsch* in 1923 (p. 23), would be unfurled for swearing-in ceremonies of new SA and SS recruits. The flag was spattered with the blood of Andreas Bauriedl, who was one of 16 men killed during the rising. The Nazi Women's Organisation, as well as the Labour Front (Nazi trade union), also took a prominent role at these rallies. On average, about half a million people participated each year in the Nuremberg rallies during the years 1933–38.

Speeches and Themes

Each rally had a theme. The development of Nazi Party policy can be traced through the speeches at these rallies.

In 1933 Hitler used the occasion to praise the German Army. In a speech delivered to the Nuremberg Rally on 23 September, 1933, Hitler assured the Army that Ernst Röhm and the SA were not attempting to take control of the Army leadership:

The 'Blood Flag' ceremony.

Source B

On this day we should particularly remember the part played by our Army, for we all know well that if, in the days of our revolution, the Army had not stood on our side, then we should not be standing here today. We can assure the Army that we shall never forget this, that we see in them the bearers of the tradition of our glorious old Army, and that with all our heart and all our powers we will support the spirit of this army.

In 1934 the rally lasted for a full week and celebrated the rise of Hitler to power. Albert Speer, Hitler's architect, was chosen to act as stage manager for the week-long pageant (show) at Nuremberg. Speer erected a stone structure 1,300-feet long and 80-feet wide, which looked like a huge altar at the Zeppelin field. A giant eagle with a 100-foot wing span and a swastika at its feet, hung above the podium. The pageant became the subject of Leni Riefenstahl's* (p. 41) film *Triumph des Willens (Triumph of the Will)*. In one of the most powerful propaganda films ever made, female director Riefenstahl made use of cheering crowds, precision marching, military bands and Hitler's closing speech to glorify Hitler and the Nazi regime.

Nazi Party Congress in Nuremberg in 1934.

Provincial Governor Adolf Wagner of Bavaria set the tone for the rally when he addressed the crowd:

Source C

The German form of life is definitely determined for the next thousand years. ... There will be no other revolution in Germany for the next one thousand years!

It was also at this rally that Dr Gerhard Wagner delivered a speech entitled 'Race and National Health', which attempted to justify the forthcoming Nazi program of **euthanasia** (the killing of the old and those that are unable to care for themselves).

Hitler's racial decrees (**Nuremberg Laws** p. 180) were announced during the 1935 rally. Hitler's main speech at the 1935 rally was delivered on 11 September. What started as a speech on cultural development, quickly turned into an attack on the Jews:

Source D

The Jews are a people of robbers. Everything that the Jew has is stolen. Foreign workmen build his temples, it is foreigners who create and work for him, and shed their blood for him. He has no art of his own: he has stolen it from others or he watched them at work and then made his copy. He cannot maintain any state for long. This is one difference between him and the Aryan.

On the 13 September Hitler ordered that a law entitled **'The Law for the Protection of German Blood and Honour'** be drawn up within 48 hours. More commonly known as the 'Nuremberg Laws', these laws deprived Jews of German citizenship and forbade marriage between Jews and Aryans.

The evils of communism and Germany's need for economic self-sufficiency were discussed at the 1936 rally. Hitler delivered a strong anti-Communist speech:

Source E

If in the West or Central Europe a single people were to become victims of Bolshevism (Communism), this poison would continue its ravages (damage), it would devastate the oldest, the fairest civilisation in the world today. Germany, by taking upon itself this conflict does fulfil, as so often before in her history, a truly European mission.

The 1938 rally (the last) concentrated on the tensions in international affairs. The title of the rally, 'First Party Rally of Greater Germany', also celebrated Germany's union with Austria in 1938. The rally was held in September against the backdrop of the 'Munich Crisis' (p. 93). Goering used the occasion to denounce Czechoslovakia for its treatment of Sudeten Germans. Sudeten Germans were a German-speaking ethnic group which for centuries belonged to the Austro-Hungarian Empire. When the Empire was divided after World War I, they found themselves in the newly-founded Czechoslovakia.

Source F

A petty segment of Europe is harassing the human race. This miserable pygmy race (the Czechs) *is oppressing a cultured people, and behind it is Moscow and the eternal mask of the Jew devil.*

Hitler also used the closing speech of the rally to send a strong message to the Czech government. He warned that if they failed to give justice to the Sudeten Germans that the Nazis would have to take action to see that they did.

On 15 August, 1939, Hitler secretly cancelled the Nuremberg Rally, which had been scheduled to begin the first week of September. Instead of marching at Nuremberg, Hitler's Army would be invading Poland. It is ironic that the theme of the proposed rally for September 1939 was to be the 'Party Rally for Peace'.

Eye-Witness Accounts

Hitler took great pride and delight in addressing the masses gathered at the Nuremberg stadium each year. Fiery speeches, marches, flags, emblems and music were used to great effect to increase national pride. William L. Shirer, an American news reporter and historian, describes one such scene in 1935:

Source G

No wonder that Hitler was in a confident mood when the Nazi Party Congress assembled in Nuremberg on 04 September. I watched him on the morning of the next day stride like a conquering emperor down the centre aisle of the great flag-bedecked Luitpold Hall while the band blared forth 'The Badenweiler March' and 30,000 hands were raised in the Nazi salute.

Hitler welcomed foreign visitors, journalists and diplomats to attend the Nuremberg Rallies. He believed that their reports would act as a source of propaganda for the Nazi Party and demonstrate to the outside world the strength and determination of the Nazi state. Virginia Cowles, a British citizen, was one such visitor to the Nuremberg Rallies.

Source H

The demonstration that followed was one of the most extraordinary I have ever witnessed. Hitler climbed to his box in the Grand Stand amid a deafening ovation (long applause), *then gave a signal for the political leaders to enter. They came, a hundred thousand strong, through an opening in the far end of the arena. In the silver light they seemed to pour into the bowl like a flood of water. Each of them carried a Nazi flag and when they were assembled in mass formation, the bowl looked like a shimmering sea of swastikas.*

Then Hitler began to speak. The crowd hushed into silence, but the drums continued their steady beat. Hitler's voice rasped into the night and every now and then the multitude broke into a roar of cheers. Some of the audience began swaying back and forth, chanting 'Sieg Heil' over and over again in a frenzy of delirium (fever). *I looked at the faces around me and saw tears streaming down people's cheeks. The drums had grown louder and I suddenly felt frightened. For a moment I wondered if it wasn't a dream; perhaps we were really in the heart of the African jungle.*

At last it was over. Hitler left the box and got back in the car. As soon as he stopped speaking the spell seemed to break and the magic vanish. That was the most extraordinary thing of all for when he left the stand and climbed back into his car, his small figure suddenly became drab and unimpressive. You had to pinch yourself to realise that this was the man on whom the eyes of the world were riveted; that he alone held the lightning in his hands.

From **Looking for Trouble** by Virginia Cowles, 1941.

Sir Neville Henderson, the British Ambassador to Germany between 1937 and 1939, attended the 1937 and 1938 rallies. He describes the atmosphere created at the Nuremberg Rallies:

Source I

His (Hitler's) *arrival was theatrically notified by the sudden turning into the air of the 300 or more searchlights with which the stadium was surrounded. The blue-tinged light from these met thousands of feet up in the sky at the top to make a kind of square roof, to which a chance cloud gave added realism. The effect, which was both solemn and beautiful, was like being inside a cathedral of ice.*

I spent six years in St Petersburg before the war in the best days of the old Russian ballet, but for grandiose beauty I have never seen a ballet to compare with it. The German, who has a highly-developed herd instinct, is perfectly happy when he is wearing a uniform, marching in step, and singing a chorus, and the Nazi revolution has certainly known how to appeal to these instincts in his nature.

From **Failure of a Mission, Berlin 1937–39** by Neville Henderson, 1940.

The following report in the *Niederelbisches Tageblatt* (Lower Elb District Daily) describes the roll call of heads of local Party groups – political wardens – at the 1936 rally.

Source J

We have witnessed many great march-pasts and ceremonies. But none of them was more thrilling, and at the same time more inspiring, than yesterday's roll call of the 140,000 political wardens, who were addressed by the Führer at night, on the Zeppelin Meadow which floodlights had made bright as day. It is hardly possible to let words describe the mood and strength of this hour... A distant roar becomes stronger and comes even closer. The Führer is there! Reich Organisational Leader, Dr Ley, gives him the report on the men who are standing in parade formation. And then, a great surprise, one among many. As Adolf Hitler is entering the Zeppelin Field, 150 floodlights of the Air Force blaze up. They are distributed around the entire square, and cut into the night, erecting a canopy of light in the midst of darkness... The wide field resembles a powerful gothic cathedral made of light. Bluish-violet shine the floodlights, and between their cone of light hangs the dark cloth of night... Twenty-five thousand flags, that means 25,000 local, district, and factory groups all over the nation who are gathered around this flag. Every one of these flag bearers is ready to give his life in the defence of every one of these pieces of cloth. There is no one among them to whom this flag is not the final command and the highest obligation... A devotional hour of the Movement is being held here, is protected by a sea of light against the darkness outside.

A report from the **Niederelbisches Tageblatt**, (Lower Elb District Daily), 12 December, 1936.

The Great Auditorium

In 1934 the architect Albert Speer began to work on the design of the great auditorium in Nuremberg. A congress hall seating 60,000 and a stadium for 405,000 was planned. The stadium was designed to enclose an area of over 11,100,000 cubic yards (the Olympic Stadium in Berlin, built in 1936, had only a volume of 9,886,800 cubic yards). In order to reflect the grandeur of the Third Reich, the buildings were to be built from marble and granite. Torchlights, floodlights and even powerful anti-aircraft searchlights were used to illuminate the stadium at night. The cornerstone of the stadium was laid during the 1937 Nuremberg Rally.

In the extract below, Albert Speer describes the extent of his plans for the great auditorium:

▲
Albert Speer, Hitler's architect.

Source K

At the Southern end of the complex was the Marchfield; the name was intended not only as a reference to the war god Mars, but also to the month in which Hitler introduced conscription. Within this enormous tract, an area of 3,400 by 2,300 feet was set aside, where the army could practise minor manoeuvres. Stands 48-feet high were to surround the entire area, providing seats for 160,000 spectators. Twenty-four towers over 300-feet in height were to punctuate these stands: in the middle was a platform for guests of honour, which was to be crowned by a sculpture of a woman. In AD 64, Nero erected on the Capitol (in Rome) a colossal figure 119-feet high. The Statue of Liberty in New York is 152-feet high; our statue was to be 46 feet higher.

contd.

The stadium was to be by far the largest structure of the tract and one of the hugest in history. Calculations showed that in order to hold the required number of spectators the stands would have to be over 300-feet high. An oval would really have been out of the question; the resultant bowl would not only have intensified heat, but produced psychological discomfort. I therefore turned my thoughts to the Athenian horseshoe shape.

From **Inside the Third Reich** by Albert Speer, 1970.

In February 1939, Hitler, in a speech to construction workers, attempted to justify the enormous cost (estimated at £250,000,000,000) involved in constructing a huge stadium in Nuremberg:

Source L

Why always the biggest? I do this to restore to each individual German his self-respect. In a hundred areas I want to say to the individual: We are not inferior; on the contrary, we are the complete equals of every nation.

Hitler also viewed the construction of a giant stadium as a future memorial to Nazi achievement, which would be preserved for generations to come, just like the ruins of ancient Rome in Italy and ancient Greece in Athens.

Source M

Hitler liked to say that the purpose of his building was to transmit his time and its spirit to posterity (future generations). Ultimately, all that remained to remind men of the great epochs (periods) of history was their monumental architecture, he would philosophise. ...

What remained of the emperors of Rome? What would still bear witness to them today, if their buildings had not survived? Periods of weakness are bound to occur in the history of nations, he argued; but at their lowest ebb, their architecture will speak to them of former glory. Today, for example, Mussolini could point to the buildings of the Roman Empire as symbolising the heroic spirit of Rome.

From **Inside the Third Reich** by Albert Speer, 1970.

Work on the stadium continued during the war, although at a slower pace due to a lack of workers and raw materials. In 1942 the giant construction cranes in Nuremberg were removed and transferred to Auschwitz concentration camp in Poland. A company called IG Farben was building a massive chemical plant there with slave labour. The unfinished stadium remained as a derelict site and a reminder of the excesses of the Nazi state for years after the war had ended.

Nuremberg Trials

Following the destruction of the Third Reich during World War II, an international military tribunal sat in Nuremberg from November 1945 to September 1946, to try major Nazi figures for war crimes. Nuremberg was chosen as the location for the trials, mainly because it had been the venue for the great Nazi Party rallies. The Allies hoped that the Nuremberg Trials would bring to a close one of the most bloodthirsty and destructive periods of German history. Albert Speer was sentenced to 20 years in prison at the end of the Nuremberg Trials in September 1946.

2. Film

Goebbels took a close interest in the German film industry. Every film screened in Germany had to be approved by his Reich Chamber of Culture. Films that were not compatible with Nazi views were banned. Examples of films banned include MGM's *PrizeFighter and the Lady*, because it starred Jewish boxer Max Baer, and *Tarzan and his Mate*, for displaying 'incorrect attitudes'.

In April 1933 Goebbels introduced the **Arierparagraph** (Aryan clause) which banned Jews from the film industry. As a result of these restrictions, many leading German film producers and actors left Germany.

Key Personality: Leni Riefenstahl

Although German films continued to be produced in Nazi Germany, little of lasting value emerged, with the exception of the films produced by Leni Riefenstahl. The first internationally-acclaimed female director, she never escaped the shadow of her role in monumental Nazi propaganda films. Her first film, **Sieg des Glaubens (Victory of Faith)** was made in 1933 at Goebbels' request. Riefenstahl found it extremely difficult to work with Goebbels. She suffered a nervous breakdown as a result of his constant meddling during the production of the film.

▲ Leni Riefenstahl (1902–2003), film director, making the film **Day of Freedom** in 1935.

In 1934 Riefenstahl was persuaded by Hitler to return to work for the Nazi Party. She went on to direct two of arguably the greatest documentaries ever made: **Triumph of the Will** (1934), which celebrated the Nazis coming to power, and **Olympia**, a record of the Olympic Games held in Berlin in 1936. Despite the support of Hitler, her relations with the Nazi hierarchy remained tense.

Albert Speer, Hitler's architect and confidant recalls:

As the only woman involved officially in the proceedings, she had frequent conflicts with the Party organisation, which was soon up in arms against her. The Nazis were by tradition anti-feminist and could hardly brook this self-assured woman, the more so since she knew how to bend this men's world to her purposes. Intrigues (plots) *were launched and slanderous* (insulting) *stories carried to Hess* (Rudolf Hess, Hitler's Deputy). *But after the first Party rally film, which convinced even the doubters of her skill as a director, these attacks ceased.*

From **Inside the Third Reich** by Albert Speer, 1970.

The centrepiece of Leni Riefenstahl's brilliant film of the 1934 Nuremberg Rally, *Triumph of the Will,* was a tribute to the soldiers of World War I, in which Hitler, like a priest, marched up the aisle, with thousands of faithful Nazi supporters standing silently to attention on both sides. The soundtrack falls silent as he lays a wreath on the tomb of the unknown soldier. In the next scene, we see Hitler preaching from a pulpit, flanked by swastika flags against a cloudless sky.

Her second great documentary, *Olympia,* was released in two parts: *Fest der Völker* (Festival of the Nations) and *Fest der Schönheit* (Festival of Beauty).

Following World War II, Riefenstahl was jailed for a brief time as she awaited trial for her role in the Nazi propaganda machine. Having been arrested in Tyrol in Austria in 1945, she was brought to a US Army base at Dachau in Germany, where she was shown photographs from concentration camps. She strongly denied that she had used gypsies from the Maxglan concentration camp as extras for her film *Tiefland* (Lowland) which she filmed in 1940. The charge was never proven and Riefenstahl was released. Although it was eventually accepted that she had never been a member of the Nazi Party, she was considered by many to be a supporter, and she found herself excluded from the film industry for almost 20 years after the war.

She died on 09 September, 2003, at the age of 101 in the Bavarian lakeside town of Pöcking.

Art, creation, is my life and I was deprived of it. My life became a tissue of rumours and accusations through which I had to beat a path. For 20 years they deprived me of my creation, everything was reduced to nothingness. I was dead.
Leni Riefenstahl.

3. The Press and Radio

Newspaper editors in Berlin had to attend daily briefings at the Propaganda Ministry, where they were told what they could or could not print. The Reich Press Law of October 1934 stated that all newspaper editors 'must possess German citizenship, be of Aryan descent and not married to a Jew'. Newspapers which failed to toe the Nazi line were shut down. Among those closed down were well-known daily papers such as the *Berliner Tageblatt* (Berlin Journal).

Goebbels viewed radio broadcasting as a major cog in his propaganda machine. In 1933, at a radio exhibition, he introduced the **'People's Receiver'** (a cheap radio receiver). Its low price was to enable the broad masses to become radio listeners.

During World War II Goebbels developed a broadcasting service directed against Germany's enemies. His most famous broadcaster was William Joyce, or 'Lord Haw-Haw' as he was known in England (p. 177).

An Historian's View on the Nazi State

There was much that impressed, puzzled and troubled a foreign observer about the new Germany. The overwhelming majority of Germans did not seem to mind that their personal freedom had been taken away, or that their life and work had become more regimented to a degree never before experienced even by a people accustomed for generations to a great deal of regimentation.

In the background to be sure, there lurked the terror of the Gestapo and the fear of the concentration camp for those who got out of line. Yet the Nazi terror in the early years affected the lives of few Germans and a newly arrived observer was somewhat surprised to see that people of this country did not seem to feel that they were being held down by a brutal dictatorship. On the contrary, they supported it with genuine enthusiasm. Somehow it imbued them with (gave them) *a new hope and a new confidence and an astonishing faith in the future of their country.*

From **The Rise and Fall of the Third Reich: A History of Nazi Germany** by William L Shirer, 1991.

Ordinary Level

Study the cartoon and answer the questions below. This cartoon was published in 1936 and is commenting on the fact that the Nazi leadership did not possess many of the traits attributed to the 'Aryan Race'.

1. According to the cartoon, what physical traits should a member of the 'Aryan Race' possess?

2. How does the cartoonist represent the teacher?

3. According to the cartoon, who is the greatest educator of the German people?

4. Which position did Goebbels hold in the Nazi Party?

5. 'It is unlikely that this cartoon would be published in Germany.' Do you agree? Give reasons for your answer.

Write a short account of one of the following:

1. Propaganda in Nazi Germany.

2. Leni Riefenstahl

3. The Nuremberg Rallies.

Higher Level

1. 'During the period 1933–39 Hitler and the Nazis turned Germany into a one-party totalitarian state.' Discuss.

2. 'The Nazi regime was sustained through the clever use of an effective propaganda machine.' Discuss.

Case Study Questions: 'The Nuremberg Rallies'

Study Sources A–M on pages 34 to 40 and answer the following questions.

Comprehension

1. In Source A, according to Hitler, what were the benefits of holding mass meetings?

2. Describe how Hitler attempted to reassure the German Army of his support in his speech to the Nuremberg Rally in 1933. (Source B)

3. According to Provincial Governor Adolf Wagner (Source C), how long would the Nazi regime last?

4. How does Hitler demonstrate his hatred of the Jews in Source D?

5. According to Hitler, what effect would the spread of communism have on Western Europe? (Source E)

6. How does Herman Goering view the state of Czechoslovakia? (Source F)

7. Read the eyewitness accounts of the Nuremberg rallies. (Sources H, I, J and K.) Briefly describe the reception that Hitler received at these rallies.

8. According to the report in the *Niederelbisches Tageblatt*, how many district groups attended the Nuremberg Rally in 1936? (Source J)

9. Describe the use of flags and lighting at the Nuremberg Rallies as outlined in Sources H, I and J.

10. In Henderson's view (Source I), what aspect of the German character did the Nazi revolution take advantage of in organising rallies such as those staged at Nuremberg?

11. What evidence is there in Source K to suggest that no expense was to be spared in the construction of a great stadium at Nuremberg?

12. What evidence is there in Source K to suggest that Albert Speer was influenced by the architecture of Ancient Rome and Greece in his design of a stadium at Nuremberg?

13. How does Hitler attempt to justify the cost of building such a giant stadium at Nuremberg? (Source L)

14. According to Hitler in Source M, what benefit would the buildings at Nuremberg have for future generations of Germans?

Comparison

1. To what extent do Hitler (Source A) and Sir Neville Henderson (Source I) agree regarding the usefulness of mass meetings?

2. Source H was written by a British citizen living in Germany, while Source J is a report from a daily German newspaper. Which of the two documents do you consider to be the more reliable? Give reasons for your answer.

3. To what extent do the eyewitnesses in Sources H, I and J agree that the Nuremberg Rally was indeed a great event?

4. How does the Nuremberg Rally compare to the Russian Ballet in St Petersburg as outlined in Source I?

5. Do you consider the eyewitness accounts of British citizens in Sources H and I to be less favourable to the Nuremberg Rally than that reported in a German newspaper in Source J? Explain your answer.

Criticism

1. Why might the newspaper report in Source J not be considered to be a fully reliable account of events? Explain your answer.

2. Can you detect any example of bias or propaganda in Source J?

3. Refer to examples of racism, bias and propaganda which are displayed in sources D E and F.

4. Albert Speer wrote Source M while serving a 20-year prison sentence in Spandau prison in Berlin after World War II. Do you consider his account to be a fair and accurate description? Explain your answer.

5. From the evidence in the eyewitness accounts (Sources G, H, I and J) do you consider the Nuremberg Rallies to be just an exercise in Nazi propaganda, or did they serve another purpose? Explain your answer.

Contextualisation

1. What was the origin of the Nuremberg Rallies?

2. What effect did the Nuremberg Laws, announced at the 1935 rally, have on Germany's Jewish population?

3. To what extent can we trace the development of both internal and foreign Nazi policy by studying extracts from speeches delivered at the Nuremberg Rallies?

4. Apart from the Nuremberg Rallies, describe one other method of propaganda used by the Nazi Party.

5. Why did the Allies consider Nuremberg to be a suitable venue to try Nazi war criminals at the end of World War II?

6. Do you agree with their choice of venue? Explain your answer.

The Communist State: Lenin in Power

Introduction

In the early years of the twentieth century, Russia was a backward country, ruled by an autocratic leader, Tsar Nicholas II. His family, the Romanovs, had ruled Russia for over 300 years. Although a Russian Parliament *(Duma)* had existed since 1905, it had no real power.

When World War I broke out in 1914, there was genuine support for the Tsar as a wave of patriotism (love of country) swept across Russia. However, the Tsar's decision in 1915 to take personal command of the Russian armed forces proved to be a major mistake.

In effect, he tied the fate of Romanov rule in Russia to the success or failure of the Russian Army in the war. Although the Russians fought bravely, they were poorly equipped, sometimes carrying only wooden farm tools into battle. As Russian casualties began to mount, the popularity of the Tsar and his family slumped, leading to their overthrow by a popular revolution in February 1917.

The Tsarist Regime was replaced by a Provisional Government, which intended to hold office until an election could be held. The Provisional Government's decision to continue in the war, along with its failure to introduce long-awaited land reform, caused it to become increasingly unpopular. It too was overthrown by a revolution in October 1917, leading to the rise to power of Lenin* and the establishment of the first Communist country in the world.

> **Autocrat:**
>
> A person who has total power.

Key Personality: Lenin

Vladimir Ilyich Ulyanov (Lenin) was born in 1870 in Simbrisk, Russia to middle-class parents. Inspired by his elder brother, who was executed in 1887 for an assassination attempt on Tsar Alexander III, Lenin became deeply involved in underground revolutionary activity. He graduated from St Petersburg University with a law degree in 1893. From 1897 to 1900 Lenin was exiled to Siberia, where he wrote his first major publication, *The Development of Capitalism in Russia.* Following his release in 1900, he emigrated to Switzerland in central Europe, where he founded and edited the Socialist newspaper *Iskra* (Spark).

In 1902 Lenin published his most important treatise, *What is to be Done?*, outlining his views on how the socialist workers revolution should happen. He argued that a small, dedicated élite should assume the leadership of the proletariat (working class) and guide them towards a Socialist revolution.

Other socialists believed that a middle-class revolution must take place in Russia before a successful working-class revolution could happen.

Lenin disagreed with this view – matters came to a head at the Congress of the Social Democratic Party in London in 1903. The Party split into Bolsheviks (majority) and Mensheviks (minority). Lenin became the leader of the Bolsheviks.

Lenin returned briefly to Russia in 1905. He was forced by the authorities to emigrate again, however, when the 1905 Revolution against the Tsarist regime failed to introduce any meaningful political reforms. He continued to develop and publish his political theories from abroad. In *Imperialism, the Highest Stage of Capitalism* (1916), Lenin blamed imperialism for the outbreak of war. In Europe, imperialism involved the possession of African and Asian colonies. His constant urgings for an end to the war persuaded the Germans to organise his return to Russia in April 1917. They hoped that he would pull Russia out of the war.

Lenin (1870–1924) in Moscow addressing supporters on the first anniversary of the Russian Revolution of 1917.

His *April Theses* called for an end to the war and the transfer of land to the peasants and all power to the soviets (workers' committees). These arguments struck a chord with the masses. Following a failed *coup* in July 1917, Lenin was forced into exile once more. He went to Finland, where he wrote *State and Revolution,* in which he justified the notion of a party dictatorship in Russia. A party dictatorship differed from a dictatorship in that the party would rule, and not just one individual.

Lenin returned to Russia in October 1917 and began a successful revolution. During the years 1917–24 Lenin and the Bolsheviks had to defend their revolution against attacks from inside and outside of Soviet Russia. During those years they also laid the basis for the development of the Union of Soviet Socialist Republics (USSR or Soviet Union), the world's first communist state.

Key Concept: Communism

Communism is the political doctrine developed by nineteenth-century political writers Karl Marx and Friedrich Engels. A communist society is one in which all economic activity is directed by the community instead of the individual. All means of production and wealth should be held in common. There is no private ownership. Land, factories, banks, etc. are held by the state for the common good of the people.

The term can also be used to describe political parties, such as the Russian Communist Party, which adopted Marx's theories and attempted to put them into practice in their own countries.

The Communist Dictatorship

Lenin's aim was to create in Russia a new form of political organisation. Democracy was to be replaced by the 'dictatorship of the proletariat (working class)'.

Following Lenin's successful Bolshevik Revolution in October 1917, he set about forming a government. On 15 November, 1917, elections were held for a new Constituent Assembly (Parliament). Of the 707 deputies elected, 380 were members of the Socialist Revolutionaries and 175 were Bolsheviks. Unlike the Bolshevik Party, where support came mainly from industrial towns and cities, the Socialist Revolutionaries were largely a rural party, supported by peasant farmers. Lenin refused to accept the result and had the assembly dissolved on 06 January, 1918. A few days later the Congress of Soviets (representatives of city and village soviets) was declared to be the highest organ of power in Russia.

> **Counter-revolutionary:** Someone who is opposed to a previous revolution.

The Constitution

In July 1918 a new constitution was agreed. It established Russia as a Soviet Federal Socialist Republic. Power was vested in the All-Russian Congress of Soviets. This Congress elected an Executive Committee of about 200 members, which in turn appointed the Council of People's Commissars (Government Ministers). The Council was dominated by the Bolshevik Party, which was now known as the Communist Party, giving them control over Russia.

From this point on there was to be only one party, the Communist Party. All other parties were considered to be counter-revolutionary. The real political power lay with the Politburo, the central committee of the Communist Party.

The Cheka

The first Soviet state security organisation, the *Vecheka* (stands for All-Russian Extraordinary Commission for Combating Counter-revolution and Sabotage), more commonly known as the *Cheka*, was created in December 1917. This new secret police force was under the control of Felix Dzerzhinsky. The *Cheka's* task was to root out and destroy all critics of the Communist Party. Counter-revolutionaries, newspaper editors and liberals all suffered at the hands of the *Cheka*. The old restrictions on people's lives that existed during the Tsarist regime continued, and many more were introduced. Between 1918 and 1922 over 140,000 people were executed by the *Cheka* in what became known as the 'Red Terror'.

▲ Felix Dzerzhinsky (1877–1926), leader of the Cheka Secret Police.

Lenin's Reforms

In the early years of Communist rule, Lenin issued a series of reforming decrees (laws) in an effort to transform Russia into a Communist society:

- An eight-hour day was introduced for all industrial workers. Workers elected factory committees that were given far-reaching power.

- Lenin's 'Decree on Land' abolished private ownership of land. Land was redistributed without compensation.

- Women were given the vote and gender equality was guaranteed.

- Universal free education was introduced and a major campaign was launched to combat adult illiteracy.

- All ranks and titles were abolished.

- Civil marriages became compulsory.

Despite these reforms, which brought about a greater distribution of wealth in Russia, opposition to Communist rule continued to grow.

▲
Trotsky (left) beside an armoured train. His skilful leadership of the Red Army ensured victory for the Communists in the Russian Civil War of 1918–20.

Opposition to Communist Rule

The seizure of power by the Communists, and their refusal to accept the result of the 1917 election, led to the rise of opposition to the Communist dictatorship within Russia. During the years 1918–20 Russia drifted into a bitter civil war. The 'White Russians', which included members of the Socialist Revolutionaries, liberals, nationalist groups (which aimed to break away from Russia), and ex-officers of the Tsarist Army, sought to overthrow the Communist Party. However, there was much division, friction and lack of co-ordination among the leaders of the Whites. They never fought as a unit, as each leader had his own agenda. Some supported the restoration of the Tsar, while others wanted the return of the Constituent Assembly.

On the other hand, the 'Red Army' (Government forces) was united under the skilful leadership of Leon Trotsky. By mid-1920 its numbers had swelled to 3.5 million. Trotsky's tactical genius greatly contributed to their success in the Civil War at the end of 1920.

Economic Difficulties

By 1921 Russia was on the verge of economic collapse, partly because of the Civil War, but also because of Lenin's policy of **'War Communism'**. War Communism is a term used to describe emergency economic measures introduced by Lenin during the Civil War (p. 159). In rural areas all grain had to be given to the state. Government forces went into villages seizing crops and livestock, sometimes leaving very little behind for the peasant's own needs. These measures proved to be most unpopular and led to peasants growing less and hiding their crops. Attempts by the Red Army and the *Cheka* to seize food by force met with stiff resistance. The result was famine, which was made worse by a severe drought during 1920–21. People fled from the countryside in search of food in the cities. There were widespread disturbances, the most serious of which took place at the Kronstadt naval base in March 1921.

Note!

The Russian economy under Lenin's rule will be dealt with in greater detail in Chapter 11.

The Kronstadt Revolt, March 1921

The sailors at the naval base at Kronstadt had been among the greatest supporters of the 1917 Revolution. Kronstadt was a naval fortress on an island in the Gulf of Finland. Traditionally, it had served as the base for some of the Russian Fleet to guard the approaches to the city of St Petersburg. However, by 1921 the sailors had grown tired of the ruthlessness of the Communist dictatorship. In March 1921 they organised one of the most effective demonstrations against Communist rule. They demanded an end to the Communist Party dictatorship. They wanted free elections, freedom of speech and the right of all socialist parties to participate in government. In the extract below, which is taken from a pamphlet called 'What Are We Fighting For?' published by the Kronstadt Temporary Revolutionary Committee, 08 March, 1921, some of their grievances are presented:

The sickle and hammer, the symbols of the Communist Party.

> *The glorious symbols of the workers and peasants – the sickle and hammer – have actually been replaced by the communist authorities with bayonet and the barbed window for the sake of preserving the calm, carefree life of the new bureaucracy of Communist commissars and officials.*
>
> *To the protest of the peasants, expressed in spontaneous* (unplanned) *uprisings, and of workers, who are compelled to strike by the circumstances of their life, they answer with mass executions and bloodthirstiness, in which they are not surpassed by the Tsarist generals.*
>
> *In this sea of blood the Communists are drowning all the great and glowing pledges* (promises) *and slogans of labour's revolution.*
>
> *There can be no middle ground. Victory or death!*

On 15 March, 1921, Trotsky issued a warning to the sailors and workers at Kronstadt, demanding that they end their revolt immediately. When they failed to respond, the Red Army launched an assault on the base and the rising was crushed with much bloodshed. In the extract below, a Red Army general describes how the sailors fought to the bitter end:

The sailors fought like wild beasts. I cannot understand where they found the might for such rage. Each house where they were located had to be taken by storm. An entire company fought for an hour to capture one house and when the house was captured it was found to contain only two or three soldiers at a machine-gun.

The Kronstadt Revolt served as a warning to Lenin. He realised that it was time to compromise, claiming that Kronstadt 'was the flash which lit up reality better than anything else'. Lenin therefore abandoned War Communism and introduced the New Economic Policy (NEP p. 160), through which compulsory seizing of grain ended. Peasants had to pay a tax on foodstuffs, but were allowed to sell their surplus grain.

Repression Continues

Lenin's timely retreat on the economic front was not mirrored on the political side. The NEP was accompanied by increased discipline within the Party. At the Tenth Party Congress in March 1921, Lenin announced an end to factionalism (division) within the Communist Party. Political debate within the party was to end:

We have allowed ourselves the luxury of discussions and disputes. Discussion means disputes; disputes mean discord; discord means that the Communists have become weak.

Following the Tenth Party Congress, censorship was tightened and the number of political prison camps increased from 84 in 1920 to 315 by 1923.

The Orthodox Church

The Russian Orthodox Church came under severe attack during Lenin's leadership. In 1921, the teaching of religion to anyone under 18 was banned. The *Komsomol* (Communist Youth Movement), founded in 1918, issued pamphlets encouraging atheism (non-belief). Religious services were banned. Churches were ransacked and looted and later turned into museums. Church lands were taken over by the state and many leaders of the Orthodox Church, including the Head of the Russian Orthodox Church, Patriarch Tikhon, were jailed.

Zhenotdel (Women's Bureau)

Zhenotdel, the Communist Party's Women's Bureau, was established in 1920 to encourage women to play a more active part in both the political and economic life of the country. Aleksandra Kollontai, a close personal friend of Lenin, became its first director. Their inspectors visited factories to make sure that laws intended to protect women's rights were being enforced. Divorce was made easier and contraception and abortion became freely available. Marriage, which was considered to be a middle-class institution, was not encouraged.

The Soviet Constitution, 1923

In 1923 a new constitution established the Union of Soviet Socialist Republics (**USSR** or Soviet Union). It was a federal system composed of four Republics: Russia (Russian Soviet Federal Socialist Republic), Byelorussia, Transcaucasia and the Ukraine. Although each Republic had a degree of self-government, the Communist Party and the All-Union Congress of Soviets linked them all to Moscow.

Lenin's Last Testament

In July 1918, Dora Kaplan, a member of the Socialist Revolutionary Party, shot Lenin. Although he survived the attack, which left two bullets lodged in his body, he never fully recovered. In 1922 he suffered a stroke, which ended his day-to-day participation in Government.

Fearing that the end was near, in December 1923 Lenin wrote his 'Last Testament', in which he reflected on his achievements and outlined his thoughts on the future of the Soviet Union. He feared for the future, believing that a growing bureaucracy (civil service) was draining the old revolutionary spirit. He seemed to have little confidence in his Government Ministers' ability to succeed him. He criticised each major figure (See Document Question p. 55). In the 'Testament' Grigori Zinoviev and Lev Kamenev were both condemned for their opposition to the plans for the October Revolution in 1917. Nikolai Bukharin was considered to be too young and too academic. Lenin admired Trotsky's ability as an organiser, but regarded him as arrogant, self-righteous and incapable of working with others.

However, his most severe criticism was levelled at the General Secretary of the Communist Party, Josef

▲
Lenin and Stalin. This picture was used by Stalin to show his close friendship with Lenin. In fact, the photograph is not real.

Stalin* (Chapter 5), whom he believed to be crude and over-interested in power. Lenin recommended that Stalin be removed from his post.

The Death of Lenin

Lenin died on 21 January, 1924. As a sign of respect, his body was embalmed (preserved) and placed in a mausoleum in Red Square. Under Lenin's able leadership, the Bolsheviks strengthened their power and remained in control during difficult times. Although the Communist state was brutal, Lenin's Government did introduce many worthwhile improvements. Unemployment was eliminated, factory conditions improved and education was provided for all children. Despite his many theories and writings, Lenin was essentially a pragmatist (realist) who was willing to adapt socialist ideas to suit circumstances in Russia.

Two Views on Lenin

Activity

Do you agree with either of these viewpoints? Why?

Their (Russian people) *worst misfortune was his birth and their next worst was his death.*   Winston Churchill*, British politician, future Prime Minister.

Lenin did more than any other political leader to change the face of the twentieth-century world. The creation of Soviet Russia and its survival were due to him. He was a very great man and even, despite his faults, a very good man.   A.J.P. Taylor, historian.

? Questions

Ordinary Level

Write a short account on Lenin's involvement in Russian affairs using two of the following headings:

1. Lenin's Reforms.

2. The Kronstadt Revolt, 1921.

3. Lenin's 'Testament'.

Higher Level

1. Discuss Lenin's management of Russian affairs during the period 1920–24.

2. 'By the time of his death in 1924, Lenin had made considerable progress in transforming Russia into a socialist state.' Discuss.

Document Question
Higher and Ordinary Level

Read the document below, taken from Lenin's 'Last Testament' and answer the questions that follow:

Comrade Stalin, having become General Secretary, has concentrated an enormous power in his hands; and I am not sure that he always knows how to use that power with sufficient caution. On the other hand, Comrade Trotsky is distinguished not only by his exceptional abilities – personally he is, to be sure, the most able man in the present Central Committee – but also by his too far-reaching self-confidence and a disposition (character) *to be too much attracted by the purely administrative side of affairs.*

These qualities of the two most able leaders of the present Central Committee might, quite innocently, lead to a split; if our Party does not take measures to prevent it, a split might arise unexpectedly. I will not characterise the other members of the Central Committee as to their personal qualities. I will only remind you that the October episode of Zinoviev and Kamenev was not, of course, accidental, but that it ought as little be used against them personally as the non-Bolshevism of Trotsky.

Stalin is too rude, and this fault, entirely supportable in relations amongst us Communists, becomes insupportable in the office of General Secretary. Therefore, I propose to the comrades to find a way to remove Stalin from that position and to appoint to it another man who in all respects differs from Stalin only in superiority, namely more patient, more loyal, more polite and more attentive to comrades, less capricious (changeable).

1. According to Lenin, how has Stalin abused his position of power since becoming General Secretary of the Party?

2. What are Trotsky's 'exceptional abilities'?

3. What fears does Lenin express about the future leadership of the Party?

4. What course of action does Lenin recommend in relation to Stalin's role in the Party?

5 The Stalinist State

Key Personality: Stalin

Stalin was born Iosif (Joseph) Vissarionovich Dzhugashvili, in Georgia in 1879. He was one of the few Bolsheviks who could claim to have emerged from a truly working-class background. His father was a shoemaker. His mother wished for him to become a priest and in 1894 he entered a seminary in Tiflis. Stalin was expelled from this school in 1899 for spreading Marxist theories (ideas put forward by Karl Marx). In 1904 he became an active member of the Bolshevik Party, adopting the code name 'Stalin' (man of steel). He organised bank robberies and gambling dens to boost Party funds. His actions soon brought him to the attention of Lenin and in 1912 he became a member of the Central Committee of the Party.

Stalin only played a small role in the 1917 Revolution, but he was later to distinguish himself as a military leader during the Russian Civil War. He led the defence of Tsaritsyn, which was later renamed Stalingrad in his honour.

During the early years of the Bolshevik Government, Stalin was put in charge of some

Stalin (1879–1953), the Soviet dictator.

of the more ordinary tasks, earning him the nickname 'The Great Blur'. However, by 1922 he emerged as the General Secretary of the Party. Stalin used this appointment to place loyal followers in key Government positions. He did this in anticipation of a takeover bid on the death of Lenin. He created a Party bureaucracy which was totally loyal to him.

Lenin became increasingly alarmed at Stalin's ruthless ambition, and in his 'Testament' of 1923 he suggested that he should be removed (p. 55).

However, Lenin failed to make a clear choice for the leadership in his 'Testament'. Although he praises Trotsky's ability as an organiser, he also recognises his shortcomings. Trotsky's gruff manner and self-righteousness made it difficult for others to work with him.

Power Struggle

When Lenin died in January 1924 it was unclear who would be his successor. A number of factors gave Stalin the advantage. Trotsky had few friends in the Communist Party. He had been a late convert as he had been a member of the Mensheviks until 1917, and was therefore distrusted. Trotsky believed in the theory of a 'Permanent Revolution', and that the Soviet Union should encourage communist revolts in capitalist countries. Stalin pointed out that such revolts had little support and that they had already failed in Germany and Hungary in 1919. This type of action, he feared, could also lead to the Soviet Union's involvement in foreign wars, for which they were not prepared. On the other hand, Stalin believed in **'Socialism in One Country'**. The Soviet Union had to strengthen its power and become an industrial giant before it could begin a communist crusade abroad. Stalin's policy was much more popular with the Russian people, who were weary of war and revolution.

Trotsky's arrogance made him many enemies and other leading Bolsheviks believed that he would form a dictatorship if he came to power. For that reason, a triumvirate, or collective leadership, of Stalin, Kamenev and Zinoviev emerged. Trotsky was stripped of his leadership of the Red Army in 1925, exiled to Alma Ata in Central Asia in 1928 and expelled from the Soviet Union altogether a year later. He eventually settled in Mexico, where a Stalinist agent murdered him in 1940.

With Trotsky sidelined, Stalin now turned on Zinoviev and Kamenev. His policy was to 'divide and conquer'. Stalin discredited each of them in turn and by 1928 he had outwitted all his rivals and become the undisputed leader of the Soviet Union.

Stalin in Power

A Totalitarian State

From 1928 onwards Stalin exercised increasing control over the Soviet Union. The **NKVD** (stands for 'People's Commisariat for Interior Affairs' or Internal Affairs Commission) merged with the *Cheka* in 1934 to become the new all-union NKVD, which acted as a secret police force. Its role was to seek out and destroy any opposition to Stalin. The NKVD operated beyond the law, sending millions of people to labour camps *(gulags)*. Up to two million died from hardship, hunger and disease in these camps.

The Army was brought under close Party control. Military commanders worked alongside Communist Party political advisors. Strict censorship was imposed on the media. Although every adult had the right to vote, only members of the Communist Party could stand for election. Unlike Lenin's regime, where a certain level of debate within the ranks of the Communist Party was tolerated, the Stalinist state increasingly became dominated by one man – Stalin. From 1928 until his death in 1953 he imposed his will on the citizens of the Soviet Union.

Note!

Stalin's economic policies will be dealt with in Chapter 11.

Case Study: The Show Trials, 1936–38

At first, the repression was directed against those outside the Party, but it was soon to extend to those within the Communist Party whom Stalin distrusted or saw as potential rivals to his leadership. During the years 1934–38 Stalin purged (removed) from positions of power within the Soviet Union anyone he suspected of being disloyal. These purges reached their climax in a series of 'Show Trials' during the years 1936–38. Show Trials are trials held by totalitarian governments for political reasons. They are not designed to find out the truth, but rather to fool the public and foreign observers into believing that those condemned as enemies of the state are guilty.

The Great Purges

Although there had been purges of the Bolshevik Party in the 1920s, the 'Great Purges' of the 1930s were much more severe.

The reasons for the purges were as follows:

1. To eliminate potential opponents of Stalin's regime, such as those who supported Trotsky or the 'Old Bolsheviks' of Lenin's rule.

2. Stalin's state of mind; he suffered from paranoia (unfounded fear) and imagined that there were plots to overthrow him. His daughter, Alliluyeva, hinted at this:

Source A

As he'd got older my father had begun feeling lonely. He was so isolated from everyone that he seemed to be living in a vacuum. He hadn't a soul he could talk to. It was the system of which he himself was the prisoner and in which he was stifling from emptiness and lack of human companionship.

From **Twenty Letters to a Friend** by Svetlana Alliluyeva, 1968.

Nikolai Bukharin, a leading theorist and editor of the Communist newspaper *Izvestia* (News) during the years 1934–36, believed that Stalin's jealousy played a major part in his decision to purge senior members of the Communist Party. Bukharin had supported Stalin, rather than Trotsky, to be Lenin's successor. However, Bukharin had fallen out of favour by 1929 and he became a victim of Stalin's Show Trials in 1938.

Source B

Stalin is unhappy at not being able to convince everyone, himself included, that he is greater than everyone else. If someone speaks better than he does, that man is for it! Stalin will not let him live, because that man is a constant reminder that he, Stalin, is not the first and best. He is a narrow-minded, malicious (cruel) man – no, not a man, but a devil.

Bukharin speaking in Paris in 1936.

Stalin used the murder of the very popular leader of the Leningrad Soviet, Sergei Kirov, in 1934 as an excuse to unleash his reign of terror. Following Kirov's death, Stalin introduced a series of purges by issuing the following directive:

Source C

I. *Investigative agencies are directed to speed up the case of those accused of the preparation or execution of acts of terror;*

II. *Judicial organs are directed not to hold up the execution of death sentences pertaining to crimes of this category in order to consider the possibility of pardon because the Presidium of the Central Executive Committee USSR does not consider as possible the receiving of petitions of this sort;*

III. *The organs of the Commissariat of Internal Affairs are directed to execute the death sentences against criminals of the above-mentioned category immediately after the passage of sentences.*

Bukharin noticed a hardening of political attitudes following the death of Kirov:

Source D

Kirov stood for the idea of abolition of the terror, both in general and inside the Party. Kirov's line of thought ran as follows: as the economic situation continued to improve, the broad masses of the population would become more and more reconciled to the Government; the number of 'internal foes (enemies)' would diminish. It was now the task of the Party to rally those forces which would support it in the new phase of economic development, and thus to broaden the foundation upon which Soviet power was based.

After Kirov's assassination, the trend was in quite the opposite direction: not toward reconciliation inside the Party, but toward intensification of the terror inside the Party to its logical conclusion, to the stage of physical extermination of all those whose Party past might make them opponents of Stalin or aspirants to his power (those who want to take his power). Today, I have not the slightest doubt that it was at that very period, between the murder of Kirov and the second Kamenev Trial, that Stalin made his decision and

contd.

mapped out his plan of 'reforms'. The determining reason for Stalin's decision was his realisation, arrived at on the basis of reports and information reaching him, that the mood of the majority of the old Party workers was really one of bitterness and hostility toward him.

The conclusion he (Stalin) drew from all this was certainly daring: if the old Bolsheviks, the group constituting today the ruling caste (class) in this country, are unfit to perform this function, it is necessary to remove them from their posts, to create a new ruling caste.

Bukharin's words as in **Letter of an Old Bolshevik: The Key to the Moscow Trials,** by Menshevik historian Boris Nicolaevsky, 1938.

Purge of Party Members, 1934–36

Following the death of Lenin, Stalin announced an increase in the size of the Party. He filled the Party with his supporters. By 1934, when he was firmly in power, there was no longer the need for a large Party that was difficult to control. On 21 April the Central Committee of the Party issued a resolution detailing six categories of 'undesirable' members who should be purged from the party.

1. Enemies of Communism engaged in stirring up discord in the Party.

2. Hypocrites, who at heart wished to destroy Party policy.

3. Those who disregarded Party discipline.

4. Bourgeois (middle-class) degenerates.

5. The over-ambitious and the careerist.

6. Moral degenerates, such as drunkards and idlers.

The NKVD imprisoned or shot thousands of Party activists. By 1939, some 850,000 Party members had been purged in what became known as the 'Great Terror'.

Source E

Note!

Nadezhda Mandelstam (Source E) was the wife of Osip Mandelstam, a Russian poet and writer who was sent to a labour camp during the period of the purges. Osip Mandelstam died in captivity in 1938.

The principles and aims of mass terror have nothing in common with ordinary police work or with security. The only purpose of terror is intimidation. To plunge the whole country into a state of chronic fear, the number of victims must be raised to astronomical (huge) levels, and on every floor of every building there must always be several apartments from which the tenants have suddenly been taken away. The remaining inhabitants will be model citizens for the rest of their lives.

From **Hope Against Hope: A Memoir,** by Nadezhda Mandelstam, 1971.

The Show Trials

The most prominent members of the Party were condemned in a series of 'Show Trials', the first of which took place in August 1936. Nikolai Yezhov, the Commissioner for Internal Affairs or Head of the NKVD, purged the top members of the Party. Leading members of the Government and former colleagues of Lenin, essentially anyone who could be seen to be a potential threat to Stalin's leadership, were put on trial.

Of the many trials that took place, the following were the most important.

The Trial of the Sixteen, August 1936

In the 'Trial of the Sixteen', former prominent members of the Bolshevik Party, including Zinoviev and Kamenev, were charged with collaborating with foreign powers to overthrow Stalin. The accused all confessed to these unfounded charges of treason, and were subsequently shot in the cellars of Lubyanka prison in Moscow.

The interrogation of prisoners by the NKVD was often accompanied by physical torture or threats against the prisoner's family. These measures were designed to make the prisoner confess to made-up charges and to connect others with their 'treasonous' crimes. Zinoviev admitted during his trial:

Collaborating:
Passing information to the 'enemy'.

Interrogation:
Getting information from a person by asking questions in a formal, usually harsh way.

Treason:
Acting against the interests of king/queen or state.

Source F

My defective Bolshevism became transformed into anti-Bolshevism and through Trotskyism I arrived at Fascism.

Kamenev stated:

Is it an accident that alongside of myself and Zinoviev are sitting emissaries (representatives) *of foreign secret police departments, people with false passports, with dubious* (uncertain) *biographies and undoubted connections with the Gestapo? No, it is not an accident.*

▲
Andrei Vyshinsky pronouncing the death sentence at the end of the first of Stalin's Show Trials in 1936.

The Trial of the Seventeen, January 1937

Other leading members of the Communist Party, such as Yuri Pyatakov, Grigori Sokolnikov and Nikolai Muralov, suffered a similar fate during the 'Trial of the Seventeen'. The charges were much the same as in the previous trial. The defendants were accused of attempting to overthrow the Soviet system by carrying out acts of sabotage and of being agents of Leon Trotsky. Among the defendants was Karl Radek, Soviet Russia's leading political writer. The Chief Prosecutor, Andrei Vyshinsky, bullied the accused and concluded his case with a demand to 'Shoot them like mad dogs!'

No evidence that could be proven was produced at these trials. A hotel in Copenhagen, where some of the defendants had allegedly met Trotsky, had actually closed several years prior to the supposed meeting. Most of the defendants were condemned to death and executed. A few, such as Radek, were sentenced to long prison sentences from which none emerged alive.

Source G

An American cartoon depicting Stalin's 'Show Trials'.

The Secret Trial of Marshal Tukhachevsky and the Army Generals, June 1937

Between the second and the third Show Trial there occurred a secret purge of the General Staff of the Red Army. Stalin feared the power of the Red Army. He became convinced that it was plotting his downfall. On 11 June, 1937, it was announced that eight top Soviet military commanders, including Assistant War Commissar Marshal Tukhachevsky, had been found guilty by a military court and were sentenced to death. Stalin's distrust of Tukhachevsky seems to have been encouraged by the Nazis. They leaked false documents in the belief that Tukhachevsky's downfall would severely weaken the Russian Army. Many other high-ranking officers soon suffered a similar fate: three out of the five Marshals; 50 of the 57 Corps Commanders; 154 of the 186 Divisional Commanders.

Marshal Mikhail Tukhachevsky (1893–1937), top Soviet military commander, who had a secret trial in June 1937 and was executed with seven other Generals for treason.

The Red Army was severely damaged by these purges. Following the Finnish Government's refusal to agree to a revision of the country's borders with the Soviet Union, the Red Army attacked Finland. This Winter War with Finland of 1939–40 clearly revealed the lack of skill in the Red Army. It took 15 weeks of fierce fighting for Soviet forces to defeat a poorly-armed Finnish Army. The disastrous Soviet military reversals during the first two years of World War II can also be blamed to a certain degree on the destruction of the officer class of the Red Army. These officers were replaced with more junior and inexperienced commanders. Unlike the political leaders, all of the executed Soviet military leaders had their names cleared in the post-Stalinist era and the charges against them were declared to be entirely false.

The Trial of the Twenty-one, March 1938

The third and last Show Trial was the most sensational. Among its defendants were a group of the Soviet Union's highest-ranking politicians and officials: Nikolai Bukharin, a leading Bolshevik scholar; Aleksei Rykov, the Chairman of the Council of People's Commissars, and HG Yagoda, a former head of the secret police. Bukharin had opposed Stalin's policy of collectivisation[+] (p. 161), believing that working with the *Kulaks* (middle-class farmers), rather than killing them, would result in increased agricultural production.

Source H

> *The investigation has established that on the instruction of the intelligence services of foreign states hostile to the USSR the accused organised a conspiratorial group named the '[Anti-Soviet] Bloc of Rights and Trotskyites', the object of which was to overthrow the socialist state system existing in the USSR and to restore capitalism and the power of the bourgeoisie* (middle class) *in the USSR.*
>
> From the charges read out at the Trial of the Twenty-one

▲
Nikolai Bukharin (1888–1938), a leading Bolshevik scholar, was a victim of Stalin's last Show Trial in March 1938.

During the trial, Bukharin and his comrades were shown as double agents. Bukharin strongly denied the charges and attempted to challenge the state prosecutor, Vyshinsky. Bukharin wrote to his wife shortly before his death:

Source I

> *I feel my helplessness before a hellish machine which has acquired gigantic power, and which uses the Cheka's former authority to cater to Stalin's morbid suspiciousness. Any member of the Central Committee, or any member of the Party, can be rubbed out, or turned into a traitor or a terrorist.*

Rykov was the first to break down and plead guilty. He then proceeded to act as a witness for the prosecution by denouncing the others, who in turn confessed to the charges. Shortly before the end of the trial he wrote a letter to the court pleading for mercy:

Source J

I ask you to believe that I am not a completely corrupt person. In my life there were many years of noble, honest work for the revolution. I can still prove that even after having committed so many crimes, it is possible to become an honest person and to die with honour. I ask that you spare my life.

Rykov's pleas failed to impress Vyshinsky, who at the end of the trial demanded the death penalty for all those charged:

Source K

'The Bloc of Right and Trotskyites', the leading members of which are now in the prisoners dock, is not a political party but a band of criminals, and not simply criminals, but criminals who have sold themselves to enemy intelligence, criminals whom even ordinary felons (criminals) *treat as the basest, the lowest, the most contemptible, the most depraved of the depraved* (evil). *The whole country, from young to old, is awaiting and demanding one thing: the traitors and spies must be shot like dirty dogs.*

By the end of 1938, all the members of Lenin's *Politburo*, except Stalin and Trotsky, had been executed. Of the 139 Central Committee members in 1934, over 90 had been shot.

   Stalin also used the last Show Trial to purge the purgers. By 1938, fearing the spread of Nazism, Stalin realised that he now needed the support of the Army. He blamed the previous purges on the excesses of his Commissioner for Internal Affairs, Yezhov, and on the former NKVD chief, Yagoda. Stalin's trusted henchman, Lavrentii Beria, who became the most feared man in the Soviet Union, replaced Yezhov. Beria remained in office until after the death of Stalin in 1953.

Eye-Witness Accounts

Foreign observers were invited to attend the Show Trials. However, very few left with the impression that the trials had been conducted in a fair and open manner. In the extract below, Fitzroy MacLean, a British diplomat who observed the 'Trial of the Twenty-one' in March 1938, describes the conduct of the Show Trial:

Source L

The prisoners were charged, collectively and individually, with every conceivable crime: high treason, murder, espionage (spying) and all kinds of sabotage. They had plotted to wreck industry and agriculture, to assassinate Stalin, to dismember the Soviet Union for the benefit of their capitalist allies. They were shown for the most part to have been criminals and traitors to the Soviet cause ever since the Revolution – before it even. The evidence accumulated filled no less than fifty large volumes. One after another, using the same words, they admitted their guilt: Bukharin, Rykov, Yagoda. Each prisoner incriminated his fellows and was in turn incriminated by them. There was no attempt to evade responsibility. They were men in full possession of their faculties; the statements they made were closely reasoned and delivered with every appearance of spontaneity. And yet what they said, the actual contents of their statements seemed to bear no relation to reality.

As the trial progressed, it became ever clearer that the underlying purpose of every testimony was to blacken the leaders of the 'bloc', to represent them, not as political offenders, but as common criminals, murderers, poisoners and spies.

The Impact of the Show Trials

Source M

This cartoon was published by a Russian refugee living in Paris in the 1930s.

▲
Visit the USSR's pyramids.

As World War II approached, the purges and Show Trials were brought to an end. The leadership of the Communist Party, which had borne the brunt of the

▲ Prisoners from slave labour camps building the White Sea Canal, c. 1938. Although thousands of prisoners lost their lives during its construction, it proved to be too shallow for ships from the Baltic Sea.

purges, had been transformed. A new generation of Party members, who could be relied upon to support Stalin unquestionably, emerged. These included Zhdanov, Khrushchev and Molotov.

As many as 20 million may have been shot, arrested or sent to forced labour camps during the purges. Millions of people were sent to the *'Gulag Archipelago',* a network of forced labour camps, which stretched across the north of the Soviet Union and into Siberia. Inmates were cruelly treated, given small rations and expected to work up to 16 hours a day.

The purges also had a negative effect on foreign relations. Stalin was viewed by the western democracies as a ruthless killer. This was at a time when Stalin hoped that he could co-operate with European democratic powers to prevent the spread of Fascism (p. 1).

It was not until 1956 (three years after Stalin's death) that the leadership of the Soviet Union questioned many of Stalin's policies and condemned the Stalinist state. On 25 February, 1956, Nikita Khrushchev (Stalin's successor as leader of the Soviet Union), in a secret speech to the 20th Party Congress of the Communist Party, denounced the crimes of Stalin:

Source N

Stalin acted not through persuasion, explanation and patient co-operation with people, but by imposing his concepts and demanding absolute submission to his opinion. Whoever opposed this concept or tried to prove his viewpoint and the correctness of his position was doomed to removal from the leading collective and to subsequent... physical annihilation (total destruction). *This was especially true during the period following the 17th Party Congress, when many prominent Party leaders and rank-and-file Party workers, honest and dedicated to the cause of Communism, fell victim to Stalin's despotism* (dictatorship).

Facts prove that many abuses were made on Stalin's orders without reckoning with any norms of Party and Soviet legality. Stalin was a very distrustful man, sickly suspicious; we knew this from our work with him. He could look at a man and say 'Why are your eyes so shifty today?' or 'Why are you turning so much today and avoiding to look me directly in the eyes?' The sickly suspicion created in him a general distrust even toward eminent (well-known) *Party workers whom he had known for years. Everywhere and in everything he saw 'enemies,' 'two-facers' and 'spies'.*

The Show Trials and the 'Great Purges' in general were designed to instil in the masses the belief that there was only one man who stood above any suspicion and on whom the security and future of the Soviet Union depended. By associating the country's survival with his personal power, Stalin believed that it would buy him security against any attempt to overthrow him.

Source O
This cartoon was published by David Low in Britain in 1930.

What does this cartoon tell you about the cartoonist's opinion of Stalin's state of mind?

Key Concept: Personality Cult

'Personality Cult' is a phrase used to describe a form of political leadership in which the public is constantly reminded of the goodness and achievements (real or invented) of the leader.

Using a clever propaganda machine, Stalin was presented to the Russian people as a warm, modest and sincere man committed to the good of the people. Towns, cities and streets were named after him. His role in the 1917 Revolution was exaggerated, while all accounts of Trotsky were removed from history books. He even wrote a book about himself describing his great achievements. His opponents were airbrushed (removed) from Russian history (see pictures on p. 68).

The cult of Stalin was reinforced though the arts, education and youth movements. The following extract is from a speech by a writer to the Congress of Soviets in 1935. The speech was published in *Pravda,* the paper of the Communist Party:

Thank you Stalin. Thank you because I am so well and joyful. No matter how old I become, I shall never forget how we met Stalin two days ago. Generations to come will regard us as the happiest of people because we lived in the same century as Stalin, because we were privileged to see Stalin, our inspired leader.

The men of all ages will carry your name, which is strong, beautiful, wise and marvellous. Your name is engraved on every factory, every machine, every place on earth, and in the hearts of all men.

Every time I have found myself in his presence I have been overcome by his strength, his charm, his greatness. I have experienced a great desire to sing out, to shout with joy and happiness. And when the woman I love presents me with a child the first word it shall utter will be: Stalin.

▲
Lenin addressing a workers' meeting shortly after the Revolution, with Trotsky standing on the steps of the stage.

▲
Trotsky has been removed from this photograph. Why do you think this was done?

The 1936 Constitution

Stalin claimed that the 1936 Constitution was the most democratic in the world. Everyone over 18 could vote in a secret ballot. A new parliament was introduced, the Supreme Soviet. It consisted of two houses: the Soviet of Nationalities, which was elected by the various republics, and the Soviet of the Union, which represented the people. Although the Constitution seemed to be liberal and democratic, it was not. There was only one political party, the Communist Party. Only those supported by the Party were allowed to stand. As Secretary of the Party, Stalin had complete control.

Socialist Realism

Stalin discouraged individuality in the arts. Writers, artists and musicians were encouraged to follow a style known as 'Socialist Realism', which sought to depict the achievements of the Soviet Union since the 1917 Revolution. Art and literature was to assume a social function, as Stalin explained in 1932:

The artist must give first priority to the truthful presentation of life, and if he truly portrays our life, then he cannot but note, cannot but show, that it leads to socialism. This will be socialist art. This will be socialist realism.

Monumental murals showing smiling workers toiling hard for the state appeared on walls throughout the Soviet Union. Artists who failed to conform were denounced and found it impossible to work. The *Komsomol* (Communist Youth) disrupted plays that did not meet with the ideals of Socialist Realism.

Education

Under Stalin, the Soviet education system developed rapidly. By the mid-1930s, the Soviet Union had one of the most organised state education systems in the world. Nursery schools were provided for the under-threes, while those aged between three and seven attended infant schools. Attendance at secondary school was compulsory for students between the ages of eight and 15. Young people were encouraged to enter higher education, and adult education was provided for working men and women. By 1936, the Soviet Union's higher education system was producing a large number of graduates in the form of engineers, scientists and doctors.

Although education was used as a vehicle for state propaganda, the illiteracy rate dropped to about 20% of the population by 1940. By the time of Stalin's death in 1953, the Soviet Union was almost universally literate.

Youth Movements

In common with other dictatorships, young people were encouraged to enrol in youth organisations. From the age of four onwards, children could enrol in the **'Little Octobrists'**. At the age of nine they progressed to the **'Lenin Pioneer Organisation'** where they were organised into brigades that took part in political activities. Between the ages of 14 and 28 they became eligible to join the **Komsomol**, the main youth movement within the Soviet Union. Membership of the *Komsomol* brought with it many advantages. Members found it easier to reach positions of management within industry, they were more likely to receive higher educational scholarships and it often opened the way to membership of the Communist Party.

Marriage and the Family

By 1930 Stalin had become increasingly concerned at the decline of the family in Soviet society. By 1934, in Moscow, 37% of all marriages were ending in divorce. Therefore there was a change in the Communist Party's attitude towards women in the Stalinist state, and traditional family values were re-introduced in Soviet society. Women were once more expected to play a central role in the family. In 1930, the *Zhenotdel* (women's bureau) was closed down as a huge propaganda campaign was launched emphasising that the ideal woman could be a good wife and mother, as well as being a good worker. Marriage became popular once more, divorce rates declined, and abortion and contraception were frowned upon.

Soviet Foreign Policy, 1918–39

Russia was left isolated after World War I. The Allies were annoyed with Russia's withdrawal from the war in 1917, and its separate peace treaty with Germany at Brest-Litovsk in 1918. Neither Germany nor Russia was invited to Versailles in 1919. It was natural then that Europe's outcasts would come together.

The Treaty of Rapallo, 1922

Germany and the Soviet Union signed the Treaty of Rapallo in 1922. The terms of this treaty promised closer economic and political links, as well as the rejection of financial claims on both sides. A secret clause to the treaty allowed German aircrews to train on Soviet territory. This allowed Germany to evade the terms of the Treaty of Versailles, which stated that Germany was not allowed to have an air force.

Between 1922 and 1925 the European powers gradually recognised the Soviet Union and began to open trading links.

However, when Germany joined the League of Nations in 1926, its relationship with the Soviet Union cooled. Germany was no longer isolated in Europe and so didn't need the Soviet Union as a friend. Although Stalin signed the Kellogg Pact in 1928, which outlawed war as a way of solving disputes, he once more found the Soviet Union isolated when Hitler came to power in 1933. Stalin became alarmed and feared the development of an anti-Communist alliance. He now decided to abandon his policy of isolation and make new efforts to gain allies.

Collective Security

Hitler's plans to destroy communism and his wish to expand eastwards *(Lebensraum)* were direct threats to Soviet security. Stalin's Foreign Minister, Maxim Litvinov, decided that steps must be taken to stop the Fascist menace. He believed that the Soviet Union should co-operate with the European democracies in an effort to stand up to Hitler. This 'collective security' would act as a warning to Hitler as it could involve him in a war on two fronts. A number of steps were taken:

- In September 1934 the Soviet Union joined the League of Nations.

- In May 1935 a Franco-Soviet Pact was signed, promising mutual assistance to Czechoslovakia in the event of a German invasion. This was to prevent Germany from expanding eastwards.

- In 1936 Litvinov suggested that left-wing parties in European countries co-operate with non-Fascist parties to stop the rise of Fascism. Accordingly, coalition governments, or 'popular fronts', were elected in France and Spain in 1936.

▲
Maxim Litvinov (1876–1951), centre, Soviet Foreign Minister 1930–39, argued for a policy of 'collective security' against Hitler.

The Spanish Civil War, 1936–39

In 1936 a bitter civil war broke out in Spain when General Franco's right-wing Nationalist forces attempted to overthrow the newly-elected Popular Front Government. The Nationalists received aid from Fascist Italy and Nazi Germany. The Republicans (Government Forces) received aid from the Soviet Union as well as anti-Fascist volunteers from other countries who were organised into units called **'International Brigades'.** Stalin sent 900 tanks and 1,000 planes to the Spanish Republicans. Although the Soviet Union did not send any troops to Spain, the ***Comintern*** (or Communists International, established in 1919 to bring about Communist Revolution in other countries) was used to recruit volunteers for the International Brigades.

It was in Stalin's interest to prolong the Civil War. He hoped that a war of attrition (a war in which one side wins by wearing the other side down with repeated attacks) in Spain would keep Hitler's forces occupied in the west and delay any plans that Hitler had for invading the Soviet Union. He supplied the Spanish Republicans with enough weapons to defend their strongholds, but he never gave sufficient arms to tilt the balance in their favour.

The Munich Agreement and the End of Collective Security

When Hitler turned his attention to Czechoslovakia in 1938, the Franco-Soviet Pact was put to the test. Much to Stalin's disappointment, France tamely followed Britain's policy of appeasement. Appeasement is the policy of giving in to the demands of aggressive powers in order to avoid war, as long as these demands are reasonable. The Franco-Soviet Pact came to an end when France, Britain, Italy and Germany met at Munich in September 1938 to decide the fate of Czechoslovakia. Hitler had made sure that the Soviet Union was not invited, thus creating a split between the Soviet Union and France. Stalin indicated that he would fight for Czech Independence, but the Czechs decided to trust the Western powers and agreed to accept the terms of the Munich Agreement (p. 93).

German Foreign Minister Ribbentrop signing the Nazi-Soviet Pact on 23 August 1939, with Stalin (right) and Molotov, the Soviet Foreign Minister (second from right) looking on.

The Nazi-Soviet Pact, August 1939

Following Hitler's invasion of Czechoslovakia in March 1939, France and Britain guaranteed Poland's frontiers, as it seemed the next most likely target for Hitler's expansion, although neither country could achieve much without the support of the Soviet Union. Stalin was now faced with the choice of an agreement with Britain and France, or one with Germany. Stalin was suspicious that the Western powers would ultimately abandon the Soviet Union in the event of German aggression. A change of course in Soviet foreign policy was signalled when Stalin replaced his Foreign Minister, Litvinov, the architect of collective security, with Vyacheslav Mikhailovich Molotov.

Frustrated by Western appeasement, Stalin chose to sign a pact with Germany. On 23 August the German Foreign Minister, Joachim von Ribbentrop, arrived in Moscow. Following a three-hour meeting, Molotov and Ribbentrop agreed on a ten-year non-aggression pact between the Soviet Union and Germany, known as the Nazi-Soviet Pact. A secret clause to the agreement placed Estonia, Latvia, Finland and the eastern part of Poland within the Soviet sphere of influence and Lithuania and western Poland within the German sphere.

For Stalin, the Nazi-Soviet Pact allowed him vital breathing space. He hoped that a future German invasion would be delayed until at least 1943. By then

Stalin's Third Five-Year Plan (p. 165), which concentrated on the arms industry, would be complete. The Red Army also needed more time to re-structure and re-organise following Stalin's purge of the Army in 1937. The Nazi-Soviet Pact came to an end when Hitler launched the German invasion of Russia, Operation Barbarossa (p. 108) on 22 June, 1941.

An Historian's View on the Stalinist State

Josif Stalin probably wielded (held) *more power than any other tyrant in history. He ruled by means of terror and through a government apparatus that he dominated. He tolerated no threat to his power, real or imaginary, and his leadership went unquestioned. The severity of his regime brought death and suffering to millions. He imposed his policies on every aspect of the nation's life and robbed the Russian people of the ability to think for themselves. Stalin's totalitarian rule was based on a style of government that was elaborate, heavily bureaucratised and over which he exercised dictatorial power. This meant that when he died, he left the country with no durable* (lasting) *form of government.*

From **Years of Russia and the USSR, 1851–1991** by David Evans and Jane Jenkins, 2001.

? Questions

Ordinary Level

Study the cartoon and answer these questions.

1. This cartoon was drawn in 1939. To which alliance is the cartoon referring?

2. Why does the cartoonist wonder how long the honeymoon will last? Explain your answer.

3. Why are Stalin and Hitler considered to be an unlikely match?

WONDER HOW LONG THE HONEYMOON WILL LAST?

Write a short account on one of the following:

1. Stalin's Show Trials.

2. The cult of Stalin.

Higher Level

1. Assess the impact that Stalin had on the Soviet Union and its people.

2. 'From the death of Lenin, 1924, up to Hitler's invasion of the Soviet Union, 1941, Stalin consolidated his personal power and transformed the USSR.' Discuss.

Document Question
Higher and Ordinary Level

Case Study Questions: 'Stalin's Show Trials'

Study Sources A–O on pages 58 to 67 and answer the following questions.

Comprehension

1. Describe Stalin's state of mind as outlined in Source A.

2. According to Bukharin in Source B, what type of personality does Stalin have?

3. What kind of punishment did Stalin demand for those convicted of acts of terrorism? (Source C)

4. According to the information in Source D, how did the mood within the Communist Party change following the death of Kirov in 1934?

5. According to Bukharin (Source D) why did Stalin feel that the majority of the old party represented a threat to his authority?

6. In Source E, what method was to be used to create a state of fear in the Soviet Union?

7. In Source F, to what crimes did Kamenev and Zinoviev admit?

8. In Source G, what message is the cartoonist attempting to get across regarding the conduct of the Show Trials?

9. In Source H, what was the main charge brought against the defendants at the Trial of the Twenty-one, March 1938?

10. According to Source H, what was the objective of the 'Anti-Soviet Bloc of Rights and Trotskyites'?

11. In Source K, what sentence does the Chief Prosecutor, Vyshinsky, demand for the accused at the end of the trial?

12. According to Fitzroy MacLean (Source L), what was so strange about the way the defendants admitted their guilt?

13. In source L, how does Fitzroy MacLean describe the purpose of the Trial of the Twenty-One?

14. In Source M, what impression does the cartoonist give in relation to Stalin's rule of the Soviet Union?

15. According to Khrushchev (Source N), what kind of people fell victim to Stalin's purges?

16. In Source O, whose bust is sitting on the chair as Stalin prepares to shoot himself?

Comparison

1. Compare the various arguments put forward as possible causes for Stalin's reign of terror as outlined in sources A, D and E.

2. Compare the attitudes displayed by Bukharin (Source I) and Rykov (Source J) to the Trial of the Twenty-one.

3. To what extent do Sources G and L agree regarding the conduct of the Show Trials?

4. To what extent do Sources A, B and N agree that Stalin's state of mind was a main cause for his decision to purge the party? Explain your answer.

5. How do the views in Sources H and L compare regarding the charges that the defendants faced during the Trial of the Twenty-one?

6. Explain why it should be considered unusual that the authors of Sources H and N seem to be in agreement regarding their view on Stalin's purges.

Criticism

1. Do Sources G, M and O (cartoons) provide any useful evidence about Stalin? Explain your answer.

2. Do you consider these sources to be a fair reflection of the Stalinist state? Explain your answer.

3. Could Sources G, M an O be considered to be examples of anti-Soviet propaganda?

4. Look at the titles on the notebooks the reporters are holding in Source O. What does the cartoonist think of the accuracy of the Soviet press reports?

5. Study Sources K and L. Which of these two sources is the more reliable? Explain your answer.

6. Source E was written by Nadezhda Mandelstam, whose husband Osip had been a victim of Stalin's purges. Do you consider this source to be reliable? Explain your answer.

7. Explain why the content of Sources F and J may not represent the truth.

Contextualisation

1. From your knowledge of the period, what effect did Stalin's Show Trials have on life within the Soviet Union?

2. To what extent could the Show Trials be blamed for Soviet military difficulties during 1939–40?

3. How did the conduct of the purges and Show Trials effect Soviet foreign policy during the period 1934–39?

4. Apart from the purges and Show Trials, briefly explain some other policies followed by Stalin which aimed to control the life of the citizens of the Soviet Union.

5. How does the Stalinist state's repression of the people compare with other totalitarian states during the inter-war period 1920–39? (Higher Level only)

6 The Third French Republic, 1920–40

Aftermath of World War I

The Third French Republic had come into being in 1870, following France's defeat in the Franco-Prussian War. Despite many difficulties, it survived until the German invasion of France in 1940, during World War II.

The President was head of state in the French Republic. This person was chosen by members of the Parliament, rather than by the general public. The Parliament consisted of two houses, the Upper House (Senate) and the Lower House (Chamber of Deputies). The Chamber of Deputies was elected by universal male suffrage (vote). Women did not have a vote in France until 1945. The President had the power to appoint a Prime Minister, who in turn nominated members from the Chamber of Deputies to form a Council of Ministers (Government).

Inter-War Politics, 1919–39

Political divisions caused much instability in France during the period 1870–1914, but these were temporarily set aside during World War I (1914–18). French politicians of different opinions stood side by side to face a common enemy. However, once the war was over, France returned to the normal process of politics and the old divisions emerged once more.

Although France was among the victors of World War I, its losses in manpower and its economic destruction made it seem like a hollow victory. An entire generation of males had been wiped out. The industrial region of France, which was mainly concentrated in the northeast, had been destroyed by four years of warfare.

Throughout the inter-war years, 1919–39, the Third French Republic was ruled by a series of coalition governments. Between 1918 and the fall of the Third Republic in May 1940, France had seen 44 different governments and over 20 Prime Ministers. Most of these governments involved a combination of left-wing Socialist and Communist parties, or strongly Conservative, Nationalistic parties.

The Bloc National, 1919–24

During World War I French politics was dominated by George Clemenceau. Nicknamed *Le Tigre* (The Tiger) and *Le Père la Victoire* (The Father Victory), he had led his country to victory in 1918. Clemenceau expected to secure a large electoral victory when France went to the polls in November 1918. When

> **Republic:**
> A state in which the system of government is based on the idea that every citizen has equal status. There is no king or queen or royal titles in a republic; power is held by the people through their elected representatives.

George Clemenceau (1841–1929) led his country to victory in 1918, but resigned in 1920.

Édouard Herriot (1872–1957), French Prime Minister from 1924–26.

the results were announced, his Bloc National, a coalition of centre and right-wing parties, secured only 400 of the 616 seats in the Chamber of Deputies.

In 1920 Clemenceau resigned as Prime Minister and stood for the office of President. Surprisingly, Paul Deschanel defeated him. Despite great admiration for Clemenceau's contribution to victory in World War I, many senators and deputies believed that he would be too strong a president. They feared that he would interfere too much in government affairs and thus reduce the power of the Chamber of Deputies. His open hostility to religion also made him unpopular with sections of the right wing.

A period of instability followed Clemenceau's resignation. A series of prime ministers came and went: Alexandre Millerand (January 1920 to September 1920), Georges Leygues (September 1920 to January 1921), Aristride Briand (January 1921 to January 1922).

Some form of stability returned with the election of Raymond Poincaré, an anti-Socialist lawyer, as Prime Minister in January 1922. Poincaré saw himself as the champion of the middle classes. He sought to protect small businessmen and shopkeepers, who were becoming increasingly alarmed at the rise in inflation. However, in 1923 he lost considerable support when economic weakness required him to introduce tax increases. Poincaré was forced to resign in June 1924 when the Senate rejected his tax proposals.

Cartel Des Gauches, 1924–26

In the 1924 election the *Cartel des Gauches* (Alliance of the Left) swept to power, winning 328 seats to the Bloc National's 226. The *Cartel* was an alliance between the Radical Party in the centre, and the Socialist Party on the left. The lower middle class of shopkeepers and farmers supported the Radicals. They opposed state control over industry. Industrial workers and peasants largely supported the Socialists and they called for state intervention in the economy. Despite these differences, the new Prime Minister, Radical Édouard Herriot, managed to hold a government together for two years.

As soon as the *Cartel* came to power, it was met by a severe economic crisis. The crisis had been caused by years of economic mismanagement. Since 1921 government expenditure had exceeded income by between seven and 12 billion francs per year.

Herriot and the Radicals refused to consider the introduction of higher taxes. He attempted to overcome the crisis by borrowing money, which only made the budget imbalance much worse. This led to the collapse of the French Franc:

December 1920	90 Francs	= £1 sterling
December 1925	130 Francs	= £1 sterling
July 1926	240 Francs	= £1 sterling

The different parties in the *Cartel* could not agree on a solution to the crisis. The Socialists pushed for a tax on capital (property and land), which would increase the burden on the rich. Herriot eventually gave in and sought to introduce a 10% tax on capital. His proposal met with horror in Conservative circles. Herriot was forced to resign from office in April 1926 when the Senate rejected his tax proposals.

The Government of National Union, 1926–32

In July 1926 Raymond Poincaré returned to power leading a Government of National Union, which included five former prime ministers and members of all parties except the Socialists. As well as being Prime Minister, Poincaré was also the Minister of Finance. Due to the poor economic situation, he was allowed to rule by decree (without the agreement of Parliament) and bypass Parliament in order to introduce emergency legislation. He quickly set about increasing taxes. Foreign loans were secured and he stabilised the then French currency, the franc, by reducing its value to one-fifth of its pre-war rate. French goods became more competitive on the world market. Although the measures were harsh, the general public saw that they were necessary.

The Government spent 80 billion francs on reconstruction in the northeast. German reparations largely financed the reconstruction. Another success story was the motor car industry, which expanded greatly during this period. By 1929 France ranked as the second largest car manufacturer in the world.

The late 1920s also saw much needed social reform. After years of social neglect, a national insurance scheme for old-age pensions and sick benefits was approved by Parliament in 1928.

The Great Depression

With the onset of the Wall Street Crash in 1929 (p. 135), political instability returned once more to France. The Great Depression had a major effect on the French economy. The cancellation of American loans to Germany meant an end to German reparation payments to France. The devaluation of the franc, which had led to economic success in the late 1920s, also had its drawbacks. France became a dumping ground for cheap foreign goods. Exports dropped by 40% between 1929 and 1932.

In 1932 a Radical Government under Herriot returned to office. However, the Government fell once again when Herriot attempted to deal with the economic crisis. He introduced a budget based on cuts in expenditure coupled with a tax increase. He also lost popularity when he refused to stop the payment of France's World War I debts to the USA.

The Growth of Fascist Leagues

In such conditions many felt that democracy as a political system was failing in France and they began to look increasingly towards extremist organisations that promised action and firmness. This led to an increase in support for Fascist and semi-Fascist organisations known as 'leagues'.

Action Française (French Action)

Charles Maurras was one of the most influential league leaders. He founded his radical right-wing movement, *Action Française*, in 1905. It was anti-Communist and anti-Semitic. Supporters included many of the old gentry who had always disliked the republican system. It also drew recruits from the professional classes and included small businessmen, shopkeepers and artisans, whose social and economic status had been declining. Many right-wing journalists also joined or supported *Action Française.*

Jeunesses Patriotes (Patriotic Youth)

Founded by the Conservative Deputy Pierre Taittinger in 1924, the *Jeunesses Patriotes* modelled themselves on Mussolini's Fascist movement. Its members wore blue raincoats and berets. Much of its support was drawn from right-wing activists in universities. By 1933 it boasted a membership of almost 100,000.

Solidarité Française (French Solidarity)

Solidarité Française was founded in 1935 by François Coty, the perfume and cosmetics millionaire. He used his wealth to promote his anti-democratic and anti-Semitic views through his newspaper *L'Ami du Peuple* (The Friend of the People).

▲
Charles Maurras
(1868–1952), who founded
Action Française, an influential
Fascist league, in 1905.

Croix de Feu (Cross of Fire)

The *Croix de Feu* was one of the largest of the leagues. Headed by a retired Lieutenant, Colonel de La Rocque, it was mainly composed of ex-servicemen. Although it was fiercely anti-Communist, unlike the other leagues it was not anti-Semitic. De La Rocque, who had a gift for public speaking, attracted wealthy backers and the *Croix de Feu* had become a mass movement by 1933.

Apart from the activities of the leagues, the Paris press stirred up right-wing opinion. Traditional right-wing newspapers such as *Le Matin* (The Morning) and *Le Journal* (The Daily) were augmented by a series of new weekly publications such as *Candide* and *Je Suis Partout* (I Am Everywhere). These newspapers specialised in slandering Republican politicians of the left and centre.

The part played by the journalists of the right, many of whom ended as collaborators of the Nazis in the Second World War, in sapping the moral fibre and powers of resistance of the Third Republic, can hardly be exaggerated.

From **A History of Modern France** by Alfred Cobban, 1974.

The Stavisky Affair, 1934

In 1934 the Stavisky Affair provided the far right with an opportunity to attack the parliamentary democratic system, which they so much hated.

In January 1934 Serge Stavisky, a financier of Russian-Jewish origin, was arrested by police in Chamonix. He was released shortly afterwards, but was found dead a few days later, apparently having shot himself. Few French people believed the suicide story, as evidence emerged detecting fraud going back to 1926. Right-wing newspapers claimed that Stavisky was murdered to prevent him from naming government ministers, judges and members of the police, who were all involved in his swindles.

In 1926 Stavisky had been arrested and charged with the theft of seven million francs. However, his trial was postponed nine times between 1926 and 1933. The public prosecutor in Paris, who had ordered the delay of Stavisky's trial on several occasions, happened to be the brother-in-law of the Radical Party Prime Minister Camille Chautemps. Suspicions of Government involvement in his death strengthened when Chautemps refused to hold a public enquiry into Stavisky's death.

On the evening of 06 February, 1934, the right-wing leagues poured onto the streets of Paris and prepared to attack the Chamber of Deputies. Fourteen people were killed and 200 were injured before the riot was crushed. Three days later the Communists attempted a *coup* of their own, by marching through Paris and calling for a general strike.

▲
Right-wing demonstrators on the Champs Elysées, Paris in February 1934, just before disturbances break out.

Chautemps resigned as a result of the scandal. To appease the leagues, a right-wing politician, Gaston Doumergue, was appointed Prime Minister. He attempted to restore confidence in Government by ordering a full investigation into the Stavisky affair. However, the result of the enquiry was open to doubt.

The Popular Front Government, 1936

In an effort to stem the growth of the Fascist leagues, the French parties of the left pooled their resources during the April 1936 election and formed a Popular Front Government. Its leader was the socialist Léon Blum. The election saw a swing to the left with the Popular Front gaining 380 seats against 237 seats to the combined right-wing parties.

The Popular Front's slogan, **'Bread, Peace and Liberty',** had echoes of Lenin's *April Thesis* of 1917 (p. 48). Although the French Communists supported Blum's Government, they refused to serve as Government Ministers.

The alliance of the left came into existence for a number of reasons. Firstly, the emergence of the right-wing leagues frightened the left. Secondly, Stalin, who was becoming increasingly worried about the rise of Hitler, encouraged a policy of collective security against Fascism. The Soviet Union's Foreign Minister, Maxim Litvinov, advised Communists in Europe to join with the democratic parties to resist Fascism.

The Matignon Agreement

On coming to power, Blum faced serious economic problems. His Government had to deal with a series of strikes and sit-ins. Industrial resentment was fuelled by the lack of social and industrial legislation since 1919, coupled with the slowness of France's economic recovery in the mid-1930s.

Throughout May and June, the trade union organisation brought economic activity to a standstill.

Blum called a conference at the Prime Minister's residence, the Hotel Matignon. An agreement involving trade unions, employers and the Government was signed in June 1936.

The Matignon Agreement included the following provisions:

• Wages for civil servants and industrial workers were to be raised by 12%.

• Annual paid holidays and a 40-hour working week were made compulsory.

- Munitions factories were nationalised (taken over by the state).
- There was to be closer state supervision of the Bank of France.
- All workers should go back to work (as agreed by the trade unions).

The Matignon Agreement did not have the stimulating effect on the French economy that was expected. It was bitterly opposed by employers, who were shocked that the Government had 'given in' to industrial militancy. Production also dropped due to the introduction of a 40-hour week. Prices continued to rise and Blum also had difficulty finding money to finance the reforms and had to resort to Government borrowing.

Socialist Léon Blum (1872–1950) addressing a meeting. Blum led a Popular Front Government from April 1930 to June 1937.

The Fall of the Popular Front

In 1937 a weakening economy forced Blum to call a halt to his reforms. He now found himself in an impossible position. Both the left and right wings attacked his policy for either going too far or not going far enough. A recurrence of strikes showed that the Popular Front had failed to bring industrial peace. A popular slogan began to circulate declaring **'Better Hitler than Blum'**.

In June 1937 Blum demanded special emergency powers to allow the Government to repay its debts. When the Senate refused his request, Blum had little option but to resign.

Government of National Defence, 1938–39

In April 1938, after several changes of government, Edouard Daladier, a Socialist who was more moderate than Blum, formed a Government of National Defence. Faced with a worsening international situation, Daladier managed to retain sufficient support until the outbreak of World War II in 1939.

French Foreign Policy, 1919–39

Between 1919 and 1939, France had two main foreign policy objectives: to make Germany pay reparations for war damage, and to protect French security for the future.

Poincaré's Policy of Coercion

German attempts to avoid payment of reparations were met by a French policy of coercion (force), which was largely associated with Raymond Poincaré.

When Germany failed to pay its instalment of reparations in 1923, Poincaré sent French troops into the industrial Ruhr region. When French troops shot a number of protesters in the Krupp steelworks in Essen, German workers began a policy of passive resistance (strikes etc.). This harsh French policy met with little approval in Britain. France lost much international support and eventually had to agree to an international conference, held in London in 1924. The result of these talks was the Dawes Plan, which involved a restructuring of Germany's reparations. In return, France agreed to withdraw its troops from the Ruhr.

On the security front, France fared no better. An Anglo-American guarantee of a military alliance with France, given in 1919 at the Versailles Conference, was not honoured. The US refused to join the League of Nations as it did not wish to be dragged into another European war. In addition, Britain slipped back into isolation after the war.

France sought to strengthen its security by concluding a series of agreements with Central and Eastern European powers: Poland in 1921, Czechoslovakia in 1924, Romania in 1926 and Yugoslavia in 1927. However, only the treaty with Poland contained a clear commitment to military action in the event of a war with Germany.

▲
Raymond Poincaré
(1860–1934) sent French
troops into the Ruhr in 1923,
when Germany failed to pay
its instalment of reparations.

Briand and Conciliation

The French foreign policy of coercion was abandoned after 1924 in favour of a more conciliatory (peace-making) approach. The new policy, based on improved Franco-German relations, is usually associated with Aristide Briand. He was the French Foreign Minister for most of the period between 1924 and 1929. Briand, along with Gustav Stresemann, the German Foreign Minister, managed to improve Franco-German relations.

In 1925 France and Germany signed the Treaty of Locarno, in which Germany accepted as permanent its existing borders with France and Belgium. As a result of this new understanding, France agreed to allow Germany join the League of Nations in 1926.

The Kellogg-Briand Pact of 1928, which was signed by both France and Germany, rejected war as a way of solving disputes.

Appeasement

The coming of Hitler and the Nazis to power in Germany in 1933 altered the situation dramatically. Pierre Laval, the French Foreign Minister in 1935, believed that France was weaker than Germany and so France should negotiate. French diplomats tended to leave much of the negotiations with Nazi Germany to the

▲
Aristide Briand (1862–1932),
the French Foreign Minister
who favoured a conciliatory
approach to Franco-German
relations.

British, who were committed to a policy of appeasement throughout the 1930s. The French were unwilling to take any action without British support (p. 93).

The Maginot Line

Laval and his successors also placed great faith in the 'Maginot Line' as a means of defending France. In the 1930s an immense unchanging line of fortifications, named after the French Defence Minister André Maginot, was constructed along the Franco-German frontier. The Maginot Line, with its huge guns, concrete bunkers and underground railways, ignored the changing reality of modern warfare. Colonel Charles de Gaulle argued in his book *Vers l'Armée de Métier* (The Army of the Future) that aerial bombardment and powerful tank divisions (units) would make the Maginot Line useless. De Gaulle tried to persuade both soldiers and civilians that tanks would be a better defence system than large troop battalions and military fortifications, but his efforts were in vain.

The Maginot Line was an immense static line of fortifications named after the French defence minister André Maginot. It was constructed in the 1930s along the Franco-German frontier. The French believed that the German Army would 'bleed itself dry' trying to breach this defence system.

The Stresa Front

Laval also devoted much effort to establishing good relations with Mussolini. In 1935 the Stresa Conference in Italy was attended by Britain, France and Italy. They agreed to show a common front in protesting against Hitler's plans to re-arm Germany. This agreement seemed encouraging for France. However, when Mussolini invaded Abyssinia (Ethiopia) in 1935 the 'Stresa Front' fell apart.

Laval, who was anxious to please Mussolini, persuaded the British Foreign Secretary, Samuel Hoare, that Mussolini should be given two-thirds of Abyssinia. When news leaked out of the Hoare-Laval Pact, the British public were so outraged that the agreement had to be thrown out. Mussolini was outraged by the collapse of the Pact, and also with the introduction of economic sanctions against Italy. The result of the collapse of the Hoare-Laval Pact was that Italy now moved closer to Germany.

France now turned eastwards to the Soviet Union for security. In May 1935 a Franco-Soviet Pact was signed whereby each country promised mutual assistance in the event of Hitler invading Czechoslovakia. However, the Pact did not involve any Franco-Soviet military staff talks, so there was no firm plan put in place. It fell apart in 1938 when the Soviet Union accused France of abandoning Czechoslovakia during the Munich talks (p. 93).

The Outbreak of War

When war broke out in September 1939, France pinned its hopes on the Maginot Line, believing that Germany would bleed itself dry trying to breach this awesome defence system. In May 1940, German Panzer Columns (armoured tank columns) caught France unprepared by bypassing the Maginot Line and invading France through the Belgian part of Ardennes (a forested hilly region extending over parts of Belgium, France and Luxembourg). France could offer little effective resistance against the German advance and surrendered on 22 June, 1940. This brought the Third French Republic to an end.

? Questions

Ordinary Level

Write a paragraph on one of the following:

1. The effect of World War I on France.

2. The Stavisky Affair.

3. The Matignon agreement.

4. French foreign policy in the inter-war period.

Higher Level

1. Discuss the strengths and weaknesses of the Third French Republic during the period 1920–39.

2. 'France was a deeply divided country during the inter-war years.' Discuss.

3. Discuss the internal and external difficulties faced by the Third French Republic during the period 1920–39.

7 Nazi Foreign Policy, 1933–39, and the Drift to War

Hitler's Aims and Objectives

From the outset, Hitler and the Nazi Party had very clear foreign policy objectives. Their main aims were:

- An end to the Treaty of Versailles.
- The creation of a Greater Germany, which would unite all German-speaking peoples in Europe *(Großdeutschland)*.
- The movement of Germany's borders eastwards *(Lebensraum)*.

Key Concept: Lebensraum

The term *Lebensraum* (living space) was used by the German Nazis to justify their claim to large areas of Eastern Europe. They said the land was needed to cater for the growing German population. Hitler also had his eye on the rich grain and oil fields of western Russia, so that he could accomplish German *'autarky'* or self-sufficiency. In line with the Nazi theory on race, it seemed natural to them to demand land from those who they considered to be the 'inferior' Slav peoples of Eastern Europe.

Germany Leaves the League of Nations, October 1933

In 1933, at a disarmament conference organised by the League of Nations in Geneva, Hitler suggested that everyone disarm down to the level set for Germany in the Treaty of Versailles. France strongly objected to this. Britain proposed a compromise: Germany would wait for four years and then be given permission to rearm. Hitler rejected this and withdrew Germany from the League of Nations, claiming that he was the only person at Geneva who was serious about disarmament. He attempted to soften the blow by offering to re-enter the League if Germany's request for equality in armaments was recognised. It was not.

Pact with Poland, 1934

In January 1934 Hitler lulled the Poles into a false sense of security by signing a ten-year Non-Aggression Pact with them. Under the terms of this Pact, Hitler agreed to respect Poland's present borders. At this stage Poland saw Stalin as a greater threat than Hitler. Other European democracies wrongly interpreted this agreement as a sign of Hitler's peaceful intentions. German demands for the return of Danzig and the Polish Corridor had always been regarded as a serious danger to European peace. Danzig was the provincial capital of West Prussia until 1919, when the Treaty of Versailles made it a free city within the Polish borders. The Polish Corridor was a strip of German territory awarded to newly-independent Poland by the Treaty in order to give them access to the sea (see map p. 94).

▲
Austrian Prime Minister, Engelbert Dollfuss (1892–1934) was murdered by Nazi sympathisers in July 1934.

The Dollfuss Affair in Austria, 1934

Hitler's foreign policy suffered a major setback in 1934. In July of that year the Austrian Prime Minister, Engelbert Dollfuss, was murdered by Nazi sympathisers. Mussolini feared a Nazi *coup d'état* in Austria. He hoped that an independent Austria would act as a buffer between Italy and Germany. Mussolini also feared that Hitler might attempt to incorporate the German-speaking people in the north of Italy into the Third Reich. Some 40,000 Italian troops marched to the Brenner Pass to prevent a takeover. Hitler ordered the Austrian Nazis to abandon their plans for a *coup d'état*, as he was unprepared for a war at this stage. Hitler's image as a man of peace was damaged by this incident.

Germany Begins to Rearm, 1935

In 1935 Hitler openly declared his intention to rearm Germany. He declared the disarmament clauses of the Treaty of Versailles abolished, and announced the introduction of general conscription. He planned to increase the Army from 100,000, as allowed at Versailles, to 550,000. The other European powers reacted by establishing the 'Stresa Front'. Italy, Britain and France met at Stresa in northern Italy and issued a joint resolution condemning Hitler's plans. This unity did not last very long. When Mussolini invaded Abyssinia (Ethiopia) in

1935, the united front began to crumble as a rift developed between Italy, and Britain and France.

The Anglo-German Naval Agreement, 1935

Britain decided to look after its own interests. In 1935 Britain and Germany signed an agreement by which Germany would limit the strength of its Navy to 35% of the size of the British fleet. A major weakness in this agreement was the exclusion of U-boats from the deal. These boats had caused much havoc during World War I by sinking many commercial ships. Britain could also be accused of condoning a serious breach of the terms of the Treaty of Versailles, as under the terms of the treaty, Germany was not allowed to have a large navy. Hitler interpreted this agreement as a weakness in the British determination to prevent German expansion abroad.

The Saar Plebiscite, 1935

Under the terms of The Treaty of Versailles, the Saar coal-mining region of Germany was to remain under the control of the League of Nations for a period of 15 years. A plebiscite (vote) was held in 1935 to determine the region's future. The fact that a massive majority of the people of the Saar voted to return to Germany was seen as an approval of Hitler's policies.

Buffer zone:
An area of land that acts as a security zone between two rival powers.

The Rhineland, 1936

By 1936 Hitler felt that it was time to start making territorial gains. He reasoned that Britain and France were busy with Italy's invasion of Abyssinia and that it was a good time to march into the demilitarised zone of the Rhineland. Under the terms of the Treaty of Versailles, the Rhineland (a region in West Germany which bordered France and Belgium) was to be a 'demilitarised zone'. This meant that Germany was permanently forbidden to have armies or military fortifications in this region.

Hitler used the 1935 Franco-Russian Pact as an excuse, claiming that Germany was threatened on both fronts and that the Rhineland was needed as a buffer zone. On 07 March, 1936, 25,000 German soldiers occupied the Rhineland. Hitler had

▲
German troops crossing the Rhine as they advance to occupy the Rhineland on 07 March, 1936. No military action was taken by either France or Belgium in response to Hitler's occupation of the Rhineland.

ordered his troops to withdraw if France or Belgium showed any sign of resistance. He was pleasantly surprised when nothing happened. Hitler also felt justified in his actions, as his Generals had advised against occupation at this time. The occupation of the Rhineland marks the beginning of a more aggressive German foreign policy.

▲
The **Stuka** dive-bomber technique was perfected during the Spanish Civil War, 1936–39. Hitler sent such planes to Spain in support of Franco and his forces.

The Spanish Civil War, 1936–39

Relations between Nazi Germany and Fascist Italy improved when they both supported Franco in the Spanish Civil War of 1936–39. Hitler sent 16,000 soldiers, one tank battalion and 11 aircraft squadrons to Spain. He had many reasons for getting involved:

- The establishment of a right-wing dictatorship in Spain would leave France in a weak position.

- Military tactics were tested in Spain. The effectiveness of repeated aerial bombardment was clearly demonstrated during the attack on the Basque town of Geurnica in 1937. The *Stuka* dive-bomber also perfected its technique during the Spanish campaign.

- Appeasement was tested. Hitler learned that the democratic powers in Europe would not intervene to support a democratically-elected Government in Spain. While the democracies were weak and divided, the Fascists proved to be strong and united.

Appeasement, 1936–39

Appeasement is a policy that aims to settle disputes by diplomatic negotiations rather than war. This policy is largely associated with the British Prime Minister Neville Chamberlain and his Foreign Minister Lord Halifax. By the time Chamberlain came to power in 1937, the League of Nations had been weakened by the departure of Germany, Italy and Japan. A new consensus would have to be reached by European powers in order to avoid future conflicts. From 1937 to 1939 Chamberlain sought to answer German complaints by allowing Hitler to revise some of the terms of the Versailles Treaty.

A number of factors contributed to the policy of appeasement:

- Britain and France were unprepared for war. As late as 1938, Chamberlain was warned in a memo from the Army: 'Our defences are so bad that we should go to any lengths to put off the struggle.'

- A large section of British public opinion now believed that the Treaty of Versailles had been too harsh on Germany, and saw nothing wrong with Hitler's desire to unify German-speaking people in one country.

- There was a distrust of the Soviet Union in Western Europe, and many people saw Nazi Germany as a safeguard against the spread of communism.

Anschluss, 1938

In January 1938 the Austrian Chancellor, Kurt von Schuschnigg, became aware of a new Nazi plot to overthrow the Austrian Government. In an attempt to stop this he arranged a meeting with Hitler. He hoped that Hitler would give him a guarantee that he would respect Austrian independence. Instead, Hitler demanded that the Austrian Nazi, Arthur Seyss-Inquart, be given a place in government. Schuschnigg was now forced to make a difficult choice: he could either stand up to Hitler and risk a war, or give in and hope that it would postpone a German invasion. Schuschnigg gave in and Seyss-Inquart was appointed Minister of the Interior. Hitler now directed Austrian Nazis to make the country ungovernable by engaging in large-scale demonstrations and riots.

Hitler announces the incorporation of Austria into greater Germany (**Anschluss**) at a mass meeting in Vienna in 1938. He was enthusiastically welcomed by many Austrians.

In a last desperate attempt, Schuschnigg arranged for a plebiscite to be held on the question of a union with Germany. Two days before polling, Hitler massed his troops on the border and demanded that the vote be cancelled. The last thing that Schuschnigg wanted was a war in which Germans fought Germans; the Austrians and Germans shared the same race and language. To avoid such a scenario he cancelled the plebiscite, resigned, and left all power to Seyss-Inquart. Chancellor Seyss-Inquart now invited the Germans to enter Austria, the supposed reason being the need to restore law and order. On 12 March the German Army marched into Vienna. Hitler had returned to his homeland in triumph. His forces were enthusiastically welcomed by most Austrians and in a subsequent plebiscite 99.75% voted in favour of the *Anschluss* (union).

Czechoslovakia, 1938

After the union with Austria, Hitler now set his sights on the Sudetenland in Czechoslovakia, which contained over three million Germans. Fourteen days after the Anschluss, Hitler met with the Sudeten-German leader, Konrad Henlein, to discuss the **'Sudeten Question'**. In his speeches, Hitler had always placed an emphasis on the destruction of Czechoslovakia as an independent state. However, this task could prove much more difficult than the occupation of Austria, for a number of reasons.

The Czechs had a huge Army of 34 divisions. They also had an excellent intelligence network as well as the impressive *Skoda* armaments works. The Sudeten Mountains provided a natural barrier against a swift German attack. Furthermore, the 1935 Franco-Soviet Pact of mutual assistance had promised to protect Czech independence by force if necessary.

However, the Czech President, Eduard Benes, was soon to learn that his defences contained some major flaws. Although France was obliged by the terms of the Franco-Soviet Pact to defend Czech independence, military leaders in Paris were unsure if it was practical, given the strength of German fortifications along the Rhine river. The British Army was also too small to resist Hitler's advances and had to restrict itself to offering repeated expressions of loyalty to the Czech government. The Soviet Union was willing to take a stance as long as France went along with them.

In April 1938 Hitler created a crisis when he mobilised his Army on the Czech border. The Czech response was quick and decisive. Benes mobilised the Czech Army, forcing a German retreat. Publicly Hitler put a brave face on the German climb down: he declared that no aggression was intended. Privately he was enraged and told his Generals, 'It is my unalterable (unchanging) intention to smash Czechoslovakia by military action in the near future.'

Chamberlain Intervenes, September 1938

Chamberlain believed that some additional peace-making steps needed to be taken to appease the Sudeten Germans.

He flew twice to Germany in September 1938 in an effort to resolve the 'Sudeten Question' with Hitler. On 15 September they met at Berchtesgarten and agreed that Germany could take possession of those parts of the Sudetenland where the population was more than 50% German. Having secured the support of the French Premier, Daladier, Chamberlain arranged a further meeting with Hitler at Godesberg on 22 September to finalise the deal. However, he was shocked to discover that Hitler was now demanding that the entire Sudetenland be returned to Germany. A disappointed Chamberlain returned to London, and Europe prepared for war.

Britain and France Prepare for War

Britain mobilised its reserve force. Anti-aircraft guns were mounted on Government buildings and schoolchildren were evacuated to the countryside. In France, one in three Parisians fled the capital fearing a German aerial attack. Chamberlain was still unsure and expressed the reservations of many when he addressed the nation in a BBC broadcast on 27 September 1938:

> *How horrible, fantastic, incredible it is that we should be digging trenches and trying on gas masks here because of a quarrel in a far-away country between people of whom we know nothing.*

The Munich Agreement, 1938

A way out of the crisis was found when Mussolini, prompted by Hitler, hastily arranged a conference in Munich on 29 September, 1938. The leaders of the four main powers in Western Europe, Chamberlain, Daladier, Hitler and Mussolini, attended the meeting. Neither the Soviet Union nor Czechoslovakia was invited. The conference lasted until just after midnight when an agreement was finally reached.

The Agreement contained almost all that Hitler had demanded from Chamberlain at Godesberg. The Sudetenland was to be handed over to Germany by 10 October. The borders of the remainder of Czechoslovakia would be guaranteed by all four powers.

France informed the Czech representatives, who were waiting in a nearby hotel, that they would no longer abide by the Franco-Soviet Pact if they rejected the deal. Abandoned by their friends, Czechoslovakia had no option but to accept the agreement.

▲ Hitler and Chamberlain at the Munich Conference in September 1938. On his return home Chamberlain declared that the Agreement ensured 'Peace with Honour'.

'Peace with Honour'

On his return home, Chamberlain was hailed as a hero and peacemaker. He waved a copy of the agreement and declared that it was **'peace with honour, peace for our time'**. Winston Churchill* (p. 101), a strong opponent of appeasement, was not impressed with the agreement, stating that 'the German dictator, rather than snatching the victuals (food) from the table, has been content to have them served to him course by course'. In October 1938, in a debate on the terms of the Munich Agreement, Churchill predicted that Hitler would not stop with the conquest of the Sudetenland:

We have suffered a total and unmitigated (absolute) *defeat. All is over. I think you will find that in a period of time Czechoslovakia will be engulfed* (swallowed up) *in the Nazi regime. We have passed an awful milestone in our history, when the whole equilibrium* (balance) *of Europe has been deranged* (upset). *And do not suppose that this is the end. This is only the beginning of the reckoning.*

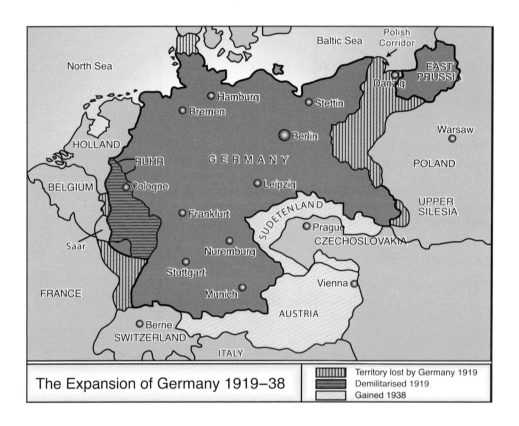

The Expansion of Germany 1919–38

Territory lost by Germany 1919
Demilitarised 1919
Gained 1938

The Occupation of Prague, March 1939

It soon emerged that Hitler was not content with the conquest of the Sudetenland, and that he was preparing for a takeover of the whole of Czechoslovakia. The remainder of Czechoslovakia began to fall apart under German pressure. Hitler encouraged Polish and Hungarian minorities within Czechoslovakia to seek unity with their mother countries, and he supported the Slovaks in their wish to establish an independent state.

In March 1939 the new Czech President, Emil Hacha, travelled to Berlin to plead with Hitler to stop interfering in Czech affairs. Hitler reacted

European History: Dictatorship and Democracy, 1920–45

furiously and declared that internal disorder in Czechoslovakia was a threat to German security. He threatened Hacha, telling him that if he failed to place the rest of his country under German control that the *Luftwaffe* (German Air Force) would bomb the capital, Prague. Fearing a massacre, Hacha placed Czechoslovakia in the hands of the Germans. On 16 March the Nazis marched into Prague.

The German occupation of Czechoslovakia marked a crucial turning point in Hitler's relations with the Western powers. Hitler could no longer claim that his foreign policy objective was only to unite German-speaking peoples. In March 1939 Sir Neville Henderson, the British ambassador in Berlin, expressed that:

▲
'Europe can look forward to a Christmas of peace', says Hitler. In this cartoon, published in the **London Evening Standard** shortly after the Munich Agreement, cartoonist David Low presents Hitler as an 'evil Santa'. Which nation is next on Hitler's list?

...by the occupation of Prague Hitler put himself unquestionably in the wrong and destroyed the entire arguable validity (strength) of the German case as regards the Treaty of Versailles.

Changes in Western Policy

On 21 March Hitler took back the Lithuanian port of Memel, which had been taken from Germany as part of the Versailles settlement. Britain and France responded by promising to aid those countries that seemed to be most at risk from future German aggression. The policy of appeasement had been abandoned. Anglo-French guarantees of aid were given to Poland, Greece, Romania and Turkey.

The Nazi-Soviet Pact, August 1939

All eyes turned to Soviet Russia. The future of Eastern Europe depended on how Stalin would react to the latest threats. At first, Stalin was anxious to forge an anti-German alliance with France, Britain

▲
Another cartoon by David Low depicting the Nazi-Soviet Pact. Which nation lies dead between Hitler and Stalin?

and the East-European states. However, Stalin did not trust Britain and France. Their previous failure to consult the Soviet Union over the Munich Agreement added to his fears. Negotiations between the Soviet Union and the Western powers made little headway due to Poland's refusal to allow Stalin access to Polish territory in the event of a German invasion. Poland and the Western powers did not trust that Stalin would leave Poland following a war against Germany.

While the Western European powers delayed taking action, Stalin turned to the Germans in an effort to buy time. On 23 August, 1939, the German Foreign Minister, Ribbentrop, arrived in Moscow. Within three hours a ten-year Non-Aggression Pact had been signed between the Soviet Union and Germany. Secretly, they had also agreed to the partitioning of Poland along the Narew, Vistula and San rivers. In the Baltic region, it was agreed that the Soviet Union could expand into Finland, Latvia and Estonia.

For Hitler, the Nazi-Soviet Pact avoided the possibility of a war on two fronts in the event of Britain and France declaring war following an invasion of Poland. Stalin gained breathing space, which allowed him time to build his defences against a future German attack.

Danzig, March 1939

Hitler's attentions now turned to Poland. On 21 March, 1939, Hitler demanded that the city of Danzig be returned to Germany. Under the terms of the Treaty of Versailles, Danzig was to remain a 'free city' under the control of the League of Nations. Hitler also demanded that Germany be given free access across the **Polish Corridor** to East Prussia.

Britain and France responded to these new German demands by pledging support to Poland in the case of a German attack. In turn, Hitler responded by cancelling both the Anglo-German Naval Agreement and the German-Polish Non-Aggression Pact. On 22 May Hitler and Mussolini signed the 'Pact of Steel', in which each side promised to support the other in the event of war.

On 22 August, 1939, Hitler discussed his plans for the conquest of Poland with his Generals:

The occasion is favourable now as it has never been. I have only one fear and that is that Chamberlain or such another dirty swine comes to me with propositions (suggestions) or a change of mind. He will be thrown downstairs. And even if I must personally kick him in the belly before the eyes of all the photographers.

No, for this it is too late. The invasion and extermination of Poland begins on Saturday morning. I will have a few companies in Polish uniform attack in Upper Silesia or in the Protectorate (Danzig). Whether the world believes it doesn't mean a damn to me. The world believes only in success.

Be hard ... Be without mercy. The citizens of Western Europe must quiver in horror.

The Outbreak of War, September 1939

Despite Hitler's statement to the Generals, he still hoped that an agreement could be reached with Britain. He delayed his planned invasion of Poland for a fortnight. On 25 August he suggested to Britain that he guarantee the security of the British Empire in return for a free hand on the continent. When Britain failed to respond, Hitler proceeded with his invasion of Poland on 01 September, 1939. On 03 September, following Hitler's failure to respond to a demand to withdraw from Poland, Britain and France declared war on Germany.

? Questions

Ordinary Level

Study the map below and answer the following questions.

1. Name the demilitarised zone marked A.

2. In what year did Hitler reoccupy this area?

3. Name area B and explain the circumstances in which it was acquired by Germany in 1938.

4. Name the city marked C. What decision was made regarding this city at Versailles in 1919?

5. What justification did Hitler put forward for claiming all of these areas?

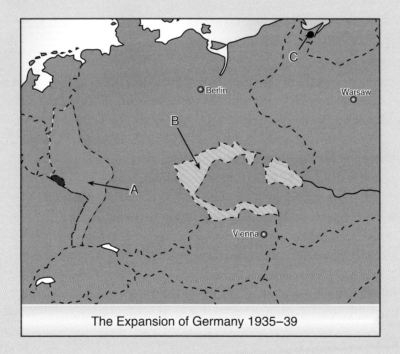

The Expansion of Germany 1935–39

Write a paragraph on one of the following:

1. The reoccupation of the Rhineland, 1936.

2. The *Anschluss*.

3. The Munich Agreement, 1938.

Higher Level

1. Trace the development of Germany's expansionist foreign policy up to 1939.

2. Discuss the reaction of European powers to Hitler's foreign policy up to the outbreak of World War II.

3. 'The outbreak of World War II was an inevitable outcome of Hitler's foreign policy.' Discuss.

Document Question
Higher and Ordinary Level

Read the document below and answer the questions that follow. The document is an extract from Paul Reynaud's book *In the Thick of the Fight 1930–45* (1955). Reynaud was the French Minister for Finance in 1938 and a member of the French delegation at the Munich Conference in 1938.

At half-past one in the morning the agreement was signed. M. François-Poncet wrote: We were bitterly aware of the cruelty of the event. Daladier shook his head, muttered, and cursed circumstances. He refused to take part in the congratulations exchanged by the other delegates. Worst, the most painful step had not yet been taken; we had now to break the news to the Czechoslovakians who were awaiting the outcome of the Conference at their hotel. Mastney, their Minister in Berlin, broke into tears. I consoled him as best I could. Believe me, I said, all this is not final. It is but one moment in a story which has just begun. Returning to our hotel at 2.30 a.m., I called Bonnet (Minister of Foreign Affairs) by telephone to inform him of what had happened. Bonnet swept aside my detailed explanations. Peace is assured, he said. That is the main thing. Everybody will be happy....

As for Hitler, he was triumphant. He had secured complete victory... The eagerness of the Allies to lick the boots of the Nazis was to exert a tremendous influence on the course of events... The Allies themselves laboured under a complete delusion (fantasy). Following his dream, Chamberlain stayed at Munich until the morning of the 30th. When he got back to Croydon, he stated Peace has been won for a generation.

1. Compare and contrast the attitudes of French Premier Daladier and British Prime Minister Chamberlain to the outcome of the Munich Conference.

2. What did Paul Reynaud consider to be the most painful step at the Munich Conference?

3. Describe the terms of the agreement reached at Munich in 1938.

4. What prediction did Chamberlain make on his return to Croydon? How accurate was it?

5. What were the consequences of the Munich Agreement? (Higher Level only)

Dictators and Democrats at War, 1939–45

8

The Nazi State at War

France and Britain Declare War, 03 September, 1939

On 01 September, 1939, and without a declaration of war, the German Army invaded Poland. The Panzer tank divisions swept through Poland, while the *Luftwaffe* destroyed over half of the Polish Air Force on the ground. This ground and air offensive was known as *Blitzkrieg*[+] or 'Lightning War' (p. 204).

Unable to come to Poland's aid, France and Britain sent Hitler an ultimatum demanding his withdrawal from Poland. Last minute attempts by Mussolini to organise a peace conference failed, and on 03 September, as the ultimatum expired, France and Britain declared war on Germany. Had the French struck immediately, Hitler would have been forced to fight a war on two fronts. Instead, the French mobilised for defence rather than attack. Poland waited in vain for help. With Warsaw destroyed by aerial bombardment, Poland suffered a further blow on 17 September when the Soviet Union invaded from the East. The invaders quickly overran the Ukrainian and Byelorussian areas of East Poland. Poland's resistance ended on 06 October and a 'Polish Government in Exile' was set up in London. Germany and the Soviet Union divided Poland between them as was allowed for under the terms of the Nazi-Soviet Pact (p. 95).

A polish farmer continues to plough a field as German tanks rumble by in September 1939.

The 'Phoney War', October 1939–April 1940

After the defeat of Poland, an uneasy peace broke out. The period became known as the 'Phoney War'. For although war had been declared, no fighting had yet taken place in Western Europe. Months passed without action. Britain and France concentrated on improving their defences. Plans were made to extend the Maginot Line along the Belgian border. In Britain, air-raid shelters were built, trenches were dug and children were evacuated to the countryside.

The British still hoped that a major conflict could be avoided. Hitler also felt that Britain and France might now sue for peace as the fate of Poland had already been decided. In addition, the German Generals were warning Hitler against a winter campaign.

Invasion of Denmark and Norway, April 1940

The Phoney War came to an abrupt end on 09 April, 1940, when Hitler invaded Denmark and Norway. Denmark was overrun in a day and most of southern Norway was occupied within 24 hours. However, the British Royal Navy managed to land at Narvik in northern Norway, but had to evacuate again due to continued German aerial bombardment. Narvik fell to the Germans on 08 June.

The British Parliament had by now lost confidence in their Prime Minister, Neville Chamberlain. On 10 May he resigned and Winston Churchill took over.

Gold standard:
The use of gold as the standard value for the money of a country.

Key Personality: Winston Churchill

Winston Churchill was born 30 November, 1874, at Blenheim Palace, Oxfordshire, England, the son of Lord and Lady Churchill. Lord Randolf Churchill was a politician and Lady Churchill (Jennie Jerome) was the daughter of an American business tycoon. He had a short career in the Army from 1895–99 and saw service in India and the Sudan in Africa. As a war correspondent during the Boer War (in South Africa) in 1899, he was taken prisoner but later escaped. He entered politics in 1900 as a Conservative, but later joined the Liberals only to return again to the Conservatives at a later stage.

During World War I Churchill served as First Lord of the Admiralty (Navy), but was forced to resign following the disastrous

Winston Churchill (1874–1965) giving his famous 'V' for victory sign. His wartime speeches did much to raise morale in Britain during the darkest days of World War II.

Gallipoli expedition in 1915. Churchill is widely recognised as the man who committed British, French and, above all, untested Australian and New Zealand forces to this doomed campaign to seize control of the Dardanelles Straits and western Turkey. Over 200,000 Allied casualties occurred with many deaths coming from disease.

Churchill returned to ministerial office in 1917 as Minister of Munitions, and as Colonial Secretary from 1921 to 1922. His political career continued to be dogged by controversy, when, as Chancellor of the Exchequer (1924–25), his Gold Standard policy was partly responsible for plunging Britain into a deep recession.

During the 1930s Churchill was out of favour and out of office. Throughout these 'wilderness years' he led a forceful campaign against the Government's policy of appeasement. Following Hitler's failure to honour the terms of the Munich Agreement in 1939 (p. 93), the general public began to realise that Churchill had been correct. On the outbreak of war, Prime Minister Neville Chamberlain invited Churchill back into Government as First Lord of the Admiralty. Following Chamberlain's resignation in May 1940, there was a general agreement amongst all parties that Churchill should succeed him. In his first speech to the House of Commons as Prime Minister on 13 May, 1940, he told the British people:

> *I have nothing to offer but blood, toil, tears and sweat. We have before us an ordeal of the most grievous kind. We have before us many long months of struggle and suffering. You ask, What is our policy? I will say it is to wage war by sea, land and air, with all our might and with all our strength that God can give us to wage war against a monstrous tyranny.*

Churchill was a gifted orator (speech-maker). His wartime broadcasts did much to keep up morale in Britain and helped encourage resistance in Western Europe. His message, as given in that first speech, was simple:

> *… victory, victory at all costs, victory in spite of all terror, victory, however long and hard the road may be; for without victory there is no survival… come then, let us go forward together with our united strength.*

When the war ended in 1945, Churchill lost the general election. He became a Prime Minister again from 1951 to 1955. He was made a Knight of the Garter in 1953 and died on 24 January, 1965.

Activity

Find out about the Schlieffen Plan and compare it to Germany's invasion of Belgium/France in 1940.

Operation Yellow: Invasion of Holland, Belgium and France, May 1940

On the same day that Churchill took office, 10 May, 1940, and before the war in Norway was over, Germany attacked France and the low countries (Belgium/Holland/Luxembourg) in 'Operation Yellow'. The German attack on France bears a striking resemblance to the Schlieffen Plan of 1914. Similar to 1914, the

 102

Germans attacked France through Belgium. However, this time the Germans moved through the hilly Ardennes, rather than low-lying Flanders, and by-passed the Maginot Line. The French were not prepared for an attack here as they believed that the Ardennes would be impassable for German **Panzer Divisions.**

The conquest of Holland and Luxembourg was completed within five days. The Dutch Navy escaped to British ports. Belgium fought until 28 May when King Leopold III surrendered to the Germans.

Dunkirk Evacuation, 26 May–04 June 1940

The Germans crossed the River Meuse on 13 May, 1940, and advanced rapidly to take Amiens and the French ports of Calais and Boulogne. As France fell rapidly, the Allies' northern and southern forces were separated by the German advance from the Ardennes to the Somme. The Allied forces were now cut in two and the Allied armies in the north were being encircled.

The British forces then made a dash towards the English Channel in an effort to escape. Between 26 May and 04 June, 366,162 Allied troops were evacuated from Dunkirk, a harbour city in the north of France, by an armada of cargo-boats, trawlers, pleasure yachts and lifeboats. Hitler could have destroyed this force had he not hesitated. It is hard to understand Hitler's actions, but it may have been the result of a disagreement between Field Marshal Hermann Goering, the Head of the *Luftwaffe*, and the Army Commander, Gerd von Rundstedt. It seems that Goering wanted the honour of finishing off the Allies while Rundsredt paused to wait for infantry divisions to catch up with the tanks. While the armoured columns halted, the *Luftwaffe* attacked the forces on the beach with dive-bombers. Although almost a whole Army escaped to Britain, the Allies had to abandon thousands of tons of equipment on the beach.

▲
British troops being evacuated from the beach at Dunkirk in June 1940. Was it a victory or a defeat?

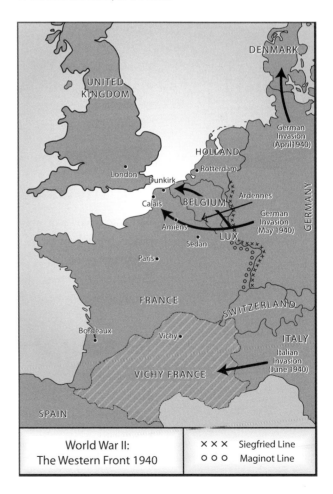

World War II: The Western Front 1940	× × × Siegfried Line
	o o o Maginot Line

Italy Enters the War, June 1940

On 10 June, 1940, Mussolini entered the war on the German side. He feared that the war would be over soon and that Italy would not get its share of the 'booty'. He stated, 'I need a few thousand dead so that I can attend the peace conference as a belligerent (nation at war).'

The Fall of France, 22 June 1940

Armistice:
A ceasefire, when fighting stops.

On 14 June the Germans entered Paris. The French Government, operating from Bordeaux in the South, struggled on until 20 June. In the same train carriage in which the Germans surrendered in 1918, the French now signed an armistice with Germany.

Two-thirds of France, including Paris and the industrial north, were now under the direct control of the Third Reich. The southeast and the French Empire in Africa were to be administered by Marshal Philippe Pétain from the capital of the unoccupied southeast, **Vichy** (Chapter 9). Pétain, who was a hero of World War I, collaborated with the Germans as he believed that authoritarian rule was the only way to restore order and pride in France. His regime was fiercely anti-Semitic and anti-Communist.

Over two million French soldiers became prisoners of war and thousands more were taken to labour camps in Germany.

Colonel Charles de Gaulle escaped to England, and on 15 June, 1940, declared himself Head of the 'French Government in Exile'. Although de Gaulle assisted Allied operations as Head of the Free French, he was never treated as an equal by Churchill, nor later by Stalin or Roosevelt.

Operation Sealion: The Invasion of Britain

Germany now dominated continental Europe. Hitler expected Britain to make peace, but when Britain refused, plans for an invasion were put in place (Operation Sealion). German troops and military equipment were assembled in French and Belgian ports. However, Germany could not hope to succeed with an invasion until they had superiority in the air.

The Battle of Britain, 10 July–31 October 1940

Herman Goering, the Head of the *Luftwaffe*, was given the task of gaining air supremacy over the English Channel. Between July and September 1940 the *Luftwaffe* launched hundreds of raids upon Britain. On 18 June, 1940, Churchill addressed the British people in the House of Commons declaring:

> *The Battle of Britain is about to begin. Let us brace ourselves to our duties and so bear ourselves that, if the British Empire and its Commonwealth last for a thousand years, men will still say, this was their finest hour.*

Although Churchill inspired the British public with his speeches, the Army lacked numbers and the Navy could not defend Britain without air cover. Only the RAF (Royal Air Force) could save Britain. When the Battle began in July, the *Luftwaffe* had the advantage in overall numbers, but the RAF were able to position their forces more effectively due to the invention of radar (p. 208), which could track German planes as they flew over the Channel.

First Phase 10 July–15 August

The *Luftwaffe* attacked British supply ships and ports. On 12 August, 200 planes struck Dover and a further 150 planes hit Portsmouth. The climax of this phase took place on 15 August, **'The Day of the Eagle',** when hundreds of German aircraft in four successive assaults attempted to break the British defences in the southeast. A surprise attack from Norway was also launched on the north of Britain. But the RAF, with the aid of radar, foresaw the attack and 75 German planes were shot down.

RAF pilots running towards their Hurricane fighter planes in the summer of 1940. 'Never in the field of human conflict was so much owed by so many to so few.' – Winston Churchill, 20 August, 1940.

Second Phase 15 August–06 September

Goering now modified his plans. He decided that operations would concentrate exclusively on attacks on RAF airfields, radar stations and aircraft factories. Between 24 August and 06 September, the *Luftwaffe* launched 35 major attacks on airports and aircraft factories. The *Luftwaffe* suffered heavy losses during this phase with 380 planes being shot down.

Third Phase 06 September–05 October

Goering again changed his plans and decided to attack London and other cities in an effort to break the spirit of the British people. This proved to be a major error, as it allowed the RAF time to recover. Between 06 September and

05 October London experienced 38 heavy daylight raids as well as several night attacks. Bombs were dropped at random. Once more the Germans suffered heavy losses. On 15 September, RAF squadrons under the command of Air Vice-Marshall Keith Park, shot down 56 German planes in two 'dogfights' lasting 45 minutes. After this defeat the Germans stopped their daytime bombing raids and returned to night attacks.

The Battle of Britain was over and the invasion plans were postponed indefinitely. While German losses totalled 1,733 planes, the RAF lost over 900 planes, and 700 pilots were killed or wounded. On 20 August, in a House of Commons speech, Churchill commented, 'Never in the field of human conflict was so much owed by so many to so few.'

The Battle of the Atlantic

When Hitler called off Operation Sealion, he decided to attack the British supply convoys. These ships crossed the Atlantic and brought vital food supplies, raw materials and military equipment back from America. German U-boats hunted these in groups known as **'Wolfpacks'.** They waited until the convoys were beyond RAF air cover before attacking.

The phrase the 'Battle of the Atlantic' refers to many incidents in the Atlantic and beyond during the course of the war. Between 1941 and 1942, over 800,000 tons of shipping was lost each month. This figure dropped to 100,000 tons a month by 1943 due to better quality escort vessels, which were equipped with radar, sonar (p. 208–09) and depth charges. By mid-1943, U-boats were being destroyed quicker than the Germans could manufacture them.

Control in The Balkans

Mussolini declared war on the Allies in June 1940. In October he invaded Greece, but was quickly forced to retreat to his base in Albania. Mussolini requested Hitler's help. Hitler was willing to help, as it would allow him the opportunity to extend his influence over the Balkans (countries on the Balkan peninsula in southeast Europe). In November, Hungary and Romania signed an alliance with Germany. This was followed in March 1941 by an agreement with Bulgaria. The following month Hitler invaded Yugoslavia and Greece. Britain rushed 60,000 soldiers from North Africa to Greece. It proved to be too little too late. By 10 May the Balkans were firmly under German control.

Wartime Alliances

Axis Powers

The label 'Axis Powers' had been used since 1936 to describe co-operation between the Fascist regimes of Italy and Germany. A full military agreement between Italy and Germany ('The Pact of Steel') was negotiated in 1939. The two Fascist leaders promised to come to each other's aid in the event of a war with a third party. It became a Tripartite Pact in 1940 following the signing of a formal military alliance with Japan. Hitler and Mussolini agreed to help Japan in the event of an attack by the USA. Following Italy's entry into the war in 1940, the meaning of 'Axis Powers' was extended to describe those countries that supported Germany during the war. Hungary, Romania and the 'puppet-state' of Slovakia joined the Pact in November 1940, while Bulgaria joined in March 1941.

Unlike the Allied Powers, the Axis partners never developed a common strategy, and they failed to match the military, industrial and economic power of the Allies.

> **Puppet state:**
> A state which has been set up under the control of a more powerful state. Although it appears to be independent, the strings are being pulled by the more powerful state, hence the term 'puppet state'.

Allied Powers

In World War II, the term 'Allies' refers to those countries which co-operated with each other against the Axis Powers. Initially, the Allied side consisted of only Britain and France. From 1941 onwards, the USA and the Soviet Union entered the conflict. Britain, the USA and the Soviet Union were the dominant Allies **(The Big Three)** and co-ordinated the progress of the war and its settlement at meetings in Tehran (Nov–Dec 1943), Yalta (Feb 1945) and Potsdam (July–Aug 1945). After the war, France was accepted as a fourth main ally. Over 50 countries entered the war at various stages on the Allied side, even though some (e.g. Latin-American countries) never sent troops into battle.

America Enters the War, December 1941

Although the USA was sympathetic towards the Allies from the start of the war, for more than two years it maintained a tactical policy of neutrality. Although, under the **'Lend-Lease Program'**, it did send generous supplies and armaments to Britain. This Program enabled President Roosevelt to transfer arms and equipment to any nation, notably Great Britain, the Soviet Union and China, deemed vital to the defence of the USA.

On Sunday 07 December, 1941, 340 Japanese planes took off from a number of large aircraft carriers and launched a surprise attack on the USA Pacific fleet at Pearl Harbour in Hawaii. The Japanese believed that if they could destroy the US base there, Japan would be free to expand throughout Southeast Asia. Within minutes, eight battleships, three cruisers and three destroyers had been sunk. Although the attack was a major blow to the US Navy, it was not fatal. The US was fortunate as its four aircraft carriers were at sea at the time of the attack. The Japanese bombers also failed to destroy Hawaii's huge oil stocks.

On the following day, the USA declared war on Japan. On 11 December Hitler and Mussolini fulfilled their obligations under the terms of the Tripartite Agreement and declared war on the USA. Britain than declared war on Japan. World War, in its true sense, had now become a reality.

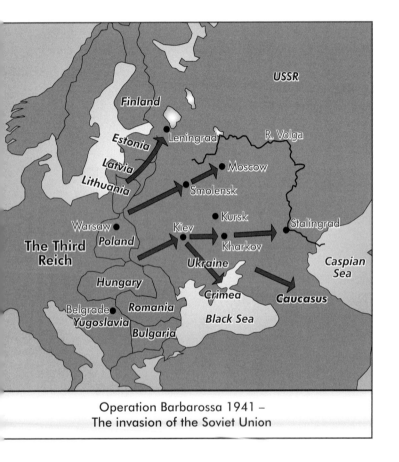

Operation Barbarossa 1941 –
The invasion of the Soviet Union

The Stalinist State at War

Operation Barbarossa: The Invasion of The Soviet Union, June 1941

'Operation Barbarossa' was the code name for the German invasion of the Soviet Union. It was the greatest single campaign of World War II, involving over three million German troops and almost five million Soviets. If Hitler could push the Russians beyond the Ural Mountains, he could obtain vital raw materials, such as oil, to sustain the war effort. The Nazi-Soviet Pact (1939) allowed Stalin almost two years to prepare for war and to restructure the Red Army, which had been devastated during the purges of the late 1930s (p. 62).

Yet when the invasion took place on 22 June, 1941, the Red Army seems to have been caught completely by surprise. Although Churchill had warned Stalin of an invasion, he refused to listen, believing that the Allies were attempting to provoke him into a war with Germany. German forces advanced on three fronts against Leningrad in the North, Smolensk and Moscow in the Centre, and the Ukraine in the South. The *Luftwaffe* quickly gained air superiority by destroying over 2,000 Soviet aircraft on the ground within the first 48 hours of the invasion.

At first the Germans advanced rapidly, overrunning the Baltic states of Estonia, Latvia and Lithuania. Within three weeks the Russian cities of Minsk and Smolensk had fallen. By September the Germans had laid siege to Leningrad and by December they were within 20 km of Moscow. Moscow's civilian population was evacuated. Over a third of the nation's industrial plants were now under German control.

'Scorched Earth' Policy

By the end of 1941 it seemed that Hitler was on the verge of attaining one of his greatest objectives – *Lebensraum* (p. 87). However, all was not as it seemed. **Marshal Zhukov,** Chief of the Red Army, led a massive counter-attack against the Germans on 05 December. Zhukov had kept the Soviet forces intact as he waited for the severe Russian winter to begin. These were similar tactics to those used against Napoleon to halt his invasion of Russia in 1812. During the summer and autumn of 1941, he ordered his troops not to involve themselves in any major military engagements against the Nazis. Instead they retreated in an orderly fashion, drawing the Germans deeper and deeper into Russia.

In Stalin's first radio broadcast of the war, he called on the Russian people to defend the Soviet Union by adopting a 'Scorched Earth' policy.

▲
Marshal Zhukov (1896–1974), Chief of Staff of the Red Army during World War II. He led the Germans into the harsh Russian winter.

In case of a forced retreat of Red Army units, all rolling stock must be evacuated; the enemy must not be left a single engine, a single railway car, not a single pound of grain or gallon of fuel. The collective (p. 161) farmers must drive off all their cattle and turn over their grain to the safe-keeping of the state authorities for transportation to the rear. All valuable property, including… metals, grain and fuel, that cannot be withdrawn, must be destroyed without fail.

In areas occupied by the enemy, sabotage groups must be organised to combat enemy units, to foment (encourage) guerrilla warfare everywhere, to blow up bridges and roads, damage telephone and telegraph lines, to set fire to forests, stores and transports. In occupied regions, conditions must be made unbearable for the enemy.

Everything of value to the enemy was destroyed – homes, factories, animals and crops – which meant that the Germans were unable to live off the land. Railway lines were lifted and bridges were blown up, making it more difficult for the Germans to gain supplies. When the Russian winter came, fuel for tanks and jeeps froze. The German Army, which had gambled on a quick victory, had not been supplied with winter clothing and many died from hypothermia and frostbite.

The early success of the German offensive had also caused the Germans to overreach themselves. Their armies were spread out and their supplies were left far behind. The Russians had destroyed the airfields as they retreated. This meant that the Nazi forces had to advance without any air cover.

The Battle of Stalingrad, 19 August 1942–02 February 1943

In the spring of 1942 Hitler decided to concentrate on capturing Stalingrad, instead of Moscow. Stalingrad stood on the River Volga, which blocked the German advance into the rich oil-fields of the Caucasus region. The German 6th Army bombarded the city to a pulp. However, the Soviets held on and counter-attacked, fighting street by street and building by building. In November 1942 Marshal Zhukov, with the aid of Generals Rokossovsky and Yeremenko, in a brilliant pincer movement, surrounded the German 6th Army and left it besieged in a ruined city during the harsh winter. The German General, Friedrich von Paulus, wanted to attempt an immediate breakout, but Hitler would not tolerate defeat and forbade such action.

▲
A German Soldier dug-in during the Battle of Stalingrad in 1940. Surrounded by snow he attempts to keep warm using blankets.

Supreme Commander to 6th Army, 24 January, 1943:
Surrender is forbidden. 6 Army will hold their positions to the last man and the last round and by their heroic endurance (staying power) *will make an unforgettable contribution towards the establishment of a defensive front and the salvation* (saving) *of the Western world.*

Hitler's communication with Paulus.

▲
Fighting in the Red October Tractor Factory in Stalingrad in 1943.

Pincer movement:
A military manoeuvre which involves splitting your forces and moving them around both sides of the enemy.

Goering ensured Paulus that he could supply his forces with 700 tons of supplies a day by air. The airdrops proved to be unsuccessful and Paulus once more sought permission to surrender. Hitler refused and in an effort to calm his General he promoted him to the rank of Field Marshal. By February 1943, 70,000 German soldiers were dead. Paulus ignored Hitler's orders and surrendered. To add to the German humiliation, Paulus became the First Field Marshal ever to be captured in battle. The Russians did not release him until 1953.

The Battle of Kursk, 05 July–15 July 1943

After the defeat at Stalingrad the Germans regrouped and attempted a new attack at Kursk. In July 1943 Field Marshals Kluge and Manstein attacked the Kursk salient (bulge) from the north and south using 1 million troops and 2,700 tanks. The largest ever tank battle commenced. The Russians were well prepared and seemed to be aware of the Nazi plans. After a seven-day battle, involving up to 6,000 tanks, the Germans were defeated.

Siege of Leningrad, 08 September 1941–27 January 1944

On 08 September, 1941, the Germans had fully encircled the Soviet Union's second largest city, Leningrad. A siege began, which lasted from 08 September, 1941 until 27 January, 1944, a total of 28 months. Over a third of the population of the city had died from the fighting or from starvation. Over 100,000 bombs were dropped on the city and up to 200,000 shells fired at it. Its survival was largely due to the determination of its people. In January 1944 the Red Army finally won and lifted the Siege of Leningrad.

Driving the Germans Out

After the Battle of Kursk, the Red Army quickly recaptured large areas of the Ukraine and Crimea. By the end of 1943 they had almost driven the Germans out of the Soviet Union. Although the British and Americans had sent some supplies to the Soviet Union by Arctic convoy to Murmansk, the Soviet victory was largely due to its own efforts.

Reasons for the Soviet Victory

- During the war Stalin abandoned his policy of persecution and called for unity. He appealed to Russian patriotism, referring to the campaign as 'the Great Patriotic War'. To restore pride and discipline in the Army, the old rank structure was reintroduced and the saluting of superiors became the accepted practice once more. Army units were named after Tsarist generals who had defeated Napoleon in a previous invasion of Russia in 1812.

- The 'Scorched Earth' policy deprived the Nazis of much needed supplies. Stalin introduced rationing to ensure that food supplies for Russians were distributed equitably. A pact of mutual assistance with Britain and the USA allowed for arctic convoys to deliver food supplies to the Soviet Union through the port of Murmansk.

- From 1938 onwards, in anticipation of an attack from the west, Stalin ordered millions of Soviet citizens and great quantities of machinery to be moved eastwards beyond the Ural Mountains. New factories, which were beyond the bombing range of the *Luftwaffe*, were established in the Caucasus region and in Central Asia. These factories produced an endless supply of arms to the Red Army during the war. Chief amongst these was the T-34 tank, which proved far superior to its German equivalent, the Panzer.

- The Germans failed to win the battle for hearts and minds in the areas they occupied. Units hand-picked from the SS and Gestapo called **Einsatzgruppen** (Task Force) treated the Russian Slavs as *Untermenschen* (sub-humans). In response to German cruelty, resistance[+] (p. 174) groups operating behind the front frustrated the German war effort by destroying lines of communication (blowing up roads, railways, etc.).

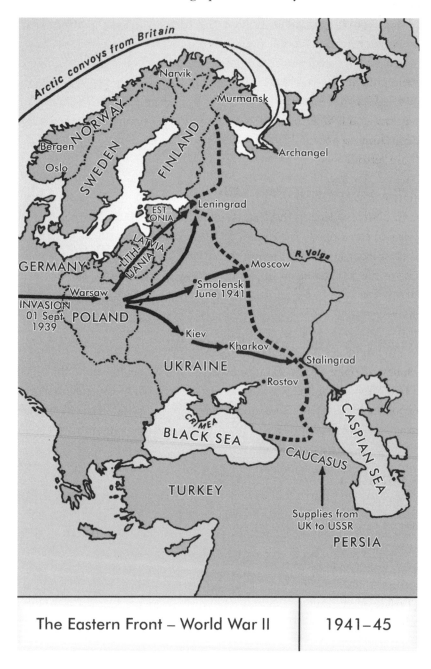

The Eastern Front – World War II	1941–45

European History: Dictatorship and Democracy, 1920–45

The Invasion of Italy, July 1943

By the end of 1943 Stalin felt that the Soviet Union was doing most of the fighting and were suffering a disproportionate number of casualties. He began to demand that Britain and America open a second front. Britain and the USA were not yet ready to start an invasion of France. When Churchill and Roosevelt met at Casablanca in North Africa in January 1943 they decided that an invasion of Italy should take place before an invasion of France.

On 10 July, 1943, the Allied armies landed in Sicily. The landings were extremely successful and the port of Syracuse was taken within two days. By September the Allies had crossed into mainland Italy. The Italian Government now changed sides. The Italian King, Victor Emmanuel, dismissed Mussolini, who was arrested and imprisoned. German commandos freed him and he was put in charge of a German 'puppet state' in the north of Italy known as the **Salò Republic,** as its administration was based in the town of Salò. Marshal Pietro Badoglio formed a non-Fascist Government for the rest of Italy. In September he negotiated an armistice with the Allies, and on 30 October, 1943, he declared war on Germany.

Hitler rushed troops to southern Italy to stop the Allied advance. The Germans fought fiercely and established a line of defences north of Naples. Heavy fighting continued throughout the winter, particularly around the Monastery of **Monte Cassino.** The Allies made slow progress as the Italian mountains and rivers made the advance more difficult. In May, the Allied armies, having built up their forces during the spring, hammered the German lines. The ruined Monastery at Monte Cassino fell at last and the Allies advanced northwards. Rome was captured in June 1944 and by the winter of that year the Allied forces were within 160 km of the River Po in Northern Italy.

The Death of Mussolini, 28 April 1945

The north of Italy was not captured until April 1945. Mussolini made a desperate attempt to escape. Franco had offered him asylum in Spain, but he hesitated too long and eventually travelled towards the Swiss border. He was captured by Italian Resistance fighters, given a brief informal trial and shot. His body and that of his mistress, Clara Petacci, were taken to a square in Milan, where they were hung upside down. Italians spat and threw rotten food at the bodies. Mussolini had admitted shortly before his death that he was the most hated person in Italy.

The Tehran Conference, 28 November–01 December 1943

In November 1943 Churchill, Roosevelt and Stalin met at Tehran. Stalin insisted that the Allies land in France to take the pressure off the Soviet Union in the east. The Allies promised that an invasion would take place in 1944. It was also agreed that an international body to replace the League of Nations should be formed after the war.

▲
General Bernard Montgomery (1887–1976) points the way for the Supreme Allied Commander General Dwight D. Eisenhower as they watch pre-Normandy training in England during World War II.

Operation Overlord: D-Day, 06 June, 1944

On 06 June, 1944, the long-anticipated Allied invasion of Nazi-held Europe took place. The code name for the invasion was 'Operation Overlord' and it began in Normandy. Much of its success was due to detailed planning, which had been taking place since late 1943. British General Bernard Montgomery and US General Dwight D. Eisenhower were withdrawn from Italy. Eisenhower was appointed Supreme Commander of the entire Allied force, while Montgomery became the Landing Force Commander.

The Germans had built strong coastal defences, known as **'The Atlantic Wall',** stretching from Holland to the Spanish coast. The RAF and the US Air Force pounded these positions night after night. They also attacked German cities in an attempt to paralyse their heavy industry. Resistance fighters within the occupied countries harassed the German troops by destroying railways, bridges and communication stations.

▲
American troops wade onto the beaches in Northern France as they leave their landing craft on D-Day, 06 June, 1944. The successful landings gave great encouragement to the population of Nazi-occupied Europe.

The Invasion

04 June Following several days of bad weather, the Meteorological Office predicted 24 hours of settled conditions, starting from late in the evening of 05 June. General Eisenhower issued the order to invade.

05 June 300 minesweepers cleared the channel to an area code-named 'Piccadilly Circus', from where 6,900 landing craft would launch an assault on five beaches code-named Utah, Omaha, Gold, Juno and Sword.

06 June

00.15 hours   British and US paratroopers were dropped into Normandy behind enemy lines to secure bridges and distract the Germans. Eisenhower also sent coded messages to the French Resistance who began a program of sabotage. In the first days of June, every bridge on the Seine below Paris was destroyed and over 950 railway lines were cut.

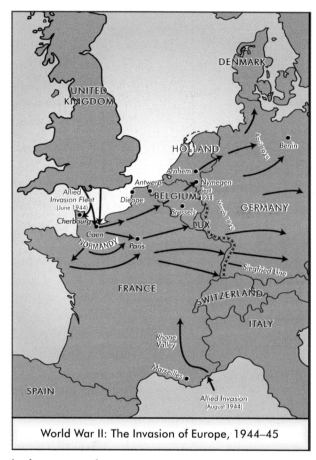

World War II: The Invasion of Europe, 1944–45

02.00 hours   Minesweepers cleared the approaches to the beaches.

03.30 hours   The naval bombardment of the beaches commenced. Twenty-three cruisers and 103 destroyers pounded the German shore defence.

06.30 hours   The first troops landed on the designated beaches. The landings were mainly successful, except at Omaha, which almost ended in failure. Cliffs enclosed the six-mile long beach. The air and sea bombardment had proven to be inaccurate and over 3,000 US soldiers were slaughtered on the beach by enemy machine gun fire.

12.30 hours   The British forces established a bridgehead on Sword Beach and were preparing to move inland.

16.00 hours   A German Panzer division stopped the British infantry three miles from the Normandy town of Caen.

19.00 hours   The Germans mounted a counter-attack on Sword Beach. The British managed to repel the attack just short of the cliffs.

24.00 hours   By midnight on 06 June over 155,000 Allied troops and over 1,000 tanks had landed in Normandy. Over 10,200 Allied soldiers and an estimated 9,000 Germans lost their lives in the assault.

> **Bridgehead:**
> A secure defensive position gained, which will help future advances.

The Allies March On

The success of the landing gave enormous encouragement to the populations of occupied Europe. By the end of July the Germans had been driven from Normandy and the Allies were advancing towards Paris. In August an Army under the command of the American General Patch landed in the South of France and opened a second front along the Rhone Valley, thus putting more pressure on the Germans. Paris was liberated on 25 August and General de Gaulle led a triumphant march through the city.

Meanwhile the Canadians, who had arrived with the American forces, were advancing rapidly along the French coast. They liberated Dieppe on 01 September, 1944. When British forces reached Antwerp in Belgium three days later, they were pleasantly surprised to discover that Belgian Resistance forces had already secured the port, which was virtually intact. The Americans had also pressed on vigorously, liberating Luxembourg on 10 September. By now they had reached the **'Siegfried Line'** (German defence line) and were preparing for an onslaught upon Germany.

The Battle of the Bulge, 16 December 1944–21 January 1945

Approaching Christmas in 1944 Hitler launched a last desperate armoured counter-attack through the Ardennes. When the assault commenced at 5.30 a.m. on 16 December along an 80-mile stretch, the Allies were taken completely by surprise. Aided by dense fog and mist, which kept the Allied Air Forces grounded, the Germans advanced quickly and forced a bulge into the Allied defensive line. However, when the skies cleared on 23 December, Allied planes inflicted heavy losses on the German armour. The German advance was eventually held and by 21 January the Germans had been driven back to their original line. The Battle of the Bulge cost Germany over 100,000 men, 1,600 planes and 700 tanks – all desperately needed to resist the impending invasion of the Reich itself. Hitler's gamble had failed.

Towards Final Victory

British and American troops crossed the Rhine in March 1945. In the meantime the Russians were not idle. Coinciding with the D-Day landings, the Red Army mounted a major offensive in the east. By the end of 1944 the Soviet Union had captured Bulgaria, Romania, most of Hungary and almost half of Poland. The Red Army continued to drive forward towards Warsaw in Poland. In August the Polish Home Army, encouraged by the Russian advance, staged an uprising against the Germans. A fierce battle lasting two months followed, in which over 300,000 Poles were killed. The Red Army failed to come to their aid, claiming that it was not possible. Although this may be true, there is also a possibility that the destruction of the Polish Home Army, which was loyal to the 'Government in Exile' in London, suited the Soviet Union. Stalin had plans for the future of Poland (p. 119).

Yalta Conference, 04–11 February 1945

In February 1945 Churchill, Roosevelt and Stalin met at Yalta in the Crimea (a peninsula of Ukraine). They agreed the following terms:

▲ Stalin, Churchill and Roosevelt at Yalta in February 1945. The seeds of Post-World War II divisions were sown at this conference.

- Germany was to be disarmed and divided into four zones, to be occupied by Britain, the USA, the Soviet Union and France.

- The countries occupied by Germany and liberated by the Allies were to be allowed to elect their own governments.

- It was agreed that the Soviet Union would recover Polish territory east of the 'Curson Line'. This was the territory that Poland had acquired from Russia during the Russian-Polish War in 1921.

- One of the greatest problems at Yalta was the question of which government should control Poland: the 'Government in Exile' in London, which Britain and America supported, or the Polish Committee of National Liberation in Lubin (outside Moscow), which the Soviet Union recognised. This question was not properly resolved at Yalta, although Stalin accepted that the 'London Poles' would be included in any new government.

- Stalin promised that the Soviet Union would join the war against Japan after the defeat of Germany.

The seeds of the post-war divisions were sown at Yalta. Roosevelt was anxious to please Stalin, as he wanted the Soviet Union to help the Americans to defeat Japan. There was very little that the US or Britain could do to stop Soviet expansion. The Soviet Union already occupied all of Eastern Europe except Greece. At the Tehran Conference in 1943, Churchill had suggested that the Allies invade Eastern Europe. This might have altered the situation, but the plan received little support from the Americans, who preferred an invasion of Italy.

The Battle of Berlin, 19 April–02 May 1945

▲
The Soviet flag being raised over Berlin after the city fell to the Russians in May 1945 in one of the bloodiest battles of the entire war.

By 11 April, 1945, American troops had reached the River Elbe and were approaching Berlin. It had been agreed that the Russians should advance on Berlin from the east. From 19 April until 01 May the Germans and the Red Army fought street by street for control of Berlin. The German forces, which included a ragbag of soldiers from the regular Army, the SS and particularly the Hitler Youth, held on until 02 May, 1945. It is estimated that over 100,000 Russians were killed during the onslaught. German soldiers, fearing revenge, attempted to conceal their identity by changing into civilian clothing. For German women, rape became a daily experience following the fall of Berlin to the Soviet Union. The Soviet commanders tolerated a certain degree of looting, and every soldier was allowed to send home a limited number of goods.

The Death of Hitler, 30 April 1945

On 30 April, 1945, as the Red Army shelled Berlin, Hitler committed suicide in his bunker not far from the *Reichstag*, where he had taken power in 1933. On the previous day he had married Eva Braun, who also killed herself. He left orders that their bodies be burned. In his 'Last Testament' he appointed Admiral Karl Dönitz to the position of Leader of the Third Reich. He refused to accept responsibility for the German defeat, claiming that the German people failed to live up to his expectations. They would deserve whatever future lay in store for them.

Admiral Dönitz surrendered unconditionally to the Allies on 07 May. Churchill declared 08 May a national holiday (**Victory in Europe Day**). The war in Europe was over.

The Potsdam Conference, 17 July–02 August, 1945

The last of the major World War II conferences took place at the former Hohenzollern (former German Royal family) Palace in Potsdam, outside Berlin. The conference lasted from 17 July until 02 August, 1945. Stalin represented the Soviet Union while President Truman represented the USA (Roosevelt had died in April 1945). Churchill came to the start of the conference, but was replaced by Labour Leader Clement Attlee nine days later, following his victory in the British general election, 26 July, 1945.

Stalin, Attlee and Truman agreed that the 'Oder-Neisse Line' should represent the new border between Germany and Poland. Germany was to be divided into four zones of occupation. German minorities living in Poland, Hungary and Czechoslovakia were to be sent home to Germany. A tribunal was to be established to try war criminals.

Stalin is generally viewed to have been the winner at Potsdam, since his control of Eastern Europe was accepted by the other leaders as being a *fait accompli*. The political differences that emerged between the leaders at Potsdam could be said to mark the beginning of the 'Cold War'.

The Potsdam Declaration

While the Allied leaders discussed the future shape of Europe at Potsdam, the war in the East against Japan continued. Initially the US planned two invasions of Japan. Southern Japan was to be taken in 1945 and the central and largest island, Honshu, in 1946. However, when it became clear that expected casualties would be very high, Truman began to consider dropping an **atomic bomb** on Japan to force a quick surrender.

On 26 July, 1945, the Allies issued Japan with a final warning. 'The Potsdam Declaration' demanded that Japan surrender unconditionally, be stripped of its empire and accept occupation until democracy could be re-established. When Japan failed to respond, Truman authorised the dropping of atomic bombs on Hiroshima (06 August) and Nagasaki (09 August), thus fulfilling his promise to the American people that he would bring the war in the East to a quick end. The Japanese surrendered unconditionally.

While the dropping of the atomic bombs was the last act of World War II, it can also be seen as the first act of the Cold War. It can be argued that Truman may have decided to drop the bomb as a warning to Stalin not to extend his power beyond Eastern Europe.

Ordinary Level

Study this cartoon, which was published in the *Daily Mail* on 23 June, 1941, and answer the following questions.

1. To which major event in World War II is the cartoon referring?

2. What document has just dropped from Stalin's hand?

3. Why was this agreement unlikely to succeed from the start? Explain your answer.

4. Why did Hitler decide to take this course of action?

5. What were the long-term consequences for Germany of Hitler's actions?

Write a paragraph on one of the following:

1. The Battle of Britain.

2. The Battle of Stalingrad.

3. The D-Day landings.

Answer one of the following:

1. How effective a wartime leader was Winston Churchill between 1940 and 1945?

2. Describe the part played by the Soviet Union in World War II.

Higher Level

1. Account for the initial success and final defeat of Germany in World War II, 1939–45.

2. Describe the part played by the Soviet Union in World War II from 1941–45.

3. Assess the part played by Winston Churchill in bringing about the Allied victory in World War II.

Document Question
Higher and Ordinary Level

Read the documents below and answer the questions that follow. Document A is an extract from Hitler's speech to his Generals on 31 January, 1943, following the surrender of Field Marshal Paulus at Stalingrad. Document B is an extract from a *communiqué* issued by Hitler to the German people on the same subject three days later.

Document A

They have surrendered there – formally and absolutely. Otherwise they would have closed ranks, formed a hedgehog (huddle), *and shot themselves with their last bullet. The man* (Paulus) *should have shot himself just as the old commanders who threw themselves on their swords when they saw that the cause was lost.*

You have to imagine he'll be brought to Moscow – and imagine that rat-trap there. There he will sign anything. He'll make confessions, make proclamations, you'll see. They will now walk down the slope of spiritual bankruptcy to its lowest depths. How can one be so cowardly? I don't understand it.

So many people have to die, and then a man like that besmirches (makes little of) *the heroism of so many others at the last minute. He could have freed himself from all sorrow and ascended into eternity and national immortality, but he prefers to go to Moscow!*

What hurts me most, personally, is that I still promoted him to Field Marshal. I wanted to give him this final satisfaction. That's the last field marshal I shall appoint in this war. You mustn't count your chickens before they're hatched.

Document B

The battle of Stalingrad has ended. True to their oath to fight to the last breath, the Sixth Army under the exemplary leadership of Field Marshal Paulus has been overcome by the superiority of the enemy and by the unfavourable circumstances confronting our forces.

1. In Document A, why does Hitler consider Paulus to be a coward?

2. In Document A, what fear does Hitler have regarding the removal of Paulus to Moscow?

3. According to Hitler in Document A, what hurts him most?

4. How does Hitler describe Paulus in Document B?

5. Explain why Hitler presented two opposing viewpoints regarding the events in Stalingrad as outlined in Documents A and B.

Vichy France 1940–45

The Fall of The Third Republic

France was a reluctant participant in World War II. The politicians were not committed to all-out war. In 1939, Daladier, the French Prime Minister, remembered the catastrophe of World War I all too well. France lost an entire generation of males during the war, and suffered major damage to its industrial region in the northeast.

Paul Reynaud (1878–1966) (right), Minister for Finance under the French Prime Minister Daladier, leaving the Elysée following a ministerial conference in 1939. He went on to succeed Daladier as Prime Minister in 1940.

The 'Joke War'

After the fall of Poland, the fighting ceased temporarily (The Phoney War). The French referred to the period between the fall of Poland in September and the summer of 1940 as *drôle de guerre* or 'Joke War'. France had declared war on Germany in September 1939 and many Parisians had evacuated. During this 'Joke War' they returned to Paris, and clubs and restaurants re-opened. Daladier wanted to preserve the French economy during this period and refused to divert resources to establish a Ministry of Munitions (a special government department which supervises the arms industry in a time of war). Efforts to introduce rationing were also opposed by the Ministry of Agriculture. Political squabbling, which had been a feature of the Third Republic, continued. Daladier and Paul Reynaud, the Minister for Finance, detested one another. In March 1940 Daladier's Government was brought down. Reynaud became Prime Minister and Minister for Defence. This Government had a majority of only one in parliament.

Even those who were not defeatists (ready to accept losing) *believed that somehow or other the war would be a bloodless one for France. Safe within the Maginot Line, the French troops would let the enemy army bleed itself white in fruitless assaults, while the Anglo-French blockade excluded the vital raw materials and slowly strangled the economy of Germany. The French and British armies, which had done practically nothing to assist the Poles, passively sat on the defensive waiting to be attacked. It was a drôle de guerre all that winter.*

From **A History of Modern France** by Alfred Cobban, 1974.

The Invasion of France

Reynaud was barely in power when the 'Joke War' came to an end. In April 1940 Hitler attacked both Denmark and Norway. On 10 May the Germans invaded Belgium and Holland. The French military leader, General Maurice Gamelin, immediately put his plans to assist the low countries into operation. He concentrated his forces on the north of France's frontiers with Belgium, but Hitler caught the French by surprise by attacking through the hilly Ardennes region (see map p. 124). By 15 May the Anglo-French forces in Belgium and Holland had been cut off from the rest of the French forces. Reynaud telephoned Churchill to say: 'We have lost the battle.'

▲
Drunken French soldiers surrendering in 1940. What does this photograph tell us about the attitude of the soldiers to the invasion of France?

Pétain Takes Over

In desperation, Reynaud sacked Gamelin and replaced him with General Weygand. In addition, Marshal Henri-Philippe Pétain, the elderly hero of World War I, now aged 84, was recalled from his role as Ambassador to Spain in Madrid to become Reynaud's Deputy.

Pétain was a French soldier who had earned a heroic reputation as the defender of Verdun in 1916 during World War I. He became Commander in Chief of the French Forces in 1917, and Marshal of France in 1918. Reynaud hoped that the old **'Conqueror of Verdun'** would revive French confidence. However, he was soon to learn that Pétain considered the war as good as lost.

"I make to France the gift of my person to help to mitigate her suffering."

▲
Marshall Henri-Phillippe Pétain (1865–1951) shown here in a wheelchair being held by a Nazi soldier. What is this cartoon trying to suggest regarding the relationship between Vichy France and Nazi Germany?

Reynaud Resigns

On 01 June the French Government was evacuated from Paris to a town south of Paris called Tours. On 14 June German forces entered Paris. The taking of Paris proved to be a shattering blow to French morale. Reynaud was now undermined by the defeatists. General Weygand by now believed that an armistice was unavoidable. He declared: 'In three weeks Great Britain will have its neck wrung like a chicken.' On 16 June Reynaud resigned from his post as Prime Minister. Pétain succeeded him. On the following day, Pétain broadcasted to the French nation, stating that the war was lost and that an armistice must be signed with the Germans.

Frenchmen… I have today assumed the direction of the Government of France. Convinced of the affection of our admirable army… convinced of the confidence of the whole nation, I give myself to France to assuage (relieve) her misfortune… It is with a heavy heart that I say we must end the fight. Last night I applied to our adversary (enemy) to ask if he is prepared to seek with me, soldier to soldier, after the battle, honourably, the means whereby hostilities may cease.

▲ General Charles de Gaulle (1890–1970) pictured in the French town of Laval soon after it had been liberated on 24 August, 1944.

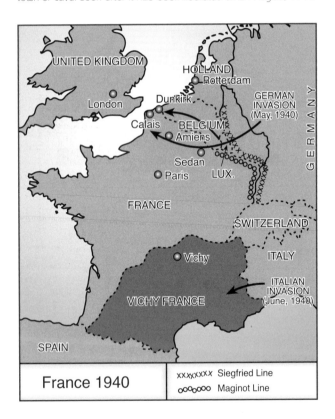

France 1940

xxxxxxx Siegfried Line
ooooooo Maginot Line

General Charles de Gaulle disagreed with the surrender and fled to England. On 18 June, 1940, in England, de Gaulle made his famous BBC broadcast declaring that he was establishing a **'Government in Exile'** and calling on all French people to continue the struggle against the Nazis. His request received very little support at home.

I, General de Gaulle, at this moment in London, invite French officers and soldiers at present on British territory, engineers, and skilled workers, to get in touch with me.
Whatever happens, the flame of French resistance must not be quenched. Nor shall it be.

Armistice

On 22 June an armistice between the French and Germans was signed at Compiègne in France. Hitler insisted on signing the armistice in the same railway carriage that Marshal Foch, Supreme Commander of the Allied Forces, had used for the German surrender in 1918.

Under the terms of the armistice, northern and western France, including Paris, were to be occupied by the Germans. The rest of France was to remain under the control of a new French regime established in the old spa town of Vichy. Pétain became the head of the new French state.

The Vichy Regime

Within ten days of coming to power, the French Chamber of Deputies and the Senate voted to give Pétain the power to draw up a new constitution. The vote was a huge majority of 569 to 80. Pétain immediately distanced himself from the Republic, declaring himself *Chief de l'État* ('Head of State') instead of President. The regime was simply named the French State. Pétain was responsible for all government appointments and the passing of laws.

Pétain stood for traditional virtues as suggested by the Vichy slogan: **'Family, Work, Country'**.

The characteristics of the Vichy regime soon emerged. It was deeply conservative and anti-democratic:

- Local councils were abolished.

- Trade unions were banned and replaced by Mussolini-type corporations, which were supposed to look after workers' rights.

- The regime moved closer to the Catholic Church; divorce was made more difficult. However, the state retained control of education.

- Vichyites (those who supported the regime) blamed the fall of France in 1940 on the Third Republic. As a result, some of its leaders were punished. Daladier and Blum were imprisoned, but had to be released in 1942 when the charges brought against them couldn't be proven. Blum was handed over to the Germans in 1942. US forces freed him from a German concentration camp in May 1945.

Anti-Semitism

Pétain's hatred of the Jews soon came to light.
- In 1940 a law removed a prohibition (ban) on racist comments in the press.

- Under the terms of the **Statut des Juifs** (Jewish Statute/Law) anyone with three Jewish grandparents was defined as Jewish. Jews were excluded from the Army, judiciary, civil service, teaching profession, the press and all elected offices.

- Assets of wealthy Jewish families, such as the Rothschilds (international Jewish bankers), were taken away.

- From 1942 onwards, the Vichy regime co-operated with the Nazis in deporting Jews to the death camps in Eastern Europe.

▲
Marshall Henri-Phillippe Pétain (1856–1951), head of the French Government after the surrender.

The Economy

The armistice had left the French with the poorest part of the land. Over 65% of French Industry and 60% of its agricultural land were now in German hands. The Germans took what they wanted, stripping occupied France of money, foodstuffs and industrial products. The invasion of France in 1940 had also disrupted the harvest. As a result, strict rationing had to be introduced in France during the winter of 1940–41.

Relations with Hitler

Pétain firmly believed that his anti-communism would be a sufficient basis on which to build a partnership between Vichy France and Nazi Germany. He was soon to learn that Hitler had no intention of treating Vichy France as an equal.

Hitler made his views clear at a meeting with Pétain at Montoire in France in December 1940. Pétain failed to achieve changes he was looking for in the terms of the armistice from Hitler. He didn't manage to secure the return of 1.9 million French prisoners of war. Hitler showed his indifference towards the Vichy Regime days later when he deported 70,000 French people from Lorraine, in northeast France, to the unoccupied zone, without consulting Pétain.

▲
Pierre Laval (right) with Catholic Bishops in Vichy. Laval became Pétain's Deputy in the Vichy Government in 1940. How do you think the Catholic Church viewed the Vichy State?

Laval and Collaboration[+] (p. 176)

The other dominant figure in the Vichy Regime was Pierre Laval, the Deputy Head of State. Unlike Pétain, Laval believed that submission was inevitable. Laval was a former Foreign Minister of France. He was a pacifist (anti-war) who had played an important role in applying the French policy of appeasement prior to the outbreak of war. From a position on the extreme left of the Socialist Party, he moved further right during the 1920s and 1930s, and became Pétain's Deputy Head of State in the Vichy Government in 1940.

Laval accepted German dominance and tried to remain on good terms with the Nazis by collaborating with them:

France was overly fat and happy. She used and abused her freedom. And it is precisely because there was an excess of freedom in all fields that we find ourselves in the present straits (trouble). It is also a fact – I say this sadly because a great calamity (disaster) has befallen us – that the existing institutions cannot be allowed to survive a disaster of this magnitude (size). Without wishing to impassion (fire up) the debate, let me remind you that too much freedom in our schools contributed to our demise (end). One word was forbidden in our schools, the word Patrie (fatherhood). Take a look at our neighbours. Italy was once on the verge of anarchy (chaos). One could walk the streets only at the risk of being assaulted by a mob bent on seizing power. In Germany, defeat had brought on misery, and misery, in turn, had brought on chaos.

Laval and Pétain had little in common. Relations between the men were always tense. On 13 December Pétain dismissed Laval as his Deputy Head of State in favour of Admiral Jean-François Darlan.

Like Laval, Darlan began by collaborating. Darlan was primarily concerned with maintaining Vichy control over French colonies. The Germans wanted bases in French North Africa and in Syria and Lebanon. Darlan thought that if he gave bases to the Germans, the colonies could remain under French control. Therefore, under the May Protocol/Agreement of 1942 he placed the French-controlled Syrian airports at the disposal of the German *Luftwaffe*. This action provoked a strong response from the British, who organised an attack on Syria with the aid of de Gaulle's Free French forces. The Vichy garrison in Syria was soon taken by the British.

Laval Returns

After the end of Vichy control of Syria, Darlan gradually moved away from a policy of collaboration. The Germans became alarmed and their Ambassador in Vichy, Otto Abetz, demanded that Pétain summon Laval back to his old job as Deputy Head of State. Pétain gave in to German pressure on 17 April, 1942. 'I am no better than a messenger boy', he privately told a colleague. Darlan, although no longer Deputy Head of State, remained Commander in Chief of the Navy.

The Occupation of Vichy France

On 11 November, 1942, the Allies landed in North Africa. The Germans now occupied the area under Vichy rule. France was now totally under German control. Despite pleas from General Weygand and others, Pétain refused to leave France to take refuge in Algeria. On 18 November, 1942, Pétain gave up all his powers to Laval. Laval joined the German side once more, saying that the Nazis were saving Europe from communism.

In reality, Laval was no more than a 'puppet' of the Nazi regime. Fritz Sauckel, who had been appointed as *Gauleiter* (Administrator) of France in June 1942, held all the power. No law could be changed without German consent. Laval spent much of his time arguing against Sauckel's demands for hundreds of thousands of French men to go to Germany as forced labourers. Of the

Activity

From your knowledge of political life within the Third French Republic 1920–40 (Chapter 6), do you consider Laval's speech to be a fair assessment of the situation?

1,575,000 demanded, Laval supplied only 785,000. However, Laval failed to stop the transportation of Jews from Vichy France to concentration camps.

The Germans also forced Laval to invite ultra-collaborators into government. In December 1943 Joseph Darnand, head of the hated *Militia* (Secret Police), became Secretary General to the Ministry of Order. In March 1944, Marcel Deat, an extreme right-wing politician and Nazi supporter, became Minister of Labour.

Resistance

Inside France, resistance to Nazi occupation grew slowly. As the deportation of workers continued, popular resistance began to emerge against Nazi oppression. Resistance forces, whose numbers were swelled by men escaping from forced labour, were pursued by the French *Militia* and German *Gestapo*. Captured, often by betrayal, they were first tortured and then sent to concentration camps (p. 174).

▲
De Gaulle marching through the Arc de Triomphe in Paris following the liberation of Paris in August 1945.

The End of Vichy

When the Allies landed in Normandy on 06 June, 1944, Pétain and Laval realised that their days were numbered. On 17 August both Laval and Pétain were forced to flee Vichy. Pétain fled to Switzerland, but was returned to France to face trial. Laval fled first to Germany and then to Spain. He too was returned to France to face trial.

At his trial, Pétain claimed in his defence that old age had weakened his ability to make good decisions. Nevertheless, he was sentenced to death. Charles de Gaulle changed his death sentence for treason to life imprisonment. He was jailed on the Ile d'Yeu, an island off the west coast of France, where he died in 1951. His role in French politics remains controversial and some still regard him as a patriot rather than a traitor.

Laval was not so lucky. He was sentenced to death by firing squad. Many others suffered a similar fate. Those who had betrayed the Republic by collaborating with the Nazis were sought out and shot. This process is known as *L'épuration* (The Purging). It is estimated that there were between 30,000 and 40,000 executions in France before Charles de Gaulle's authority became effective.

An Assessment of Vichy France

After the war, the Vichy regime continued to have its defenders. Some French people argued that state collaboration of the Vichy regime under Pétain and Laval saved the French people from even more oppression from the Nazis.

On the other hand, it is argued that the Vichy regime did little to protect its own citizens from mass deportation to Germany as slave labour. In reality, Vichy France received practically nothing in exchange for the collaboration it had voluntarily undertaken.

Questions

Ordinary Level

Write a paragraph on one of the following:

1. The fall of France, 1940.

2. Marshal Pétain.

3. The end of Vichy France, 1944.

Higher Level

1. Account for the rise and fall of the Vichy regime in France, 1940–44.

2. 'Vichy France proved to be little more than a German puppet state.' Discuss.

Read the document below and answer the questions that follow. The document is an extract from a speech given by Marshal Pétain, 11 October, 1940.

Frenchmen!

Four months ago, France suffered one of the most thorough defeats in her history. This defeat was caused by many factors, not all of which were of a technical nature. In truth, the disaster was simply the reflection, on a military plane, of the weaknesses and defects of the former regime. Many of you, however, as I well know, loved that regime. Because you exercised the right to vote every four years, you considered yourselves to be free citizens in a free state. I will thus surprise you by saying that, to an extent unparalleled (unmatched) *in the history of France, the state was at the mercy of special interests during the past 20 years. It was taken over in various ways, successively and sometimes simultaneously, by coalitions of economic interests, and by teams of politicians and syndicalists* (socialists who believed that countries should be governed by trade unions) *falsely claiming to represent the working class.*

Everything pointed to the impotence (weakness) *of a regime which repudiated* (rejected) *its very principles by resorting to emergency decree powers in the face of every serious crisis. War and defeat merely hastened* (speeded up) *the coming of the political revolution toward which the country was eventually headed. Hindered* (held up) *by such domestic political considerations, the regime was, for the most part, incapable of formulating* (planning) *and implementing a foreign policy worthy of France. Inspired in turn by a paranoid* (fearful) *nationalism or a doctrinaire* (rigid) *pacifism, characterised by lack of understanding and weakness – at the very moment when our victory called upon us to be at once generous and strong, our foreign policy could only result in disaster. It took us approximately fifteen years to fall into the abyss to which it inexorably* (inevitably) *led. One day in September 1939, without even daring to consult the Chambers, the Government declared war. This war was all but lost in advance. We had been equally incapable of avoiding or of preparing for it.*

1. What disaster does Pétain refer to at the beginning of the speech?
2. Why does Pétain consider that the French people were not entirely free prior to the establishment of the Vichy regime?
3. According to Pétain, how did the French Government deal with every serious crisis?
4. Why did Pétain consider the war 'all but lost' as soon as it was declared in 1939?
5. How successful was Pétain in restoring French national pride during the period 1940–44? (Higher Level only)

 **10** # Economic and Social Problems in Britain and Germany During the Inter-War Years, 1919–39

The European Economy in 1919

The inter-war years in Europe were marked by major economic and social problems. The twin problems of inflation and unemployment led to growing demands that governments improve and increase the social services provided for citizens.

Key Concept: Inflation

Inflation is a rise in prices and a fall in the purchasing power of money.

With the end of World War I in 1918, European governments struggled to restore normal economic activity and improve social conditions. Vast sums of money had been borrowed by European states to finance the war. High inflation swept away previously healthy currencies and weakened the European political scene. Prices were three times higher in 1920 in Britain than before the war and five times higher in Germany. Workers began to resent the widening gap between themselves and the wealthy classes.

Key Personality: John Maynard Keynes

Born and educated in Cambridge in England, John Maynard Keynes was one of the most influential economic thinkers of the twentieth century. He taught economics at Cambridge University from 1906–8. During World War I, he worked at the Treasury. He went on to represent this department as a delegate to the Paris Peace Conference in 1919.

Keynes was highly critical of the level of reparations which Germany was expected to pay. In his book *The Economic Consequences of the Peace* (1919), Keynes argued that such reparations would cripple Germany and lead to further instability. However, his views failed to make an impression

▲ John Maynard Keynes (1883–1946), one of the most influential economic thinkers of the twentieth century.

on the political leaders, who were under immense pressure from a public mood which was determined to get revenge.

After the war he continued to advise successive British governments on economic policy. Following the Wall Street Crash in 1929, and the depression which followed, Keynes argued against the belief that the economic market always had an ability to correct itself. He believed that government spending on public works could stabilise a depressed economy by creating jobs. The 'Keynesian' approach to economic stability was clearly expressed in his book *The General Theory of Employment, Interest and Money* (1936). His theories failed to make an impression on government policy during the 1930s.

The Beveridge Report, which was published in 1942, took on board some of Keynes' views. The report recommended that the British Government introduce a social insurance scheme, covering areas such as unemployment and family allowances. Keynes also had an influence on the outcome of the Bretton Woods Conference of 1944, which led to the establishment of the World Bank and the International Monetary Fund.

Keynes' arguments that government intervention could lead to full employment received a more favourable reception following World War II. His theories became the basis of government economic policy both in Britain and Western Europe until the 1970s.

Post-War Economic Problems in Britain

Britain emerged from World War I with its empire intact and its international status higher than ever. However, economically the war proved to be very expensive for Britain.

The British economy had been declining slowly before the war. Britain had slipped down the league of industrial powers. Its share of world trade was declining and exports fell dramatically during the war. In 1885 British exports amounted to 17% of world trade; by 1913 this figure had dropped to 14%. Much of Britain's industry was old fashioned and generally slow to adopt modern techniques of production. Traditional industries, such as textiles and shipbuilding, declined. This was mainly due to the rise of shipbuilding in the

United States of America and Japan. Britain also relied too heavily on the coal industry as a source of energy, while other European countries were increasingly turning to oil and hydro-electricity.

Unemployment and Industrial Unrest

The steady decline in British industry led to serious unemployment problems. A temporary boom in 1919 soon came to a halt, and by the autumn of 1920 over 1.5 million men were without work. Many soldiers who had returned home a year earlier as war heroes, now found themselves unable to find work. From then until the outbreak of World War II in 1939, British unemployment figures never fell below one million. Unemployment was most evident in the north of England and southern Wales, where the old industries were located.

The post-war period in Britain saw an increase in industrial tensions between worker and employer. As the profits made from industry dropped, employers sought to reduce wages. This is especially true in relation to Britain's coal mines. Miners were forced to accept a wage cut following an unsuccessful three-month strike in 1921. In the wake of the miners' defeat, wages were also cut in the engineering, docks, shipbuilding, textiles, printing and railway industries.

Problems in the Coal Industry

Stability seemed to be returning to Britain, as Stanley Baldwin's Conservative Government (1924–29) became the first government in the post-war period to run its full term. Industrial trouble was dying down. By 1925, days lost due to strike had dropped by 90% compared to the figure in 1921. Unemployment had also dropped. It was therefore unusual that a general strike occurred in Britain in 1926.

The roots of the general strike lay in the mining industry. Although the miners had been defeated in 1921, much bitterness remained. As the coal

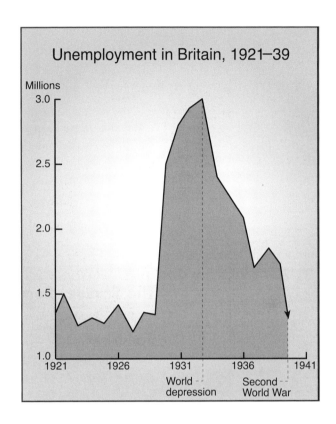

▲
Stanley Baldwin (1867–1947), Conservative Prime Minister of Britain in the 1920s.

industry continued to decline, mine owners tried to offset their losses with further wage cuts.

In June 1925 the mine owners gave notice of wage cuts and threatened the miners with a lockout if they refused to accept the new terms. The miner leader, AJ Cook, refused to accept these conditions and called on other trade unions to join the miners in a general strike. On **'Red Friday'** (31 July, 1925), he managed to persuade his colleagues in the Trades Union Council (TUC) to support the miners.

To avert a general strike, Prime Minister Baldwin intervened and established a Royal Commission to examine the problem. In the meantime, wage cuts would be suspended and the Government agreed to subsidise the coal industry for a short while out of public money.

It seemed as if the miners had won a major victory on Red Friday. In fact, Baldwin's Conservative Government was buying valuable time. It was using the time to make plans to ensure minimum disruption in the event of a general strike.

The Samuel Commission

The Government appointed Sir Herbert Samuel, a former Liberal Party minister, to head a commission to investigate difficulties in the coal industry. When the Royal Commission issued its report in March 1926, it suggested some long-term initiatives to improve the industry. However, in the short-term it suggested that there was no alternative to wage cuts. It also proposed that an extra half-hour should be added to the working week of miners in an effort to make the industry more competitive. Cook rejected the Samuel Report and adopted the slogan: **'Not a penny off the pay, not a minute of the day.'**

General Strike, 1926

On 01 May the miners went out on strike. With some hesitation, the TUC ordered the railwaymen, transport workers, dockers and printers to go out in sympathy. Over two million workers responded, and a general strike began at midnight on 03 May, 1926.

Much to the disappointment of the TUC, there was little disorder. The Government contingency plan worked well. Soldiers, police, students and other volunteers were used to drive lorries and buses, unload ships and distribute supplies. The Government organised the *British Gazette*, which was edited by Winston Churchill, to ensure the circulation of news.

The General Strike is in operation, expressing in no uncertain terms a direct challenge to the ordered government. It would be futile (useless) to attempt to minimise the seriousness of such a challenge, constituting as it does an effort to force upon some 42,000,000 British citizens the will of less than 4,000,000 others engaged in the vital services of the country.

The strike is intended as a direct hold-up of the nation to ransom. It is for the nation to stand firm in its determination not to flinch. From Winston Churchill's editorial of **British Gazette**, 06 May, 1926.

Some right-wing Conservatives, such as Churchill, wanted the Government to take tougher action against the strikers by arresting trade union leaders. Baldwin rejected such advice, fearing that it would make the situation worse. King George V also played a calming role, urging employers not to punish the workers.

In the document above, how does Churchill consider the General Strike to be a direct threat to British Democracy?

The Strike Ends

When it was clear that the Government would not yield, most trade union leaders sought an agreement. Sir Herbert Samuel acted as a mediator. He proposed the creation of a National Wages Board for the coal industry. In the meantime, miners' wages would not be reduced.

On 12 May, the TUC agreed to call off the strike. The miners had not been consulted about the decision. They felt betrayed and refused to return to work. The miners held out for a further six months. Driven by hardship, they eventually drifted back to work and faced longer hours and less pay.

The results of the strike were mixed. While it represented a defeat for trade unions, especially the miners, it also warned employers of the folly of cutting wages. In the years after 1926, wage disagreements were generally settled quickly, as employers did not want to risk another major strike.

▲ A volunteer bus driver is accompanied by a policeman as he sets out from the depot during the General Strike of 1926. Why do you think the policeman is with him?

The Wall Street Crash, 1929

The late 1920s brought some economic recovery to Britain. Unemployment fell to about one million as new investments arrived and trade was revived. All of this came to a sudden end with the collapse of the Wall Street Stock Exchange in October 1929, and with the onset of the **Great Depression.**

▲ Workers walking to work during the General Strike. This scene shows the lack of public transport.

Unemployment in the USA rose from one million in 1929 to 13 million by 1933 (more than a quarter of the workforce). The collapse of the US economy had a knock-on effect on Europe as world trade shrank to one-third of what it had been.

Key Concept: The Depression

In an economic boom, products are in demand, industry thrives and unemployment falls. In an economic slump, there is an oversupply of products and not enough money to go around. As a result, there is a fall or significant reduction in industrial or trading activity, which results in increased unemployment. When an economy fails to climb out of a slump over a number of years, it is called a 'depression'.

The severe economic depression of the late 1920s and 1930s occurred on a worldwide scale following the Wall Street Crash in 1929. The effect of the crash spread quickly throughout the world because 40% of all industrial goods were produced at that time by the USA. Factories and businesses closed and unemployment rose rapidly as American loans and investment to European countries ceased.

The Labour Government in Britain

The British general election of 1929 brought Labour back to power. Ramsay MacDonald formed a minority Labour Government with the support of 59 Liberals.

The onset of the Great Depression in October 1929 caused major problems for the Labour Government. MacDonald and his ministers were inexperienced in economic matters and had difficulty handling the problems created by the economic slump.

▲
Unemployed men during the depression, waiting for news of job possibilities outside the labour exchange.

Unemployment

Unemployment in Britain began to rise dramatically as the world moved into depression. Demand for British goods declined. Rising unemployment meant that the Government collected less money from income tax, while at the same time had to pay out more than before in unemployment benefits. By 1932 unemployment stood at 2.7 million.

Foreign businessmen, who held large amounts of money in Britain, started exchanging their pounds for other currencies such as dollars or gold. They felt that sterling was too risky to have at a time when the British economy was in sharp decline.

This caused a run on the pound (panic withdrawal of money) and threatened to cause national bankruptcy as reserves in the Bank of England ran low.

The fall of the Labour Government

Faced with this crisis, the Labour Government had two alternatives. First, it could reduce spending and borrow money from foreign banks to sort its reserves. The Chancellor of the Exchequer, Philip Snowden, as well as the Bank of England, supported this plan of action. Second, the Government could devalue the pound. This would discourage the trading of pounds for other currencies, as the pound would now buy fewer dollars. **Devaluation** could also boost trade by making British goods cheaper and more competitive on the world market.

MacDonald decided to follow the advice of the Bank of England. Taxes were raised and civil servants had their salaries reduced. Unemployment benefits were to be reduced by 10%. It was estimated that these savings would amount to £76 million.

Although the Conservative and Liberal parties supported the decision, it proved to be unacceptable to certain sections of the Labour Party and the trade union movement. Opponents of the scheme argued that the proposals placed too great a burden on working-class people. The cabinet split on the issue and MacDonald resigned as Prime Minister on 24 August, 1931.

> **Devaluation:**
> A reduction in the value of a currency against other currencies.
> For example €1 may be = $1 but if devalued, €2 could be = $1. It can often lead to an improvement in the economy as exports are then cheaper and therefore more competitive in the world market.

National Government in Britain

On the same day that MacDonald resigned, a meeting was held between the leaders of the major political parties. Consultations with the King resulted in the formation of an all-party National Government. Ramsay MacDonald, with Stanley Baldwin, the Conservative Leader, as his deputy, led this new Government. A majority of the Labour Party opposed the National Government and, as a result, MacDonald and his supporters were expelled from the Labour Party.

Election, October 1931

In October 1931 the National Government sought to receive a mandate from the British people by calling a General Election. The Labour Party, as well as a minority from the Liberal Party led by Lloyd George, opposed the National Government. The result of the election was a landslide victory for the National Government. MacDonald's

▲
National Government Leaders Stanley Baldwin (left) and Ramsay MacDonald.

National Labour Party won 13 seats, the Liberals 18 seats and the Conservatives 473 seats. The Labour Party only won 52 seats.

MacDonald remained as Prime Minister. However, the Conservatives, as the largest party, held 11 out of the 20 cabinet positions. Stanley Baldwin became the real power in the Government and the Conservative Neville Chamberlain replaced Philip Snowdon as Chancellor of the Exchequer.

Key Concept: Protectionism

Protectionism is an economic policy designed to protect home industries by imposing taxes (sometimes referred to as tariffs or duties) on imported goods. The idea is to raise the price of cheaper imported goods in order to encourage consumers to spend their money on goods produced by domestic industry. Protectionism is the opposite of free trade, a system whereby goods can come and go free from tariffs.

Economic Reforms

The National Government managed to stabilise the economy through a series of measures introduced by Neville Chamberlain.

- **Import Duties Bill**, February 1932: This bill imposed duties on certain imports. It provided protection for British manufacturers and ended a policy of free trade that had been followed by all British governments since 1846.

> **Commonwealth:**
> An association of states made up of Britain and most of its former colonies.

- A system of **imperial trading preference** was attempted. At a conference held in Ottawa, Canada, during July and August 1932, Chamberlain attempted to persuade Australia, New Zealand and Canada to reduce tariffs on trade between the commonwealth nations. The conference had only limited success, as many of the Dominions (members of the commonwealth) were reluctant to reduce tariffs as they were attempting to protect their own economies.

- An attempt was made to revive the steel industry by imposing tariffs on foreign steel. A **British Iron and Steel Federation** was formed. New steelworks were established at Ebbw Vale and Corby in Wales, but the federation was bitterly criticised for not allowing a similar plant to be built at Jarrow in the northeast of England, where unemployment was the highest in the country.

- Cheap loans were given to the Cunard Shipping Company for the construction of luxury liners such as the Queen Mary and the Queen Elizabeth.

Unemployment Continues

By the end of 1937 unemployment had fallen to 1.4 million. The economy in the midlands and the south improved dramatically. This was mainly due to the arrival of new industries, such as car manufacturing in Coventry and Oxford. However, high unemployment continued in areas that had concentrated on the older industries, such as coal mining and shipbuilding. This is known as 'structural unemployment' because it is associated with a fault in the structure of the economy, rather than with a world economic crisis.

Unemployment was mostly concentrated in the north of England, Scotland and Wales. Some towns in economically depressed areas had massive unemployment. In 1934 some 68% of the workforce in Jarrow, in northeast England, and 62% of the workforce in Merthyr Tydfil, in Wales, were unemployed.

> **Malnutrition:**
> A lack of foods needed by the body to keep it working properly.

Case Study: The Jarrow March, October 1936

Hunger Marches

To many, the 1930s became known as the 'hungry thirties'. It was during these years that many traditional industries in the northeast of England declined. Malnutrition was common amongst the unemployed.

Unemployment benefits (the dole) were low, and did little to ease the situation. Much bitterness was caused in areas of high unemployment in 1931 by the introduction of a means test, by which the income of the whole family was taken into account before a person qualified for the dole. The dole lasted for only 26 weeks. A 10% reduction of the dole in 1931 made matters worse. The **Unemployment Assistance Board** was established in 1934 to look after the needs of the long-term unemployed. The help provided by the board was totally inadequate and did little to change the

Source A

▲ This cartoon by David Low, published in 1935, is a comment on the Government's ineffectiveness in dealing with poverty. The caption refers to Neville Chamberlain, who had been Chancellor of the Exchequer from 1931–35.

miserable circumstances in which the unemployed lived. For many, the daily battle was simply to survive with some dignity. Mrs Pallas, the wife of an unemployed shipbuilder, was one such survivor, as she explains in this extract from Felix Greene's book *Time to Spare*, published in 1935:

Source B

If only we had work, just imagine what it would be like. On the whole, my husband has worked about one year out of twelve and a half. His face was lovely when I married him, but now he's skin and bones. When I married he was robust (healthy) *and he had a good job. He was earning from eight pounds to ten pounds a week. He's a left-handed ship's riveter – a craft which should be earning him a lot of money. There aren't many left-handed riveters.*

He fell out of work about four months after I was married, so I've hardly known what a week's wage was. Through all the struggling I've still not lost my respectability. About three or four years ago I could even manage to win a competition for the best-kept home for cleanliness and thrift (being careful with money). *The bedclothes were all mended, but they were clean. The originals you could hardly have known for the patches on. My children wouldn't go to school with a hole in their trousers. They come to me. My eldest boy has trousers on at the moment with six patches on them; I just tell him he'll be all the warmer, especially in the winter. My husband helps me with the darning; I do the patching. I've just put the eighth patch into a shirt of his. I take the sleeves out of one and put them in another – anything to keep going.*

In protest against such conditions, '**hunger marches**' amongst the unemployed became a feature of the 1930s. Most of these marches were organised by the National Unemployed Workers Movement (NUWM). In 1933 over 2000 workers from the north of England marched to London. Further hunger marches took place in 1934 and 1936. The most famous of these marches was the 'Jarrow Crusade' in October 1936. In the extract below, Wal Hannington, a communist and a member of the NUWM, describes how the hunger marches of 1933 forced the Government to grant some concessions to the unemployed:

Source C

The hunger march in 1933 had stimulated (encouraged) *a nationwide demand for humane treatment by the Government. The Government could not escape this; the march had been an extremely disturbing factor for them, and the agitation* (protest) *which it had aroused compelled* (forced) *them to retreat. Before the march Mr Chamberlain, the Chancellor of the Exchequer, had stated in the House of Commons, that there was no need to restore the cuts in benefit to the unemployed, as the unemployed, he claimed, were better off than they were in 1931, because of the fall in the cost of living. The march compelled him to eat these words, and when he introduced his 1934 budget, he announced that the Government had decided to restore the ten per cent cuts that had been made in the scales of the unemployed by the economy measures of 1931.*

Unemployment in Jarrow

Jarrow was a small industrial town situated six miles east of Newcastle-Upon-Tyne, in the northeast of England. Until the late 1920s, there had been plenty of work to go around at the Palmer shipbuilding yard. The yard, which had been established by Mark Palmer in the mid-nineteenth century, was, for a time, recognised as one of the best run and most up-to-date shipbuilding operations in Europe. However, stiff competition from American and Japanese shipbuilding companies eventually led to its closure in 1935. This resulted in Jarrow changing from a 'boom town' into an unemployment 'black spot'. The town was devastated by high unemployment as a result of the closure.

By September 1935, when both Jarrow's ironworks and shipbuilding yards had closed, unemployment in the town was at 72.9% of the working population. One out of two shops in the town had closed. As unemployment figures increased, poverty set in. Poor housing and malnutrition led to high infant mortality (death). The town was described at the time by one of its residents as being a 'filthy, dirty, falling down, consumptive (sick) area'. Ellen Wilkinson, the local Labour Party MP, complained:

The plain fact is that if people have to live and bear and bring up their children in bad houses on too little food, their resistance to disease is lowered and they die before they should.

From **The Town That Was Murdered: The Life Story of Jarrow** by Ellen Wilkinson, 1939.

In 1934 the English writer JB Priestly visited Jarrow. In an extract from his book, *English Journey,* which was published in 1934, he paints a depressing picture:

My guide book devotes one short sentence to Jarrow: 'A busy town (35,590 inhabitants (people)), has large iron works and shipbuilding yards.' It is time this was amended to: 'An idle and ruined town (35,590 inhabitants, wondering what is to become of them), had large iron works and can still show what is left of shipbuilding.'

There is no escape anywhere in Jarrow from its prevailing (current) misery, for it is entirely a working-class town. One little street may be rather more wretched than another, but to the outsider they all look alike. One out of every two shops appeared to be permanently closed. Wherever we went there were men hanging about, not scores of them, but hundreds and thousands of them. The whole town looked as if it had entered a perpetual (continuous) penniless bleak Sabbath (the Seventh day of the week, devoted to worship and rest). The men wore the drawn masks of prisoners of war. A stranger from a distant civilisation, observing the condition of the place and its people, would have arrived at once to the conclusion that Jarrow had deeply offended some celestial (heavenly) emperor of the island and was now being punished. He would never believe us if we told him that in theory this town was as good as any other and that its inhabitants were not criminals with votes.

A March is Organised

The march was organised by the local town council and Jarrow's Labour MP, Ellen Wilkinson. An outstanding speaker and political organiser, Wilkinson had a long tradition of fighting for the rights of the working class. She had been a strong supporter of the hunger marches organised by the NUWM in the past. She had spent a brief period as a member of the British Communist Party before being elected Labour Party MP for Middlesborough East in 1924.

On 20 July, 1936, a decision was taken at Jarrow Borough Council to organise a march from Jarrow to London to present a petition from the unemployed in Jarrow to the Parliament. In order to gain all-party support for the march, it was decided by the members of Jarrow Borough Council to organise the march independently of the NUWM, which was considered by many to have strong links with the Communist Party. Indeed, the term 'crusade' was chosen instead of 'march' to distinguish this march from similar ones organised by the NUWM.

A team of 200 marchers was chosen following medical examination. Each man had his boots soled and healed and was issued with two pairs of socks. Women were not invited to march.

Source E

At a great demonstration of the unemployed [it was] suggested that the unemployed of Jarrow should march to London and tell the people of England on their way down of the treatment they had received. That was in July 1936. Labour had just won its majority on the Town Council. The Mayor decided that

From **The Town That Was Murdered: The Life Story of Jarrow** by Ellen Wilkinson, 1939.

The Jarrow Crusade

On 05 October, 1936, 200 marchers left the town hall in Jarrow and set out on a 300-mile walk to London. They carried with them an oak box containing a petition signed by 11,000 inhabitants of Jarrow. The march was led by a mouth-organ band with a Labrador dog as a mascot. Two doctors, a barber and a group of journalists accompanied the marchers. Ellen Wilkinson, and Alderman JW Thompson, the Mayor of Jarrow, remained in touch with the marchers and participated from time to time in the march.

Source F

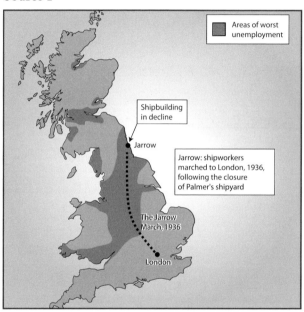

Source G

This is not a hunger march, but a protest march. The unanimity (agreement) of the protest that Jarrow is making to the rest of the country is indicated in the fact that the political parties represented on the Jarrow Town Council have agreed to bury the political hatchet to the extent of holding no elections this November. Further, although the town cannot by law spend a farthing (penny) of the ratepayers' money on this demonstration, the labours of its Mayor in the despatching of about 200,000 letters to other corporations, trade unions, co-operative societies, and similar bodies at the expense of the march fund has raised that fund to £850, and it is hoped to have the round £1,000 before the marchers reach the Marble Arch on October 31.

There is no political aspect to this march. It is simply the town of Jarrow saying 'Send us work.' In the ranks of the marchers are Labour men, Liberals, Tories (Conservatives), and one or two Communists, but you cannot tell who's who. It has the Church's blessing; in fact, it took the blessing of the Bishop of Ripon (Dr Lunt) and a subscription of £5 from him when it set out to-day. It also had the blessing of the Bishop of Jarrow (Dr Gordon).

From **The Manchester Guardian**, Tuesday 13 October, 1936.

A second-hand bus, which was bought for £20, carried essential equipment – such as blankets, waterproofs and first-aid supplies. An advance party, led by Harry Stoddart (a member of the Labour Party) and Rodney Suddick (a Conservative Party member), travelled ahead of the march arranging overnight accommodation. The standard of overnight accommodation varied considerably, depending on the generosity of those living in towns where the march stopped for the night. In Barnsley, the men were given free access by the town council to the local heated swimming pool.

The men set off at 8.45 each morning of their 25-day march to London. They walked for 50 minutes at a time followed by a 10-minute rest. Sandwiches and drinks were provided at regular intervals. In some respects many of the men were eating better food on the march than they had been used to at home:

Source H

With eggs and salmon and such sandwiches as I saw today being consumed on the menu it is emphatically (definitely) *not a hunger march. The men are doing well on it, and only two of them have fallen out for reasons of health in nearly 90 miles of marching. All the time communication is maintained with Jarrow, and if work turns up for a man on the march, back he will go to it.*

The organisation seems well-nigh (nearly) *perfect. It includes a transport wagon – a bus bought for £20 and converted – which goes ahead with the sleeping kit, waterproofs for every man worn bandolero fashion, 1s 6d pocket money and two 1p stamps a week, medical attention, haircutting (and shaving for the inexpert), cobbling, accommodation at night in drill halls, schools, church institutes, and even town halls, and advance agents in the persons of the Labour agent at Jarrow, Mr Harry Stoddart, and the Conservative agent, Mr R Suddick, who work together in arranging accommodation and getting halls for meetings.*

From **The Manchester Guardian**, Tuesday 13 October, 1936.

▲
The Jarrow Crusade, 26 October, 1936. Marchers from Jarrow approach Bedford on their way to London with their petition.

Impact of the March

The Jarrow Crusade successfully reached London on 01 November. Despite popular support, which was demonstrated throughout the march, their demonstration at Hyde Park Corner in central London was not well attended. Their decision not to march to the Parliament in Westminster proved to be a big mistake. Instead, in a more low-key approach, they allowed Ellen Wilkinson to present their petition during a debate on unemployment in the House of Commons on 04 November. In a passionate speech she called on the Government to introduce immediate measures to ease the hardship of the population of Jarrow. Her pleas fell on deaf ears. Much to the disappointment of the organisers of the march, the Prime Minister Stanley Baldwin declined to meet with a deputation from the men, claiming that he was too busy.

Although the Jarrow march gained the sympathy of the nation, the Government did little to lighten the hardship of the town. The Ministry of Labour attempted to disguise the extent of unemployment in Jarrow by merging its labour exchange with that of nearby Hebburn, a wealthier town with lower unemployment, giving the area an unemployment figure of 39%. Ellen Wilkinson complained bitterly at the failure of the Labour Party and the Trades Union Council to give adequate support to the marchers.

Source I

Quite independently of our march, unemployed from Scotland, Wales, Cumberland, Durham and Yorkshire were marching to London to expose their grievances (complaints) *against the Means Test and UAB* (Unemployment Assistance Board) *regulations. The Trades Union Congress had frowned on the marches, and the Labour Party Executive followed the lead. No one could say that the Jarrow March was 'communist-inspired', but indubitably* (without a doubt) *there were two communists in our ranks as there were several Tories. Had the Labour Party put its power behind the marches, sent out the call for solidarity* (unity) *with them, then by the time these men had reached London, not only from Jarrow, but from all parts of the country, the support that would have been roused from everywhere would have been enough to shake the complacency* (non-interest) *of the Baldwin Government.*

From **The Town That Was Murdered: The Life Story of Jarrow** by Ellen Wilkinson, 1939.

Although unemployment in Britain had fallen by the end of 1937, conditions in depressed areas continued to get worse. A recession in 1938 caused another rise in unemployment. By the end of that year the unemployment figure had risen to 1.8 million. The following tables provide an insight into the levels of unemployment in major industries and regions in Britain throughout the 'hungry thirties'.

Source J

Percentage unemployment in major industries compared to national average:

	1929	1932	1936	1938
Coal	18.2	41.2	25.0	22.0
Cotton	14.5	31.1	15.1	27.7
Shipbuilding	23.2	59.5	30.6	21.4
Iron and steel	19.9	48.5	29.5	24.8
Average for all industries	9.9	22.9	12.5	13.3

Source K

Percentage of workers in various regions of Great Britain who were unemployed:

	1929	1932	1937
London and Southeast England	5.6	13.7	6.4
Southwest England	8.1	17.1	7.8
Midlands	9.3	20.1	7.2
Northern England	13.5	27.1	13.8
Wales	19.3	26.5	22.3
Scotland	12.1	27.7	15.9

Some relief was brought to Jarrow when, in 1938, a ship-breaking yard and an engineering works were established. However, the Government had no strategy for reducing long-term unemployment. The problem continued until 1939, when concern about Nazi expansion in Europe prompted the British government to begin a rearmament program, which stimulated the economy and reduced unemployment.

This cartoon by David Low was published in 1939. It shows the relationship between the production of arms and the reduction in unemployment.

Social Change in Britain

During World War I, the British Government realised that working-class people deserved some reward for their sacrifices. The Prime Minister, Lloyd George, promised to build 'homes fit for heroes'. Throughout the inter-war period successive governments introduced legislation to reform unemployment, insurance, education, health and housing. It became the accepted policy that state intervention was necessary to introduce such reforms.

Unemployment benefit

Unemployment was the most pressing problem for governments during the inter-war period.

- The **Unemployment Insurance Act, 1920,** increased unemployment benefits from seven to 15 shillings a week for up to 15 weeks per year. This scheme included most workers with an income under £250 a year. Almost two-thirds of the workforce were now insured against unemployment.

- In 1921 Lloyd George's Government further extended the Unemployment Insurance Act. Benefits were now paid for two 16-week periods per year. The extra payments were called 'uncovenanted' benefits. This meant that the workers had not contributed anything towards them by way of social insurance. This form of payment, that later became known as the **'dole'**, was means-tested. Only those who were poverty-stricken as result of unemployment received the money. However, this represented a great step forward as the Government had accepted some responsibility for caring for the unemployed.

- The **Unemployment Act, 1934,** introduced by the National Government, allowed for benefit to be paid from the age of 14. The Act included a very strict means test whereby benefit could be refused if others in the family were working.

Housing

Although Lloyd George's promise to build 'houses fit for heroes' was not fully implemented, some progress towards the building of social housing was made.

- The **Addison Housing Act, 1919,** provided cash for local authorities to build houses for the working class. By the end of 1922, over 213,000 new houses had been built.

- The **Wheatley Act, 1924,** allowed local authorities to give yearly grants to build council houses. These houses were then rented to working-class people. Rents were fixed at pre-war levels, which made them affordable. By 1933 over 500,000 such houses had been built.

- The **Greenwood Housing Act, 1930,** provided government subsidies to local authorities for the purpose of slum clearance.

In an effort to control spending, the National Government suspended some of their schemes during the economic slump that occurred from 1931–34.

Education

The **Fisher Education Act, 1918,** was based on the belief that working-class children deserved a good education. In this Act, compulsory education was provided for all up to the age of 14. Local Authorities could also provide 'continuation schools' up to the age of 16. In addition, nurseries were to be opened for under-fives. In principle, the act was very progressive, but from 1921 onwards, as the economic situation worsened, many of the provisions of the Act were not implemented due to government cutbacks.

By 1939 only a small proportion of working-class children were finishing secondary education.

Assessment

Social conditions improved considerably during the inter-war period as a result of increased state involvement. Government spending on Social Services had increased from £22 million in 1913 to £204 million by 1935. However, the Government's failure to deal adequately with health insurance and education meant that many people living in depressed areas failed to escape the poverty trap.

Post-War Economic Problems in Germany

World War I put the German economy under huge pressure. The Allied blockade of German ports was not lifted until the Treaty of Versailles was signed on 28 June, 1919. By that time over a quarter of a million Germans had died of starvation. Under the terms of the Treaty of Versailles, Germany lost 75% of its iron ore resources, 25% of its coal deposits and 15% of its arable land.

Reparations

Germany's economic difficulties were made worse by the Allied demands for reparations (compensation) to be paid for the damage caused during World War I. In 1921 the Reparations Commission finally agreed that Germany owed a debt of £6,600 million. The money was to be repaid in yearly instalments of £100 million. The British economist John Maynard Keynes estimated that this sum amounted to three times what the German Government could actually pay. The Allies refused to accept large payments in kind (coal, iron, chemicals, etc.) for fear that it might affect their own domestic industries. The German Government had two options. They could raise taxes or borrow money to meet their annual repayments. Since raising taxes would be most unpopular, the Government decided to borrow heavily.

The Occupation of the Ruhr

At a conference in London in December 1922, the Germans protested that they could not meet their reparation payments due for the following year. The French rejected a German request for a postponement until the German currency, the mark, stabilised. When the Germans failed to pay an instalment in January 1923, the French Premier, Poincaré, lost patience and sent French troops into the Ruhr to extract payment by taking possession of supplies of iron, steel and coal.

The Germans responded through a policy of passive resistance. When German workers refused to work, French miners were sent to the Ruhr. This infuriated the German Government and they began to print money to pay the miners of the Ruhr not to work. The cost of the loss of production proved to be twice as costly to the German Government as the annual reparations.

▲ A one billion mark banknote issued on 25 October, 1923.

Hyperinflation

Borrowing and printing money sparked off the greatest inflation in German history. By 1923, some 1,783 printing presses were churning out paper notes day and night. The normal rate of exchange for the German mark was 15 marks to £1 sterling. Within a brief period the rate of exchange increased dramatically:

January 1922	760 marks	= £1 sterling
January 1923	72,000 marks	= £1 sterling
November 1923	16,000,000,000 marks	= £1 sterling

Prices increased rapidly as the value of the mark plummeted. Apples were sold for 300 billion marks a half-pound, and by November 1923 a litre of milk cost 360 billion marks. The price of a cup of coffee could double in the time that it would take to drink it. Workers insisted on being paid each morning so that they could shop at lunchtime before shopkeepers posted new afternoon prices. In the countryside many people resorted to a barter system, where they were prepared to work for food and fuel rather than money.

Konrad Heiden gives an account of the hardship caused by the inflation in his book *Der Führer: Hitler's Rise to Power*, published in 1944:

On Friday afternoons in 1923, long lines of manual and white-collar workers waited outside the pay-windows of the big German factories, department stores, banks and offices…They all stood in lines, staring impatiently at the electric clock, slowly advancing until at last they reached the window and received a bag full of paper notes…With their bags the people moved quickly to the doors, all in haste, the younger ones running. They dashed to the nearest food store, where a line had already formed…When you reached the store, a pound of sugar might have been obtainable for two millions; but, by the time you came to the counter, all you could get for two millions was a half pound, and the saleswoman said the dollar had just gone up again.

European History: Dictatorship and Democracy, 1920–45

The period of hyperinflation caused enormous hardship. As the mark became worthless, real wages declined, and life savings were wiped out. White-collar (office) workers and civil servants on fixed salaries suffered most. Middle-class support for the Weimar Republic dropped.

Not everyone suffered as a result of hyperinflation. Those with fixed mortgages and other loans were able to repay banks with the inflated currency. Industrialists were not only able to repay their debts, but were able to buy out smaller competitors who were struggling. In effect the rich got richer.

Recovery

In August 1923 the first President of the Weimar Republic, Friedrich Ebert, asked Gustav Stresemann to form a government. Under Stresemann, who had been Chancellor for a brief period in 1923 and was Foreign Minister from 1923 until his death in 1929, Germany entered a period of economic stability.

Stresemann's first step was to end the occupation of the Ruhr. He realised that if German industry continued to decline in the Ruhr, future recovery would be very difficult. Stresemann aimed to stabilise the German mark and to resume some reparation payments. He understood that Germany must demonstrate a willingness to co-operate with the payment of reparations in order to win concessions from France and Britain. Accordingly, in November 1923 Stresemann ordered an end to

▲ Gustav Stresemann (1878–1929) was asked to form a government in Germany in 1923.

the passive resistance and resumed reparation deliveries of raw materials from the Ruhr. The French and Belgians eventually left the Ruhr.

On 15 November, 1923, the President of the *Reichsbank*, Hjalmar Schacht, introduced a new mark that was based not on the value of gold, but on a mortgage of the value of all land and industry in Germany. Each *Rentenmark*, as it was known, was exchangeable for one trillion old paper marks.

The Dawes Plan, 1924

In April 1924 the American banker Charles G. Dawes unveiled a new plan to aid German economic recovery. A regular schedule of German reparations payments was established. Although the total sum of reparations was not reduced, Germany was given more time to pay. Germany was to pay £50 million per annum for the next five years. This sum would increase to £125 million from 1929 onwards.

Germany also received loans totalling 800 million marks. American financiers mainly gave the loans, as they saw Germany as a future market for American goods and investments.

The Young Plan, 1929

In 1928 Stresemann protested once more about Allied stubbornness over reparations. A committee of experts led by the American banker Owen D. Young was established to examine the situation. The Young Plan was produced in 1929; it stated that the reparations would be reduced to £2,000 million. Germany was given until 1988 to repay this money.

Stresemann stated, 'We are once again masters in our own house.' However, right-wing forces in Germany condemned the plan, claiming that it would cause the 'economic enslavement' of two future generations of Germans. They also agreed that acceptance of the plan amounted to an acceptance of war guilt. The newspaper and film magnate Alfred Hugenberg, along with Hitler, led a vigorous campaign against the plan.

Industrial Expansion and Social Improvements

By the late 1920s German industry had almost regained its pre-war levels of output. By 1927, coal had reached 79% of its pre-war level, pig iron 68% and steal 86%. Large industrial cartels, such as the United Steel Works and pharmaceutical company IG-Farben, once more dominated the scene. Social conditions in Germany also improved during the Stresemann years. Wages rose above their pre-war levels and social and health schemes were introduced.

However, the extent of German economic recovery during the period 1924–29 should not be exaggerated. By 1928 unemployment still stood at 1.8 million. The economic recovery was also over-reliant on short-term American loans.

Agriculture did not recover to the same extent as industry. Prices were slow to rise and the plight of small farmers failed to improve. Over 20% of Germany's arable land was owned by less than 1% of landowners. Hitler and the Nazi Party would eventually win much support in rural areas with their promises of agricultural reform.

From Boom to Bust

Germany's economic recovery was brought to an abrupt end with the onset of the Great Depression, following the Wall Street Crash in 1929 (p. 135). American investments in Germany ceased and loans were recalled. German exports slumped as nations moved to protect their economies. Unemployment had risen to two million by the end of 1929. By January 1933 the figure had reached six million, a third of all adult males. Banks were forced to close and once more Germans lost their savings. This depression hit Germany harder than the economic collapse of 1923.

The Rise of the Nazis in Germany

Two economic collapses in the space of six years convinced many Germans that the democratic system of the Weimar Republic had not served them well. The Grand Coalition Government – comprising three of the largest parties, the Social Democrats, the Catholic Centre Party and People's Party – was unable to agree on a solution to the crisis. The alliance fell from power in 1930 when the Social Democrats objected to the Government's plans to cut unemployment benefits and old age pensions. Moderate supporters of the Weimar Republic lacked a strong leader. Gustav Stresemann had died three weeks prior to the Wall Street Crash.

▲
Heinrich Brüning (1885–1970) formed a new government in Germany in March 1930 and became known as 'The Hunger Chancellor'.

On 30 March, 1930, Heinrich Brüning formed a new government, which attempted to stop the economic decline by introducing a deflationary budget. Taxes were raised, while wages and social welfare payments were reduced in order to cut state expenditure. The measures were extremely unpopular earning Brüning the title, **'The Hunger Chancellor'**.

Every section of public opinion seemed to be hostile to his proposals. André François-Poncet, the French Ambassador in Berlin, explained this in a report to Paris in September 1931:

> **Deflationary budget:**
> A budget which aims to reduce government spending.

The Chancellor believes he can counteract the crisis by a sharp and methodically executed deflation. He is cutting wages, salaries and pensions and thereby evoking dissatisfaction among workers, civil servants and retired persons. He is introducing price controls which anger the farmers, and controls on the banks, which elicit (bring out) the antipathy (opposition) of financial circles. He is making himself unpopular with industrialists because he wants to lower the prices of raw materials. Everybody is dissatisfied with him.

In May 1932, due to the unpopularity of his policies, Brüning was eventually forced from office. His successors, Franz von Papen and later Kurt von Schleicher, fared no better. In such circumstances the German people turned to more extreme

▲
Public work schemes, such as the building of Autobahnen (motorways), were a feature of the First Four-Year Plan, (1932–36).

▲
Dr Hjalmar Schacht (1877–1970) President of the **Reichsbank** and financial wizard of the 1930s.

parties for a solution, thus paving the way for Hitler's rise to power in January 1933 (p. 26).

Nazi Economic Policy

One of the main factors involved in the rise of the Nazi Party was Hitler's promise to end the economic crisis. Although the world depression was receding when Hitler came to power, his results still seemed remarkable. Unemployment was the greatest problem. Hitler declared on coming to power, 'History will judge us according to whether we have succeeded in providing work.' In 1933 there were six million people unemployed in Germany; by 1936 this figure had been reduced to two million, and by 1939 there was full employment. However, the revival of the German economy cannot be explained simply as a Nazi economic miracle. By the time the Nazis came to power in 1933, the world economy was showing signs of improvement.

Public Works

Under Hitler, Germany appeared to prosper. Unemployment was tackled during the years 1933–36. Great public work schemes were undertaken, such as the building of *Autobahnen* (motorways), hospitals, schools and factories. Regulations were introduced forbidding the use of machinery for road building as long as unemployment lasted. In 1934 a rapid expansion of the armaments industry began, which absorbed large numbers of workers. The introduction of conscription in 1935 also eased the unemployment situation. Marriage allowances for women who stayed at home reduced the amount of women on the job market.

Hjalmar Schacht

The most influential figure on Nazi economic policy between 1933 and 1937 was the President of the *Reichsbank*, Dr Hjalmar Schacht. Under his direction, German industry was pushed back on its feet. Government loans were provided to industrialists to encourage them to modernise their factories. All interest on foreign loans was frozen. Bilateral (two-sided) trade agreements were signed with Eastern European and South American countries, by which Germany exported manufactured goods in exchange for a supply of cheap raw materials.

Autarky

Hitler hated relying on foreign countries for essential raw materials. He planned to change this through a policy called *autarky*, which he hoped would turn Germany into a self-sufficient state. *Autarky* was the main aim of the Four-Year Plan, which was launched in 1936. Herman Goering was put in charge of this plan. German scientists attempted to produce **Ersatz,** or substitute materials. Substitutes for petrol, oil and wool were made, but they proved to be more expensive and less efficient.

The Four-Year Plan failed to meet its targets. By 1939 synthetic oil had only reached 45% of its predicted target. Germany was still importing 20% of its food and 33% of it raw materials. When this policy failed, it became inevitable that Hitler would invade the Soviet Union, which had an abundance of raw materials.

'Blood and Soil'

Despite the fact that Nazi ideology placed a huge emphasis on 'blood and soil' and the virtue of rural life, the agricultural sector remained weak. Nazi promises of agricultural reform failed to materialise. The law on the New Formation of German Peasantry, introduced in June 1933, failed to break up the large estates. The price of agricultural land doubled between 1932 and 1938, forcing small and middle-sized farmers from the market. Farm labourers earned about half the wages paid to those working in industry and trade. The number of farm labourers fell by over 300,000 in the 1930s, as many migrated to industrial towns in search of better pay.

How Successful was Nazi Economic Policy?

Undoubtedly, Nazi economic policy had its successes. Unemployment was reduced and Germany's economy revived. However, the massive cost of public works schemes and rearmament programmes could not be sustained forever. Despite huge investment in industry, Germany lacked some raw materials, such as oil and rubber. Agriculture failed to meet its targets, and Germany continued to depend on food imports. Hitler believed he could solve Germany's shortage of raw materials by extending his borders eastwards *(Lebensraum)*, where there was a greater supply of grain and oil (p. 108).

Ordinary Level

Study the cartoon and answer the following questions. This cartoon, published in the satirical (mocking) magazine *Punch*, is commentating on the formation of a National Government in Britain in August 1931.

1. Which British politician does the chemist in the cartoon represent?

2. Name the three parties that made up the National Government.

3. Why is the bottle with liberalism written on it smaller than the other bottles?

4. Why was a National Government formed in Britain in August 1931?

5. Describe two policies that were implemented by the National Government in order to improve the economic situation.

Write a paragraph on one of the following:
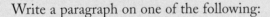
1. John Maynard Keynes.

2. The General Strike in Britain, 1926.

3. The Jarrow Crusade.

4. Hyperinflation in Germany, 1923.

Higher Level

1. Discuss the economic and social effects of the Great Depression on Britain and Germany, 1929–39.

2. Describe the strengths and weaknesses of the German economy during the period 1920–39.

3. 'Unemployment proved to be a major problem in Britain throughout the inter-war years.' Discuss.

Case Study Questions: The Jarrow March

Study Sources A–L on pages 139 to 147 and answer the following questions.

Comprehension

1. In Source A, what symbols of poor housing conditions has the cartoonist David Low placed in the yard beside the children?

2. What occupation did Mrs Pallas' husband have? (Source B) Explain why someone of that trade might have been out of work in the mid-1930s.

3. According to Source C, what was the main cause of the Hunger Marches in 1933?

4. In Source C, why did Chamberlain consider that there was no need to restore the cuts in unemployment benefit?

5. In Source D, of whom did the unemployed men of Jarrow remind the writer JB Priestley?

6. In Source E, what was the attitude of those who were better off, regarding the hunger marchers of the early 1930s?

7. Look at the map (Source F). Mention two areas where unemployment was at its highest.

8. In Source G, why does the journalist consider the Jarrow March not to be a 'hunger march'?

9. According to Ellen Wilkinson in Source I, what attitude did the Labour Party and Trades Union Congress adopt to other groups that were marching to London independently of the Jarrow Crusade?

10. Look at Source J. In which year did unemployment in the industries listed reach its peak?

11. Which of the industries listed in Source J had the highest rate of unemployment between 1929 and 1936?

12. Looking at Source K, name the region of Britain which had the lowest level of unemployment between 1929 and 1937.

13. Which region in Britain listed in Source K had the highest rate of unemployment in 1932?

14. Look at Source L. Which new industry was creating the main employment opportunities?

15. According to the cartoonist in Source L, what effect would this industry have on the population?

Comparison

1. In Source A, how does the cartoonist David Low compare the living standards of the children in the yard with those of the politicians in the car?

2. In Source B, compare the lifestyle of Mrs Pallas and her family before and after her husband lost his job.

3. In Source D, compare the descriptions of Jarrow given (i) in the guidebook and (ii) by JB Priestly.

4. Describe how the organisation of the Jarrow Crusade in Source E was different to previous marches like those outlined in Source C.

5. To what extent do sources G and I agree that the Jarrow March was not inspired by Communists? Explain your answer.

6. Compare the different attitudes to the Labour Party's support for the Jarrow Crusade as outlined in Sources G and I.

7. To what extent do sources A and C hold Neville Chamberlain, the Chancellor or the Exchequer responsible for the economic difficulties during the early 1930s?

Criticism

1. In Source A, do you consider the cartoonist to be more favourable to the people or the Government? Explain your answer.

2. Do you consider the cartoon (Source A) to be a fair reflection of the economic situation in Britain in 1935? Explain your answer. The figures in Sources J and K may help you.

3. Can you detect any signs of bias in Source C?

4. Do you consider the report in Source H to be a favourable or unfavourable account of the Jarrow March? Explain your answer.

5. Source I was written by Ellen Wilkinson, a participant on the Jarrow Crusade. How reliable do you consider her account to be? Explain your answer.

6. In Source L, do you consider the cartoonist to be favourable towards the industrialists that were creating new jobs in the arms industry?

Contextualisation

1. Give a brief description of the economic situation which led to 'hunger marches' in the 1930s.

2. Source I refers to the 'means test' and Unemployment Assistance Board. What were their functions?

3. How effective were the policies of the National Government in dealing with the economic problems of the Great Depression?

4. Briefly describe how the Nazi State in Germany dealt with unemployment during the years 1933–39.

5. Look at the figures in Sources J and K. Can you explain why the employment situation in major industries began to show signs of improvement by 1938?

11 The Soviet Economy 1920–39

State Capitalism

When the Communist Leader Lenin (p. 47) came to power in 1917, the Russian economy was in ruins. This was mainly due to years of neglect by the Tsars, as well as hardships caused by Russia's involvement in World War I. Both the industrial and agricultural systems needed urgent attention.

Under a communist system, all economic activity is brought under state control. Factories, banks and land are owned by the government for the common good of the people. However, on coming to power in October 1917, Lenin argued that this could not be achieved overnight without causing major economic disruption. Therefore, for a brief period, lasting from October 1917 to June 1918, the Communist Government allowed the existing capitalist system to remain until communism could be successfully adopted. Factories, businesses and banks were to remain in private hands subject to the watchful eye of the Communist Party. This transitional period (a brief period between change) was known as 'State Capitalism'.

War Communism

In 1918, faced by civil war, Lenin set about transforming the Russian economy. He introduced emergency economic measures, which became known as 'War Communism'. War Communism, Lenin claimed, was 'dictated not by economic, but by military needs'. It was at this time that Lenin decided to introduce communism in Russia in place of the existing capitalist system.

Land, industries and businesses were all nationalised (taken over by the state). Every factory that employed over five people fell under state control. Private trading was banned, and a 'People's Bank' was established.

The economy was administered along military lines. A supreme Economic Council *(Gosplan)* was established to plan the economy. Peasants were ordered to hand over to the state all extra grain at a fixed price. The Government declared that these drastic means were necessary to keep the economy functioning during the civil war, and to ensure that vital food supplies reached the cities.

▲ People queuing for bread during the Russian Civil War (1918–20).

Results of War Communism

By the end of the Civil War in 1920, the Russian economy was paralysed. Industrial output had fallen to less than 15% of its pre-war figure. Transport was at a halt. Foreign trade had dried up and the money system had collapsed. The black market was flourishing. The peasants were producing enough food for themselves, and refusing to supply the cities with the surplus.

The *Cheka* (secret police) (p. 49) were sent to the countryside to demand grain at gunpoint. Faced with starvation, industrial workers deserted the factories and fled to the countryside in search of food. A severe drought in 1920 made matters worse. During 1921–22 Russia suffered a terrible famine, in which over four million people died.

The result was that many Russians became disillusioned, believing that the 'People's Revolution' of 1917 had not delivered its promises. Lenin's *April Thesis* of 1917 had promised 'peace, bread and land'.

Black market:

A system whereby goods or currencies are bought and sold illegally. This usually means that they are in breach of government controls, such as rationing.

▲
Starvation victims of the Russian famine of 1921–22.

The Kronstadt Revolt

In March 1921 the sailors at the naval base of Kronstadt, who had previously been loyal supporters of the Bolsheviks (Communists), mutinied (p. 51). They demanded an end to the Bolshevik dictatorship. They wanted free elections, freedom of speech, and all left-wing parties to have the right to participate in government. The Communists were shaken by the revolt, but they reacted with extreme force and brutality. Trotsky led the Red Army to crush the revolt. Many sailors were massacred. However, Lenin realised that it was time to rethink his economic policy. He stated that the Kronstadt revolt was like 'a lightning flash which lit up reality'. In March 1921 he announced a 'New Economic Policy'.

The New Economic Policy (NEP)

Lenin's New Economic Policy (NEP) made extensive concessions to private enterprise:

- Compulsory seizure of grain was ended. Peasants now paid a state tax on foodstuffs. All surplus crops could be sold for profit on the open market.

- In industry, small private enterprise was allowed. Businesses employing less than 20 workers were returned to private ownership.

- Large industries (such as coal, steel and oil), the railway system and the banks remained in state hands. This accounted for over 90% of Russia's industry.

- Foreign investment was encouraged.

Some leading Party members, including Trotsky, saw the NEP as a retreat from communism and resented the resulting emergence of a new 'rich class'. However, Lenin realised that concessions had to be made to save the revolution. He stated that it was better at this stage to take one step back, so that two steps forward could be taken at a later date. In October 1921 Lenin explained the reasons behind the new policy to the Party faithful at a conference in Moscow:

> *We had hoped, through the decrees of the proletarian* (working-class) *government, to fund state institutions and organise the distribution of state products upon a Communist basis in a country that was petit bourgeois* (lower middle class)*! Life has shown that we made a mistake. A succession of transition periods such as State Capitalism and Socialism was required to prepare the transition to Communism. You must first attempt to build small bridges which shall lead a land of small peasant holdings through State Capitalism to Socialism.*

The NEP gradually brought a substantial recovery to the Russian economy. Foreign trade resumed, as European countries were eager to exploit a profitable Russian market. By 1926 industry and agriculture had almost recovered to the levels of 1913.

Socialism in One Country

When Lenin died in 1924, Stalin took over and replaced the NEP with a move towards a more planned economy. Stalin's economic policy during the years 1928–41 was influenced by his theory of **'socialism in one country'** (p. 57). His idea was to spread communism to other parts of the world through the example of Soviet economic successes, rather than by force. He believed that if he transformed the Soviet Union into a modern industrial power, it would act as an example of communist achievement and that this would convince others to follow a similar path. However, before Stalin could begin the industrialisation of the Soviet Union, the agricultural system would need to become more efficient.

 # Key Concept: Collectivisation

Collectivisation involved a policy of joining small and medium-sized farms into one large holding. There were two main types of collective farm:

- *Kolkhozy:* These were peasant co-operatives, where the farmers pooled their resources and sold their output to the state at fixed prices. Modern equipment for the *Kolkhozy* could be rented from motor tractor stations, which served particular regions.

- **Sovkhozy:** These were government-run state farms. Farm workers were hired as state employees. The *Sovkhozy* were not as numerous as the *Kolkhozy*, and often proved to be inefficient due to the interference of a large state bureaucracy (civil service).

Reasons for Collectivisation

(a) The production of food was not keeping up with demand in urban areas. If large-scale industrialisation was to take place, peasants would be needed to work in the factories in the cities. Agricultural production would need to become more efficient and less labour intensive.

(b) The industrialisation of the Soviet Union could only be carried out if machinery from the West was imported. This would have to be paid for through the export of agricultural goods.

(c) The existence of private land, as allowed under the NEP, ran contrary to communist beliefs.

The Russian peasants at the time can be divided into two classes, the **Kulaks,** who were prosperous, and the **Muzhiks,** who were poorer. Stalin's plan was to merge farms into large units called 'collectives'. The policy of collectivisation was tolerated by the poorer farmers, who welcomed it as giving them some form of protection against the constant threat of famine. However, the *Kulaks*, who had prospered since Lenin's NEP, bitterly opposed the system, as they had most to lose. In an attempt to defeat Stalin's plans, they cut back on production, burnt their farms and killed their livestock.

▲ A woman drives a tractor on a collective farm in Russia in 1929.

	1928	1938
Sheep	146 million	42 million
Cattle	200 million	34 million

Agricultural output fell dramatically, which resulted in a famine during the years 1932–33. Despite this, the Government insisted that the peasants supply as much grain as before to feed the cities. Stalin reacted by attacking the *Kulaks*. In 1929 he declared, 'We must break down the resistance of this class in open battle. This is the turn towards the policy of eliminating the *Kulaks* as a class.' *Kulak* families were rounded up and sent to forced labour camps *(gulags)* in Siberia and northern Russia. Millions died of disease, starvation and exposure to severe weather conditions. By 1940, 97% of cultivated land had been put into collective farms.

Results of Collectivisation

(a) The *Kulaks* as a class disappeared. It is estimated that up to 10 million *Kulaks* suffered enforced deportation, poverty or death.

(b) Many collective farms were inefficient. On the eve of the German invasion in 1941, agricultural production had not yet returned to its 1928 level.

(c) Collectivisation was enforced at a huge cost in human suffering.

(d) It caused long-term damage to the agricultural sector, which failed to meet the needs of the Soviet Union during World War II.

In the extract below, Eugene Lyons, an American journalist who was in Moscow between 1928 and 1929, describes the impact of collectivisation on rural Russia:

A population as large as all of Switzerland's or Denmark's was stripped clean of all their belongings – not alone their land and homes and cattle and tools, but often their last clothes and food and household utensils – driven out of their villages. They were herded with bayonets (blades attached to rifles) *at railroad stations, packed indiscriminately* (randomly) *into cattle cars and freight cars, and dumped weeks later in the lumber regions of the frozen North, the deserts of Central Asia, wherever labour was needed, there to live or die. Some of this human wreckage was merely flung beyond the limits of their former villages, without shelter or food in those winter months, to start life anew if they could, on land too barren to have been cultivated in the past.*

Tens of thousands died of exposure, starvation, and epidemic (widespread) *diseases while being transported, and no one dared guess at the death rate in the wilderness where the liquidated* (killed) *population was dispersed.*

The Five-Year Plans, 1928–41

Stalin promoted a **'great leap forward'** which would bring about the industrialisation of Russia. The industrialisation of Russia was also considered by Stalin to be necessary for the security of the Communist regime.

In a famous speech in 1931, Stalin declared:

> *To slow down the tempo (of industrialisation) means to lag behind. And those who lag behind are beaten. The history of old Russia shows that because of backwardness she has constantly been defeated. Beaten because of backwardness – military, cultural, political, industrial backwardness. We are behind the leading countries by fifty to one hundred years. We must make up this distance in ten years. Either we do it or they crush us.*

This industrialisation of Russia was to be completed through the implementation of a series of five-year plans.

The First Five-Year Plan 1928–33

The First Five-Year Plan was presented to the Party in 1928. It concentrated on heavy industry and on the production of goods that were necessary for the advancement of the economy. Russia's vast resources of oil and coal were to be fully exploited. New factories, power stations, roads, oil refineries and railways were built, such as the Dnieprostroi Dam and the Gorky Motor Works. A new railway linking Siberia and Turkestan was also built. Labour forces moved to new centres of industry in the Urals, Donbass and in western Siberia.

Quotas were fixed for factories and workers, but the quality of goods was initially poor due to a lack of skill. The targets set in the Plan were over-ambitious and impossible to meet. Despite these problems, production soared, and the national income rose from 27 billion roubles in 1928 to 45 billion roubles by 1932. The output of electricity almost trebled during the same years.

The Second Five Year Plan 1933–38

The Second Five-Year Plan was more realistic in its aims. The plan got off to a difficult start due to the outbreak of famine during 1932–33. Stalin now concentrated more on education and consumer goods (clothes, household goods, etc.). Schools and technical colleges were built and teaching standards were improved. Between 1928 and 1940 over 300,000 Russians graduated with engineering or industrial degrees. Heavy industry was not ignored in this plan; the production of coal and electricity continued to improve during the Second Five-Year Plan, although the performance of the oil and textile industries was disappointing. Due to the rise of Hitler in Germany in 1933, priority was given to the defence industry, which trebled its output towards the end of this plan.

With the completion of the Moscow-Volga Canal and the White Sea Canal, internal communications improved. It was also during this period that the 'Stakhanov movement' (p. 165) became a feature of Soviet economic policy.

The Third Five Year Plan 1938–41

The main objective of the Third Five-Year Plan was determined by an increasing threat from Nazi Germany. This plan was almost exclusively based on the arms industry. Factories were moved further east, beyond the Ural Mountains and even as far as Siberia. This saved Russia during World War II, as most of its factories were beyond the bombing range of the *Luftwaffe*. By 1939 a quarter of the national budget was being spent on defence. This plan was cut short by the German invasion of Russia in June 1941 (p. 108).

By the late 1930s, the Soviet Union had been transformed from an agricultural country into the second most industrialised country in the world (the US being the first). Despite some difficulties, industrial output increased dramatically during the lifetime of the five-year plans.

	1927	1930	1932	1935	1937	1940
Coal (million tons)	35	60	64	100	128	150
Steel (million tons)	3	5	6	13	18	18
Oil (million tons)	12	17	21	24	26	26
Electricity (million kilowatts)	18	22	20	45	80	90

The Stakhanov Movement

On 30 August, 1935, Alexei Stakhanov, a miner from Donbass, was reported to have cut over 100 tonnes of coal in a single ten-hour shift. His great achievement was of course artificially created. Several people stood behind him and carried out support tasks, such as the removal of the coal. Stalin made much propaganda out of this and the 'Order of the *Stakhanovites*' was born. Cash prizes, visits to the Kremlin, medals, and holidays to the Black Sea were given to those who received the award. Their names were also placed on **'Honours Boards'** in factories.

However, the movement also caused jealousy amongst teams of workers competing against each other. Sabotage was common and safety standards fell. There were 33,000 industrial accidents in the Soviet Union during the lifetime of the five-year plans.

▲
Alexei Stakhanov, a miner from Donbass, who supposedly cut over 100 tonnes of coal in a single ten-hour period in Russia during the Five-Year Plans, thus creating 'The Stakhanov Movement'.

Working and Social conditions

Other capitalist methods, such as piecework rates and bonuses, were also used to encourage the workforce. Wage differentials were introduced in 1933; those with better skills and education were paid a higher wage. If workers exceeded the yearly quota for production, 10% of the excess profits were shared amongst them. However, the quotas were usually too ambitious and workers rarely benefited.

Wages improved slowly and new housing schemes were built in cities such as Moscow. Workers' flats were usually badly built and furniture and consumer goods were scarce. Trade unions existed, but they were little more than a 'mouthpiece' for government policies.

Medical services and hospitals were free and the right to an old-age pension became law in 1936. However, money was not always available to pay for these services.

In the extract below, Andrew Smith, an American who worked in a factory in Moscow at the time, describes the living conditions of a typical industrial worker:

> **Piecework:**
> Work paid for according to the quantity of goods produced.

The room contained approximately 500 narrow beds, covered with mattresses filled with straw or dried leaves. There were no pillows or blankets… Some had no beds and slept on the floor or in wooden boxes. In some cases, beds were used by one shift during the day and by others at night. There were no screens or walls to give any privacy… There were no closets or wardrobes because each one owned only the clothing on his back.

From **I was a Soviet Worker**, by Andrew Smith, 1936.

Overview

Under the leadership of Lenin and Stalin, the Soviet Union made great strides in economic developments. In a relatively short period of time, Russia was transformed from a backward agricultural country into an industrial giant. The industrialisation of the Soviet Union during the period of the five-year plans must be seen as one of Stalin's greatest achievements. It was during this period that the Soviet Union began to emerge as one of the world's great powers. However, progress often took place at great human expense.

Ordinary Level

Study the tables below and answer the questions that follow.

Grain Harvests (millions of tons)	
1913	80.0
1922	50.3
1925	72.5

Livestock Holding (in millions)			
	Horses	Cattle	Pigs
1916	35.5	58.9	20.3
1922	24.1	45.8	12.0
1925	27.1	62.4	21.8

1. In which year did agricultural output in Russia reach its lowest level?

2. Explain why this was the case.

3. Lenin introduced the New Economic Policy in 1921. Using the data in the tables, explain the effect of the NEP on the Russian agricultural sector during the period 1922–25.

Higher Level

1. During the period 1920–39 Russia was transformed from a backward agricultural country to an industrial power. Explain how this came about.

2. Describe the economic policies followed by both Lenin and Stalin during the inter-war years.

12 Society During World War II

Introduction

World War II had a much more direct effect on the civilian populations of the countries involved than had been the case with World War I. It was a war in which the entire populations of some countries were involved, whether as members of the armed forces, workers in war-related industries, civilians suffering aerial bombardment or victims of a policy of mass extermination.

The Home Front

The phrase 'home front' refers to the civilian population, and their activities, of a country at war. The impact of the war on the home fronts of those countries involved in World War II was on a scale that had never been experienced before. There were many inconveniences. Strict **blackouts** had to be maintained at night and, due to a shortage of petrol, public transport was severely reduced. Roads and railways were needed for troop movements, and civilian travel was discouraged. There were shortages of everything from food to toiletries.

All countries at war censored the news and restricted the level of information that the general public was given. Posters constantly reminded the public that 'Careless Talk Costs Lives'. In Nazi-occupied Europe, listening to Allied radio broadcasts was an offence that could be punishable by death.

Rationing

As U-boat attacks on British shipping lanes intensified, a system of food rationing was introduced in Britain. In January 1940 a ration book was allocated to each person in the country. Coupons in each ration book could be exchanged at local shops for supplies of tea, sugar, butter, margarine, cooking fats, meat, bacon, eggs, etc. A typical adult food ration for one week was eight ounces of sugar, two ounces of butter, three ounces of cooking oil, four ounces of bacon and three pints of milk.

Fresh vegetables, fruit and sausages were not rationed, but were subject to availability. Non-native fruits such as bananas and oranges disappeared from shop shelves. Beer and tobacco were not rationed as they were considered necessary for morale. Nonetheless, these were subject to the same shortages as everything else. The quality of beer declined as oats and potatoes replaced barley.

The use of home-grown food was encouraged. As part of the **'Dig for Victory'** campaign, public parks were turned into vegetable allotments. The

Ministry of Food also set up **'British Restaurants',** which provided good nourishing meals at low prices.

Economies of all sorts were encouraged. The general public was asked to donate to the war effort through a series of appeals such as the 'spitfire fund' or 'warship week'. Donations included aluminium pots and pans.

Although rationing in Britain seems severe by today's standards, the situation in Nazi-occupied Europe was worse. The Nazis drained countries of food supplies in order to feed Germany. Denmark, France and Norway were forced to triple their export of agricultural products to Germany. Thousands also died of starvation when food supplies could not reach the civilian population due to heavy fighting in the area. In Germany, vital food supplies remained at an adequate level. Bread rations only fell from 2,400 grams in September 1939 to 2,225 grams by October 1944. Potato and vegetable consumption increased in the absence of dairy products, fish and meat. Living conditions in German cities did not really deteriorate until the massive Allied bombing campaigns of 1942–45 (p. 170).

▲
Britain's Home Guard or 'Dad's Army'.

The Home Guard

In Britain, older or less fit men joined the Home Guard, or **'Dad's Army'** as it was affectionately called. Its primary objective was to combat possible German parachute landings. Most of its members were men who were too old to fight, and boys of 17 and 18 years of age. Despite its lack of arms, it had a positive effect on British morale during the war.

The Role of Women During the War

In Britain, more and more women joined the workforce during the war, taking over jobs which had traditionally been done by men. They became conductresses, postal workers, train and tram drivers, etc. In early 1940 a new regulation required unmarried women of military age to register for national service. Many joined various auxiliary forces such as the Women's Auxiliary Air force, the Auxiliary Territorial Service and the Women's Royal Naval Service. Others worked in munitions (weapons) factories.

To help increase food production, there was the **Women's Land Army.** By early 1940 the Land Army had over 25,000 members. The largest women's organisation was the **Women's Volunteer Service,** which helped those who suffered following bombing attacks.

The situation in Germany was very different. Throughout the 1930s Hitler encouraged women to stay at home. Even during Germany's most difficult

▲
Members of the Women's Land Army receive instruction in tractor ploughing at the Somerset Agricultural Institute in May 1941.

years, 1944–45, there were fewer women in the workforce than in Britain. However, it should be remembered that Germany used thousands of foreign 'slave labourers' during the war. By 1944 one in every five workers in Germany was either a prisoner of war or a foreign worker *(Fremdarbeiter)*. During the course of the war, seven million labourers, including one and a half million women, were forcibly recruited: four million from the Soviet Union, one million from Poland and the rest from Belgium, France and Holland. The workers from Eastern Europe were denied legal rights, and were often detained in concentration camps.

As the war dragged on, women became increasingly important to the German war effort, and the Nazi Party was forced to rethink its policy on women in the workforce. By 1943 all women between the ages of 17 and 45 had to register for national service. However, only one million women were actually mobilised for war production by 1945. Over 3,500 women were trained by the SS as concentration camp guards. Their attitude and actions differed little from their male colleagues.

One positive outcome of the war for women was that they returned to German universities in large numbers, accounting for 61% of students by 1945.

War production: The production of materials needed for war, such as bombs, tanks and guns.

The Bombing of Cities

Although the Battle of Britain ended in 1941, German night-time raids continued well into 1942. These raids involved the dropping of high-explosive bombs, incendiaries (bombs designed to cause fires) and parachute mines, which devastated entire streets. The cities of London, Coventry, Sheffield and Glasgow suffered terrible damage. The civilian population sought protection in **'Anderson' huts** (which were set in the earth and covered with soil) and tube stations. Indoor steel boxes, known as **Morrison shelters,** were also used. Although over 44,000 civilians were killed during these raids, they failed to break the spirit of the people. Instead, a type of communal spirit grew, and the civilian population felt a certain empathy with the soldiers on the 'front-line'.

In the extract below, from his book *Child at War*, George Macbeth describes how, as a child in Sheffield, he viewed the German air raids of 1940:

In the morning, I would walk along Clarkehouse Road with my eyes glued to the pavement for shrapnel (fragments of a bomb). *It became the fashion to make a collection of this, and there were few days when I came home without a pocketful of jagged, rusting bits, like the unintelligible pieces from a scattered jigsaw of pain and violence.*

Of course we didn't see them as this at the time. They were simply free toys from the sky, as available and interesting as the horse chestnuts in the Botanical Gardens, or the nippled acorns in Melbourne Avenue.

From 1942 onwards, the German civilian population suffered a similar fate to their counterparts in Britain, as the Allies launched huge night raids on German industrial cities. The most devastating raid occurred on Dresden during 13–14 February, 1945. Over 50,000 people, mainly civilians, were killed in a firestorm following a raid in which over 800 British bombers dropped 2,600 tons of explosives on the centre of the city. Dresden's population had been swollen by refugees who had fled before the Soviet advance, and by those who had evacuated previously-bombed cities.

▲ A Glasgow family walk with their belongings down a street destroyed during German air raids.

Evacuation

▲
Evacuee children boarding a train in Britain in 1938.

Britain

The earliest plans for the evacuation of children from London were made in 1938, when Chamberlain threatened war with Hitler over his plans to takeover the Sudetenland in Czechoslovakia. The Government established an **Imperial Defence Committee,** which produced a report greatly exaggerating the predicted numbers of casualties. The report estimated that Britain would suffer almost one million deaths and over one million injured during the first two months of war. High-risk areas were identified, and safer areas in the countryside were prepared to receive a large influx of people.

When the war broke out in September 1939, the evacuation plan was immediately put into action. Thousands of children were escorted by their parents and teachers to train and bus stations to be sent to foster homes in the

The Blitz:

The Blitz refers to the German air raids on London, Coventry and other industrial cities in Britain during 1940–41.

countryside. Each child carried a case with a change of clothing and their gasmask in its cardboard box. A label was attached to their coat detailing their name, age, address and new destination.

The operation lasted three days, within which 827,000 children, 103,000 teachers and social workers, 524,000 mothers and babies, 13,000 expectant mothers and 7,000 people with disabilities were evacuated.

Many of the evacuees returned to the cities during the period of the Phoney War (September 1939 to May 1940), when the expected air raids failed to materialise. However, a new evacuation had to be quickly organised with the onset of the *Blitz* (p. 105) in September 1940.

The number of evacuees rose or fell depending on the intensity of bombing campaigns. The greatest mass departure from London took place during the summer of 1944, when German VI Rockets began to rain down on the city.

France

In France the evacuation was not so orderly. In June 1940 some five million people in Northern France fled their homes in an effort to avoid the advancing German Army. The evacuees received little help from the Government, which also fled Paris on 10 June. In Versailles a notice on the town hall stated, 'The mayor invites the population to flee.' The population of southern French cities swelled, causing administrative and social problems for the local councils.

The *Exode* ('Exodus' or mass departure), as it was known, did not last very long. Following the signing of the armistice on 22 June, the Germans allowed most of the evacuees to return home.

The Soviet Union

In the Soviet Union, large sections of the population were moved eastwards in a military/economic plan which sought to place Russian industry beyond the bombing range of the German Air Force. Between July and November 1941, over 1,503 factories were moved. The evacuation of Russian industry had largely been completed by the summer of 1942. Once the factories were up and running and the necessary industrial skills acquired, women replaced their husbands and brothers, who were urgently needed at the front.

Refugees

From the moment Hitler came to power in 1933, people began to flee Germany. By the end of that year, over 65,000 refugees had left the country. Most of them settled in France. Between 1933 and 1939, over 56,000 refugees from Nazi Germany, Austria and Czechoslovakia fled to Britain. The majority of these were Jewish, although small numbers of political opponents of the

Nazis also sought safety in Britain. In April 1933 the British Jewish community informed the Government that they would meet the cost of incoming Jewish refugees. From 1934 onwards those fleeing Germany had to pay a very high **'emigration tax'**. As a result, most refugees arriving in their adoptive countries had very little money.

After the outbreak of war in 1939, it became almost impossible to escape from Germany or Eastern Europe as a refugee. By May 1940 the number of refugees entering Britain was very small. Over the next five years less than 6,000 refugees escaping Nazi-occupied Europe managed to get to Britain. By 1935 British public sympathy for the plight of refugees had begun to decline. Some politicians and newspapers were openly hostile:

> *Once it is known that Britain offers sanctuary* (safety) *to all who care to come to Britain, the floodgates will open and we will be inundated* (flooded) *by thousands seeking a home.* From **Daily Mail**, 1935.

The British Union of Fascists blamed refugees for taking away the jobs of 'British workers'.

Jewish emigration to Palestine also became an issue for the British Government. Palestinian Arabs, worried about their future, began to protest. The British Government was anxious to maintain friendly relations with Arab governments in the Middle East in case of war in that region. In 1937 Britain limited the number of Jewish refugees allowed to travel to Palestine to no more than 10,000 over the following five years.

In July 1938, an international conference on refugees was held at Evian in France. The conference failed to agree to a settlement, as most countries were not prepared to allow an intake of a large number of refugees.

▲
German soldiers arresting Jews in Budapest for deportation to concentration camps in 1943.

Sympathy for Jewish refugees increased from August 1942 onwards as news of the deportation of Jewish people to ghettos reached Britain. However, on 30 December Anthony Eden, the Foreign Secretary, informed the War Cabinet that Britain could admit only a further 1,000–2,000 refugees. In April 1943, as a result of public pressure, the British Government organised another international conference on refugees; this time in Bermuda. Once more the conference ended in deadlock when the governments refused to commit themselves to accept large numbers of refugees.

As the tide turned in World War II, a short-lived organisation called the **United Nations Relief and Rehabilitation Organisation** was formed in 1943. Between 1943 and 1946 this organisation helped over 30 million refugees and displaced people worldwide who had been left homeless following the end of World War II.

Key Concept: Resistance

Resistance movements sprang up at the same time in all the occupied countries. These secret networks carried out acts of sabotage, blew up bridges and destroyed railway and telephone lines. They also provided help for Allied airmen who landed in the occupied territories.

For the first two years of war, resistance movements were badly organised and failed to make any real impact on the Nazi occupation. However, from 1942 onwards, as the economic situation worsened, resistance movements began to gain more support.

The **British Special Operations Executive** (SOE), together with the **American Office of Strategic Services** (OSS), made contact with resistance movements and supplied some of them with arms and munitions. Some resistance groups used less dangerous techniques, such as 'go slow' campaigns. The Czechs were best at this, remaining friendly to the Germans while performing inefficient work.

French Resistance

France had a number of resistance movements, covering a whole range of political opinion from left to right. They formed armed fighting groups called the *Maquis* (after a type of foliage in Corsica, behind which resistance fighters on the island used to hide). Charles de Gaulle, who had established a French 'Government in Exile' in London, attempted to co-ordinate the different groups. In his book *Mémoires de Guerre (War Memoirs)*, 1954, de Gaulle outlined the role of resistance movements:

We envision (imagine) *nothing less than an organisation that will permit us simultaneously* (at the same time) *to inform Allied operations by providing intelligence about the enemy, to arouse resistance to the enemy in every region and to equip every sympathetic force that will, at the proper time, participate, at the Germans' rear, in the battle for liberation in order to prepare for our country's restoration to health once victory has been achieved. France must be brought back into the war, thus to participate in the final victory. During the first stage, information networks must be established for the benefit of the Allied chiefs of staff. A second should consist of sabotage of the enemy war machine wherever it may be and rejection of any compromise with the occupying authority and its accomplices. A third should see the organisation and training of military forces to attack the enemy as the Allies advance, to hinder his defence and to promote a climate of national unanimity* (agreement) *for the restoration of the nation's economy and of fundamental* (basic) *freedoms.*

In 1943 Jean Moulin, a colleague of de Gaulle, brought most of the various resistance groups together when he founded the National Resistance Council. A combined staff was created for this underground army under the command of General Charles Delestraint. The French Resistance received a setback in June 1943 when Moulin was arrested. He was tortured and later killed by the Nazi Klaus Barbie (the infamous 'Butcher of Lyon').

In Denmark, anti-Nazis used a campaign of civil disobedience and strikes to protest against German occupation. When the Nazis ordered Danish Jews to wear a yellow star, the non-Jewish Danish King appeared wearing a yellow star of his own. Danish resistance movements managed to smuggle most of the nation's 5,000 Jews to safety in neutral Sweden.

Josip Broz (Tito) and Resistance in Yugoslavia

When Yugoslavia fell to the Germans in April 1941 a communist leader, Josip Broz, later nicknamed 'Tito', formed a nationwide resistance group known as the **Partisans.** They quickly established themselves as Europe's most effective guerrilla army. Tito had gained military experience fighting for the Republican side in the Spanish Civil War. By the end of 1942, Tito's Army had 28 brigades, each with 3–4,000 men and women. Tito instructed his forces not to engage in major battles with a superior German Army, but to wage a 'guerrilla war' in the countryside.

Tito's efforts were extremely successful and the German Army was driven out of most of Serbia by the end of September 1941. In response, the German General Keital ordered that 50–100 civilians be executed as punishment if any one German soldier died.

Between 1941 and 1943 Tito and his Army fought off five German offensives. From late 1943 onwards his forces received arms from the Allies. Tito eventually drove the Germans out of all of Yugoslavia by March 1945, becoming the only resistance leader to liberate his own country without front-line military help from the Allies.

The civilian population often suffered because of the activities of resistance groups. The Nazis took their revenge for successful attacks by resistance movements. They wiped out the Czech village of Lidice and murdered 340 of its inhabitants, sending the rest to concentration camps or for re-education with German families. They also massacred 642 men, women and children in the French village of Oradour-sur-Glane. The town was then looted and every building burnt.

German Resistance to Hitler

Even within totalitarian Germany, small resistance groups emerged. Many of these groups came from amongst younger members of German society. Members of such groups adopted the Edelweiss flower as their symbol in

▲
Marshal Tito, (1892–1980), the Yugoslav Communist Leader in the 1940s.

Guerrilla army:
An irregular, or unofficial, army that engages in quick 'hit and run' attacks against its perceived enemy.

common with a Catholic group of resisters based in Bavaria – the **Edelweiss Pirates.** The *Gestapo* broke up this group, but they re-formed and spread to other parts of Germany, particularly to industrial cities. In Cologne in 1944, 12 members of the Edelweiss Pirates were publicly hanged as an example to other youths.

Other groups included *Die Mute* (The Courage) in Leipzig, the 07 Group in Munich and the *Verband* (Association) from the foothills of the Alps in Germany. The most organised and political of the youth movements was the **White Rose,** which was based in Munich University under the leadership of Hans and Sophie Scholl. They published and distributed anti-Nazi leaflets. A White Rose leaflet of June 1942 condemned the slaughter of Jews during the Polish campaign. From the beginning, their campaign lacked security and their openness brought them to the attention of the *Gestapo.* In February 1943 Hans and Sophie Scholl, along with other members of the group, were arrested and executed. This ended the most significant youth revolt against Nazism.

The most notable adult resistance group was the *Kreisau* **Circle,** which was named after the estate owned by their leader, Count Helmuth von Moltke. The *Kreisau* Circle held secret conferences in 1942 and 1943, where they discussed the future of Germany after the collapse of Nazism. Many of its members were connected with an unsuccessful Army plot to kill Hitler in July 1944. Most of its leaders, including von Molke, were executed in the purge that followed the failed plot.

Although these resistance groups failed to have any major impact on the fall of Nazism, they became a source of inspiration for future generations of Germans, by reminding them that not everyone obediently followed Nazi beliefs.

Key Concept: Collaboration

In the countries they occupied, the Germans appealed to those sympathetic with the Nazi cause to assist them in their task. These people, who co-operated with the enemy, were known as 'collaborators'.

Many of the collaborators were people of German descent *(Volkdeutsche)* who lived outside the Reich. These people found themselves part of racial minorities in new countries following the redrawing of Germany's boundaries by the terms of the Treaty of Versailles. German minorities in Poland and Czechoslovakia felt mistreated in their adopted nations, and welcomed the Nazi conquest.

Other collaborators were nationals of the occupied countries who volunteered to help the Nazis either out of enthusiasm for Nazi ideology, or self-interest. For others, anti-Semitism or anti-communism drew them towards the Fascist ranks.

Quisling and Collaboration in Norway

Following the German invasion of Norway in April 1940, Vidkun Quisling, the leader of the right-wing **Nasjonal Samling** (National Unity), the Norwegian National Socialist Party, declared himself Head of Government. He commanded little support within Norway and was forced to stand down after a brief period in power. However, the German occupation allowed him to head a 'puppet' Government from 1942 to 1945.

The name 'Quisling' became a new name for 'traitor'. He was sentenced to death by firing squad for collaboration after the liberation of Norway.

▲
Vidkun Quisling (1887–1945) (right) declared himself Head of Government following the German invasion of Norway in April 1940. Himmler, the SS Leader, is seated left.

French Collaboration

Collaboration in France occurred on a large scale. Marshal Pétain, supported by Laval and Darlan, imposed a right-wing semi-Fascist regime in the unoccupied Vichy France (Chapter 9).

Others in the occupied zone also exhibited open admiration for Nazism. Amongst the groups that collaborated was the PPF (*Parti Populaire Francaise* or French Popular Party) led by Jacques Doriot. Doriot organised the 'League of French Volunteers against Bolshevism' to fight against the Russians on the Eastern Front. He fled to Germany after the Normandy landing, where he was killed in an Allied air raid. Others joined the *Milice,* an auxiliary police force that committed horrifying atrocities.

> **Puppet government:**
> A government that is set up to serve the purposes of a foreign government.

The Ustasa and Croatian Collaboration

Ante Pavelić, Leader of the Croatian Fascist movement, was chosen by Mussolini to run a 'puppet' government in the new independent state of Croatia, between 1941 and 1945. He organised the *Ustasa,* a terrorist movement that massacred thousands of Serbs, Jews, gypsies and communists. The actions of the *Ustasa* were so bad that even the Germans became uneasy. At the end of the war, Pavelić escaped to Argentina, where he remained until his death in 1959.

Lord Haw-Haw and Collaboration

William Joyce, who was nicknamed 'Lord Haw-Haw' by a *Daily Express* journalist because of his aristocratic nasal drawl, was one of the most colourful wartime collaborators. He was born in New York and raised in Ireland and

England. In 1937 he formed the right-wing British National Socialist Party. Joyce fled to Germany shortly before the outbreak of the war and offered his services to the Nazis. Throughout the war, he broadcast humorous anti-British propaganda from Radio Hamburg, which extended his nickname to 'Lord Haw-Haw of Hamburg'. His programme was widely listened to in Britain, more out of amusement than belief.

He was arrested in Germany by Allied forces in May 1945 and extradited to Britain. Although he claimed German citizenship, he kept his British passport, which secured a conviction for treason. He was hanged in Wandsworth Prison in January 1946. His last public message, reported by the BBC, said that, 'In death as in life, I defy the Jews who caused this last war, and I defy the powers of darkness they represent.'

Revenge

When the war ended, resistance groups sought revenge against those who had collaborated with the Germans. This was particularly true in France. While the Government tried leading collaborators, many others were summarily executed (executed without government sanction). In some cases girls who had made friends with the German Army had their heads shaven, and they were excluded from their communities. Charles de Gaulle disliked the persecution of collaborators, but could do little to halt it. It is estimated that there were between 30,000 and 40,000 summary executions in France before proper authority was re-established.

▲
Belgian women getting their heads shaved as a punishment for associating with German soldiers.

Ordinary Level

Study the photograph and answer the questions below. The photograph shows British women working in a factory that manufactured barrage balloons (helium-filled balloons designed to prevent low-level bombing) in 1942.

1. Describe how the women in the photograph are dressed.

2. Why did the number of women working in factories increase dramatically during the war years?

3. The scene in the picture above would not have been as commonplace in Germany. Explain why this was the case?

4. Write a short account of 'The Role of Women in the Workforce During World War II'.

Write an account of 'Society During World War II' using three of the following headings:

1. Rationing

2. Evacuation

3. Refugees

4. Collaboration

5. Resistance

Higher Level

1. Compare and contrast the experiences of the civilian population in at least two of the countries involved in World War II.

2. Discuss the impact of World War II on society using three of the following headings: Rationing; Evacuees; Refugees; Collaboration; Resistance.

13 Anti-Semitism and the Holocaust

Key Concept: Anti-Semitism

Anti-Semitism is a term used to describe prejudice against the Jews. Anti-Semitism can often be confined to a non-violent dislike of Jews, but in Hitler's Germany it took on a more evil and violent form, leading to the organised mass extermination of many European Jews during World War II.

Persecution of the Jews in Germany

Hatred of the Jews was always a major force behind the growth of support for Nazism in Germany. Accounting for less than 1% of the German population, Hitler held the Jews responsible for most of Germany's difficulties during the inter-war period (1919–39). He appealed to a long-standing prejudice against the Jews that had existed in Germany, Poland and Russia for centuries. Much of the hatred towards the Jews was fed by jealousy associated with their commercial success in Europe.

> **Prejudice:**
> When someone is prejudice, they have a set opinion about something. It usually means that the opinion is negative.

Anti-Jewish Laws

As soon as they came to power in 1933, the Nazis passed anti-Jewish laws, removing Jewish property and depriving Jews of civil rights by banishing them from public life, business activity and eventually life itself.
The main anti-Jewish laws included the following:

- In April 1933 there was an official boycott of Jewish shops. Jews were driven out of the civil service, the judiciary and the teaching profession. A quota system for Jews was introduced into schools and universities. This system allowed only a small number of Jews into these institutions.

- In September 1935 the **Nuremberg Laws** forbade marriages between Aryans and Jews in order to prevent the birth of *Mischlinge* (children of mixed race unions).

- In 1936 Hitler allowed a brief interval in his anti-Semitic campaign, as he feared that the Olympic Games in Berlin might be boycotted.

- By 1937 Jewish businesses could be seized without legal justification. Jews were no longer allowed to enter public parks, attend cultural events or keep pets.

> **Boycott:**
> Refuse to have any dealings with a person, movement or event.

- On 09 November, 1938, the killing of the German Ambassador in Paris by a Jew caused a wave of organised attacks and violence against the Jews in Germany. By the end of *Kristallnacht* (Night of the Broken Glass) more than 20,000 Jews had been imprisoned, dozens killed and many had fled the country.

- In 1939 a curfew was forced on Jews and they were not allowed to leave their houses after dark. Jews were also banned from using public transport or owning a bicycle or a radio.

▲ Smashed windows of Jewish shops on the morning after *Kristallnacht*, 09 November, 1938.

Up to the outbreak of war in 1939, the Nazi regime did all it could to encourage Jews to emigrate. Half a million Jews lived in Germany in 1933. By 1939 more than 360,000 had succeeded in emigrating. Others were unable to leave due to a lack of money and the inability to pay a tax levied on emigrants. Most European countries also imposed a quota on Jewish immigration and refused to accept those who were penniless.

With the outbreak of war in 1939, Nazi policy towards the Jews entered a new and more radical phase. At the outset there was no plan for dealing with the millions of Jews who fell into German hands in Poland and Western Europe. At first the Germans restricted themselves to legal measures, based on laws similar to those already passed in Germany. Jews were banned from public office, had their property seized, and were forced to live in designated areas or 'ghettos'.

The Ghettos

In 1940 ghettos or **'Jewish Residential Districts'** were established throughout Nazi-occupied Eastern Europe. All Jews had to move into these poorer city districts. The ghetto was sealed by police and enclosed by a wall and barbed wire. The largest ghetto was in Warsaw in Poland with 450,000 inhabitants. Anyone who attempted to leave could be shot on the spot by guards. Overcrowding and unsanitary living conditions led to the death of thousands in the ghettos – 96,000 in the Warsaw ghetto alone.

As the war proceeded, various plans were drawn up by the Nazis to clear Europe of its Jewish population. The German SS Chief of Reich Security, Reinhard Heydrich, created a scheme in 1939 whereby all European Jews would occupy eastern lands in a reservation between the rivers Vistula and Bug. This plan was abandoned early in 1940 due to transportation difficulties.

In March 1940 Hitler suggested a plan which would involve the transportation of four million Jews to Madagascar in southern Africa. In preparation for this scheme, 6,500 German Jews were transported to the South of France under the control of the Vichy Government. Transportation difficulties came into play again, and this plan was not carried through.

▲ The sign reads 'Jews are not welcome in this town'.

Einsatzgruppen (Task Forces)

The invasion of the Soviet Union in 1941 brought yet another increase in the level of Nazi persecution directed at the Jews. Hitler ordered the execution of all communists and Jews caught behind enemy lines. Mobile SS Special Task Forces *(Einsatzgruppen)* followed the advancing Army and began the systematic extermination of Soviet Jews. By early 1942 the *Einsatzgruppen* had killed over 500,000 people in Poland, the Ukraine and Russia.

Key Concept: The Holocaust

The 'Holocaust' (from the Greek, *holos* (completely) *kaustos* (burnt)) refers to the systematic attempt by the Nazis to destroy European Jews.

On 30 January, 1939, Hitler informed the *Reichstag* that if 'international Jewish financiers forced a war on Germany… it would end with the annihilation (total destruction) of the Jewish race in Europe'. By the time the war ended in 1945, he had gone a long way towards keeping his word.

The **'Final Solution'** was the name of the Nazi plan to kill all of the Jews in Europe. It began to develop early in 1942. On 20 January Heydrich chaired a conference at Wansee, a Berlin suburb,

Polish Jews being rounded up in the Warsaw ghetto, April 1943. This small boy was lucky, he survived and now lives in America.

during which it was formally agreed to introduce a policy to deport European Jews to the East and exterminate those who were too weak to work. The participants, 15 in all, included representatives of the SS and the Nazi Party as well as various state ministers. The task of rounding up millions of Jews was left to Adolf Eichmann, an SS officer and head of the 'Jewish Evacuation Department'.

Extermination Camps

Extermination camps were quickly organised during 1942. Bergen-Belsen (Germany) opened its gates in March, Sobibor (Poland) in April, Auschwitz (Poland) in June and Treblinka (Poland) in July. Eichmann and his agents in the occupied territories sent Jews by the millions to concentration camps. Transports arrived regularly at Auschwitz, the main extermination camp, where up to 10,000 people were sent to the gas chambers each day.

Jews sent to Auschwitz, who were considered incapable of working (infants, the elderly, pregnant women, those with disabilities and the sick), were immediately sent to the gas chambers. The others were sent to adjoining work camps where they remained until they were weakened by exhaustion.

In March 1942 a second camp was opened nearby at Birkenau. This was a huge complex, which housed 200,000 prisoners and was equipped with four crematoria. A third camp, a labour camp that made synthetic rubber, operated by IG Farben, was opened in October 1942 nearby at Monowitz.

Joseph Mengele – the 'Angel of Death'

Joseph Mengele, the notorious Auschwitz doctor, carried out racial experiments on prisoners. In an attempt to create a race of blue-eyed Aryans, he experimented on Jewish identical twins. No information of much medical value came from his trials. Mengele, the 'Angel of Death', escaped to South America after the war, and became one of the most hunted Nazi war criminals. It is believed that he died in a drowning accident in Brazil in 1979.

The way we selected our victims was as follows: Two SS doctors on duty in Auschwitz examined the arriving transports. The prisoners had to pass by a doctor, who signalled his decision as they walked by. Those fit to work were sent into the camp. Others were sent immediately to the extermination facilities. Children of tender years were exterminated without exception, as they were unable to work due to their youth.   From a statement made by the Commandant of Auschwitz, Rudolf Höss, at his trial in Cracow, 1946.

Other European Countries

In Central Europe, only the Romanian Government co-operated with the Nazis in rounding up Jews and sending them to concentration camps. Parts of Yugoslavia and Greece under Italian control escaped the extermination campaign until they were occupied by Germany following Mussolini's fall from power in 1943.

Hungarian Jews were protected by their Government until the spring of 1944, when the Germans occupied the country. By June of that year, Eichmann had transported 350,000 Hungarian Jews to Auschwitz, where 250,000 of these were gassed within 46 days of their arrival.

Death Marches

By late 1944 the 'Final Solution' began to grind to a halt because labour shortages became a problem. As the Soviet Army rolled into Eastern Europe in 1945, the Nazis attempted to cover their tracks by forcing the inmates of camps to march westwards. When the Red Army crossed the River Vestula in Poland in January 1945, Heinrich Himmler ordered the evacuation of concentration

▲
Roll call at Sachsenhausen concentration camp near Berlin in February 1941. These prisoners had to stand for over six hours in the biting cold of winter as they waited for the camp commandoes to capture an escaped prisoner. This kind of group punishment often lasted well into the night, and great numbers of the waiting men dropped or died from exhaustion.

camps in Poland, including Auschwitz. Hundreds of thousands of prisoners died from exhaustion and hunger on these 'Death Marches'.

It is estimated that by the end of the war, more than six million Jews had been murdered, three million of whom had been Polish. The total pre-'Final Solution' Jewish population in the countries occupied by the Nazis had been eight million. Others, such as Romanian gypsies and Soviet prisoners of war, suffered a similar fate.

How Much Did Hitler Know?

As early as 1922, Hitler explained his plans for the Jews during a magazine interview with the journalist Josef Hell:

Once I really am in power, my first and foremost task will be the annihilation (total destruction) *of the Jews. As soon as I have the power to do so, I will have gallows built in rows – at the Marienplatz in Munich, for example – as many as traffic allows.*

Then the Jews will be hanged indiscriminately, and they will remain hanging until they stink; they will hang there as long as the principles of hygiene permit. As soon as they have been untied, the next batch will be strung up, and so on down the line, until the last Jew in Munich has been exterminated. Other cities will follow suit, precisely in this fashion, until all Germany has been completely cleansed of Jews

As cited in **Hitler and the Final Solution** by Gerald Fleming, 1984.

From evidence in the extract below, it seems that Hitler was kept well informed of Nazi activities in Eastern Europe:

Continuing reports on the work of the 'Einsatzgruppen' in the East should be provided to the Führer. For this purpose, especially interesting illustrative material, such as photos, posters, flyers and other documents are needed. If such material can be obtained or produced, I ask that it be sent as soon as possible.

Telex from Heinrich Müller, Head of the Gestapo, to Special Units, 01 August, 1941.

By 1942 Hitler had referred to the destruction of European Jews in no fewer than four speeches. In December 1942 the leader of the SS, Himmler, sent Hitler a detailed report of the work of the *Einsatzgruppen*, detailing the deaths of 336,211 Jews in Russia.

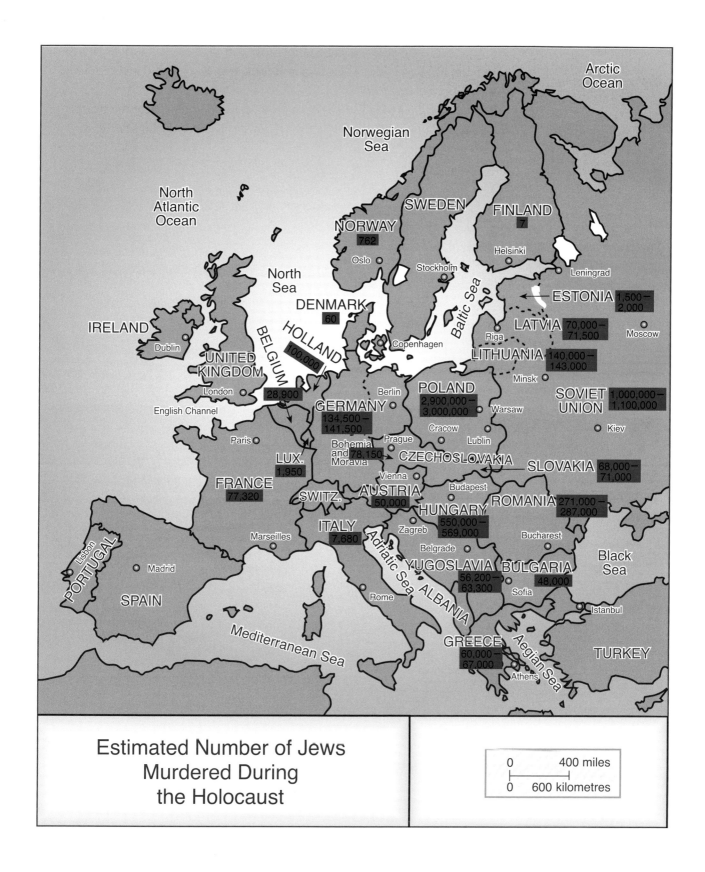

Estimated Number of Jews
Murdered During
the Holocaust

0	400 miles
0	600 kilometres

No detailed paperwork relating to the 'Final Solution' exists. In 1943 Martin Bormann, head of Hitler's Secretariat ordered that all correspondence relating to the 'Final Solution' be verbal.

It is also difficult to believe that many ordinary Germans were totally ignorant of the 'Final Solution'. Deportations took place during daylight hours. Jewish neighbours vanished without trace. German soldiers on leave from the front also carried stories of mass executions taking place in the East.

We are fighting this war today for the very existence of our people. Thank God that you in the homeland do not feel too much of it. The bombing raids, however, have shown what the enemy has in store for us if he had the power. Those at the front experience it at every turn. My comrades literally are fighting for the existence of our people. They are doing the same as the enemy would to us. I believe that you understand me. Because this war in our view is a Jewish war, the Jews are primarily bearing the brunt of it. In Russia, wherever there is a German soldier, the Jews are no more.

From a letter by a German Soldier to his wife, September, 1942.

? Questions

Ordinary Level

Explain the following key concepts:

1. Anti-Semitism

2. Holocaust

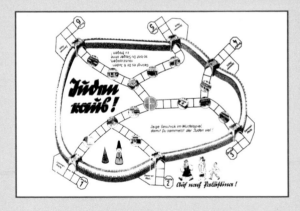

Study this picture of a children's board game called 'Jews get out'. The winner is the child who manages to chase six Jews from their businesses and homes (represented by the circles in the centre).

1. What was the purpose of allowing children to play such a game?

2. What does this picture tell us of the German attitude towards the Jews?

3. Mention two other ways in which the Nazis attempted to arouse hatred toward the Jews in Germany.

Higher Level

1. Explain how Nazi persecution of the Jews became more extreme between 1933 and 1945.

Following the Wansee Conference in 1942, Adolf Eichmann summarised the discussions in a document. In the extract below, which is taken from Eichmann's document, he discusses the meaning of the 'Final Solution'. Read the document below and answer the questions that follow.

> *As a further possible solution, and with the appropriate authorisation by the Führer, emigration has now been replaced by evacuation of Jews to the East.*
>
> *However, this operation should be regarded only as a provisional option, though in view of the coming final solution of the Jewish question it is already supplying practical experience of vital importance.*
>
> *In the course of the final solution and under appropriate direction, the Jews are to be utilised for work in the East in a suitable manner. In large labour columns and separated by sexes, Jews capable of working will be dispatched to these regions to build roads, and in the process a large number of them will undoubtedly drop out by way of natural attrition* (wearing away). *Those who ultimately should possibly get by will have to be given suitable treatment because they unquestionably represent the most resistant segments and therefore constitute a natural elite* (select few) *that, if allowed to go free, would turn into a germ cell* (origin) *of renewed Jewish revival.*
>
> *In the course of the practical implementation of the final solution, Europe will be combed through from West to East. The evacuated Jews will first be taken, group after group, to so-called transit ghettos, from where they will be transported further to the East. The onset of the individual major evacuation moves will largely depend on military developments. In regard to the manner in which the final solution will be carried out in those European territories which now either occupy or influence, it has been suggested that the pertinent* (relevant) *specialists in the Foreign Office should confer with the appropriate official of the Security Police and the SD* (Security Service).

1. What evidence is contained in this document to suggest that Hitler was aware of the 'Final Solution' to the 'Jewish question'?

2. How are the Jews to be utilised during the first stages of the evacuation to the East?

3. Why are the Jews who survive this first stage considered to be such a threat to society?

4. Describe the planned process for the evacuation of the Jews to the East as outlined in the document.

5. At no point does the document refer to the killing of Jews. Why was this the case?

6. Account for the effect of the 'Final Solution' on Europe's Jewish population. (Higher Level only)

14 Church-State Relations under Mussolini and Hitler

'Honeymoon Period'

At first, the Christian Churches in both Italy and Germany were not too alarmed at the rise of Fascism. Indeed many Church leaders viewed the Fascist state as an important defence against the spread of Communism from the East. However, this 'honeymoon period' between Fascist dictators and Christian Churches became strained as the true nature of Fascism began to unfold.

The Catholic Church and Mussolini

To begin with, Mussolini was hostile to the Catholic Church. In 1919 he declared, 'We are the heretics (non-believers) of all Churches.' He soon realised that this policy made little sense in a loyal Catholic country such as Italy. From 1921 onwards, he began to woo the Catholic Church. On coming to power in 1922, he ordered the introduction of religious instruction into schools and universities. Obscene publications and swearing in public were banned, as was the sale of contraceptives. By 1926 the Fascist state and the Catholic Church had developed friendly relations. While the Catholic Church was critical of Fascist violence, it was thankful that a more dreaded enemy, Communism, was being held back.

A full reconciliation with the Church came in 1929, when Mussolini succeeded in solving a 60-year dispute between Church and state. Church/state relations had been strained since Italian troops had captured Rome in 1870, during the unification of Italy.

Negotiations on the **'Roman Question'** between Mussolini and Cardinal Gaspari, the Vatican Secretary of State, began in 1926. Talks continued in secret for a number of years. Telephone taps on the Vatican kept Mussolini informed on how far the Church was prepared to go in order to reach a settlement. The Vatican wanted a figure of 4,000 million lire as compensation for territory confiscated by the Italian state in 1870. On 11 February, 1929, the Vatican and the Fascists eventually reached a compromise and signed the Latern Treaty.

The Latern Treaty 1929

The terms of the treaty included the following provisions:

1. The Vatican was recognised as an independent state.

2. Mussolini agreed to pay 750 million lire to the Vatican as compensation for the loss of the Papal States in 1870.

3. Catholicism became the official religion of the state.

4. The Catholic Church agreed to recognise the authority of the Italian state for the first time since the unification of Italy in 1870.

Catholic Church cardinals join Mussolini in the Fascist salute.

Most people were delighted with it. He [Mussolini] himself looked back on his conciliation (reunion) with the Church as his masterpiece and it was undoubtedly an immense political success that won him the enthusiastic acclamation (praise) of the great bulk of Catholics.

From **Mussolini** by Denis Mack Smith, 1982.

This Treaty gave the Fascists an air of respectability both at home and abroad. Mussolini saw the treaty as one of his greatest successes. Pope Pius XI was also delighted with the agreement claiming, 'We have given back God to Italy and Italy to God.'

Catholic Action

Shortly after the signing of the Latern Pact, Mussolini's attitude towards the Church created some tension in relations with the Vatican. Speaking in 1930, Mussolini claimed that as a result of the Latern Treaty, the Catholic Church was no longer free, but subordinate to the state. Pope Pius XI saw things differently of course, and condemned the 'pagan worship of the state' by the Fascists. Calls by the Church to have its own say in education were dismissed by Mussolini. His refusal to allow a lay organisation, **Catholic Action,** to continue with its work in social affairs, in trade unionism and in organising sporting activities for Italian youths, also became an issue. Following a meeting between the Pope and Mussolini in the Vatican in 1932, Pius XI was persuaded by Cardinal Gaspari and Cardinal Pacelli (future Pope Pius XII) to give way on the matter. The cardinals viewed a conflict with Fascism as unimportant, as the real enemy was Communism. An uneasy peace followed until 1938.

Manifesto Della Razza

Mussolini's decision to introduce a **'Charter of Race'** *(Manifesto della Razza)* in 1938 led to a renewal of tensions between the Catholic Church and the state. Marriages between Italians and those of 'non-Aryan' race were forbidden. Foreign Jews and those who had entered the country after 1919 were to be expelled. Jews were forbidden to become teachers, lawyers or journalists.

Mussolini's decision to attack the Jews had more to do with his wish to pacify the Nazis, than any deep-rooted hatred of the Jews. The manifesto (policy) was never strictly enforced. Nonetheless, the racial laws were strongly condemned by Pope Pius XI. Mussolini responded by reverting to his earlier policy of anti-clericalism. He acknowledged publicly that he was a non-believer and told a cabinet meeting in 1939 that Islam was perhaps a more effective religion than Christianity. However, as was often the case with Mussolini, his words were stronger than his actions. When some younger members of the Fascist Party attempted to launch a church-burning campaign, Mussolini moved swiftly to stop such action.

▲
Pope Pius XII (1876–1958) passing through a crowd in Rome in May 1940.

Relations with Pius XII

In March 1939, following the death of Pope Pius XI, Cardinal Pacelli was elected Pope as Pius XII. Although Pius XII did not meddle as much in politics as his predecessor, he too proved to be an annoyance to Mussolini. He repeatedly advised Mussolini of the necessity to maintain neutrality in the war. The Vatican newspaper, *L'Osservatore Romano,* published articles that were clearly anti-Fascist in tone. In May 1940 it printed messages of sympathy from the Pope to the King of Belgium, the Queen of Holland and the Grand Duchess of Luxembourg, following the Nazi conquest of their respective countries. Following Italy's entry into the war in May 1940, Mussolini warned the Papal Nuncio (ambassador) in Rome that the paper would be banned if it continued to print anti-Fascist political comment. *L'Osservatore Romano* reluctantly gave in to his wishes.

Church-State Relations and Hitler

National Socialism and Christianity are irreconcilable (unable to exist together).
From a speech by Adolf Hitler in 1941.

Although Hitler was baptised a Catholic, he had nothing but contempt for religion. The Nazis viewed the Catholic and Protestant Churches as potential threats to their regime.

The Catholic Church

The Catholic Church was not unduly alarmed at the rise of Hitler. In 1931 it lifted a ban on Catholics joining the Nazi Party. Two years later it signed a concordat (agreement between Church and state) with Hitler, by which priests would not interfere with politics and in return Hitler would allow the Church to regulate its own affairs. Franz von Papen (Deputy Chancellor of the Third Reich 1933–34) and Eugene Pacelli (then the Papal Nuncio in Berlin) signed the Concordat in July 1933.

The National Government sees in both Catholic and Protestant Churches the most important factors for the maintenance of our society. It will respect the agreements concluded between them and the state. Their rights will not be touched. It will guarantee their due influence in education. The struggle against the materialistic ideology and for the establishment of a real national community is in the interests of the German nation as much as of our Christian faith.
From Hitler's Reichstag speech, 23 March, 1933.

Although this agreement seemed to work at the start, tensions arose from time to time as Hitler limited the power of the Church through his control of newspapers, youth movements and the education system.

In December 1936, the Bavarian Catholic bishops, voicing their concern that the Nazi Government was not operating within the spirit of the Concordat, issued a statement:

After the deplorable (terrible) *fight carried on by communists, free thinkers and freemasons against Christianity, we welcomed with gratitude the National Socialist profession of positive Christianity. Our Führer, in a most impressive speech, acknowledged the importance to the state of the two Christian Churches and promised them his protection. Unfortunately, men with considerable influence and power are operating in direct opposition to those promises and seek to rid Germany of the Catholic Church and instead promote a united Church in which the confession of faith will be meaningless.*

Encyclical:

Papal letter to all Bishops of the Roman Catholic Church.

Hitler's racism also angered Pope Pius XI, and in 1937 he issued his encyclical *Mit Brennender Sorge* (With Burning Anguish). In it he condemned the Nazi failure to honour the Concordat. The encyclical accused the Nazis of breaking the Concordat and of sowing 'the seeds of suspicion, discord, hatred and calumny (slander) and of secret and open fundamental hostility to Christ and His Church'. The Pope was probably about to publish a second encyclical condemning Hitler's anti-Semitism when he died in 1939.

Cardinal von Galen

In 1941 Cardinal Galen of Münster in Germany spoke out against the Nazi practice of **euthanasia** (killing the old and very sick). Galen saw euthanasia as a crime and reported the Nazis to the civil police. His protest met with such public approval that Goebbels warned Hitler not to arrest him. As a result of Galen's intervention, the Nazis ended the policy of euthanasia.

While the Nazis tolerated a certain amount of opposition from the higher ranks of the Church, many priests were imprisoned in Dachau Concentration camp as a result of their opposition to Nazi policies.

The Protestant Churches

Key Concept: Reichskirche (State Church)

In 1933 the process of *Gleichschaltung* (co-ordination) (p. 29) was strictly applied to the Protestant Churches. Germany had 28 different types of Protestant Church. Hitler decided that it would be easier to control them if they were merged into one large state Church *(Reichskirche)* under the leadership of one Reich Bishop, Pastor Ludwig Müller. In July 1933 representatives of the various Protestant Churches wrote a constitution for a new *Reichskirche*. The new Church was formally recognised by the *Reichstag* on 14 July, 1933.

The Confessional Church

Most of the Protestant Churches accepted Nazi domination, but some individuals, such as Pastor Martin Niemöller, a former U-boat officer, denounced the Third Reich and refused to be associated with the *Reichskirche*. In May 1934, at a synod (council) of Protestant leaders, Professor Karl Barth and Niemöller formed a group known as the 'Confessional Church'. In 1936 the Confessional Church wrote an open letter to Hitler, objecting to his interference in religious matters and also to his anti-Semitic policies. The Nazi reaction was swift. One of the leaders of the Confessional Church, Dr Friedrich Weissler, was taken to Sachsenhausen concentration camp and executed. Hundreds of pastors, including Niemöller, were put in concentration camps, while others, such as Barth, went into exile. Niemöller remained jailed in Dachau until its liberation in 1945.

▲
Dietrich Bonhoeffer (1906–45), a leading theologian and anti-Nazi who was arrested in 1943 and executed in 1945. This photograph was taken in 1935.

Dietrich Bonhoeffer

Leading theologians, such as Dietrich Bonhoeffer, were forbidden from speaking in public. He refused to be silenced. During the war, Bonhoeffer made contact with anti-Nazi movements. He was arrested by the SD (Nazi Intelligence agency) in 1943 and executed in Flossenbürg concentration camp in April 1945.

Jehovah's Witnesses

Jehovah's witnesses also suffered oppression. They were jailed when they objected to military service on religious grounds. In 1943 Jonathan Stark, a leading member of the Jehovah's witnesses, was arrested for refusing to take an oath of honour to Hitler, as well as refusing to do military service. He was sent to Sachsenhausen concentration camp, where he was hanged in 1944.

Christian Churches' Response to Nazism

Following World War II, many attacks were made on the leadership of the Christian Churches for their failure to condemn the Nazi regime in a strong and open manner. This attack was especially directed against Pope Pius XII. Although he was aware of the extermination of the Jews, he told a meeting of Cardinals in June 1943 that a public condemnation could lead to a further backlash against the Jews. Church leaders also feared that their own followers would face persecution from the Nazis in response to any statement of condemnation they might issue. However, the cautious approach of Church leaders did not stop individual priests, nuns and ministers from sheltering thousands of Jews throughout Nazi-occupied Europe in their churches, convents and monasteries.

? Questions

Ordinary Level
Write a short account on Church/state relations in either Italy or Germany.

Higher Level
'The relationship between the Churches and the Fascist states was often strained.' Discuss.

Read the document below, which is an extract from a list of 30 guidelines issued to the Protestant Church in Germany by the Nazi government in July 1933:

1 *The National Reich Church of Germany categorically claims the exclusive right and the exclusive power to control all churches within the borders of the Reich: it declares these to be national churches of the German Reich.*

6 *The National Church has no scribes, pastors, chaplains or priests, but National Reich orators are to speak in them.*

13 *The National Church demands immediate cessation* (end) *of the publishing and dissemination* (distribution) *of the Bible in Germany...*

14 *The National Church declares that to it, and therefore to the German nation, it has been decided that the Führer's* Mein Kampf *is the greatest of all documents. It not only contains the greatest, but it embodies the purest and truest ethics for the present and future life of our nation.*

18 *The National Church will clear away from its altars all crucifixes, Bibles and pictures of saints.*

19 *On the altars there must be nothing but* Mein Kampf *(to the German nation and therefore to God the most sacred book) and to the left of the altar a sword.*

1. According to the information in the document, who controls the activities of all churches within Germany?

2. Describe some of the restrictions placed by the Nazis on religious freedom as outlined in the document.

3. From your knowledge of the period, explain briefly how the Protestant Churches in Germany reacted to Nazi control. (Higher Level only)

15 Anglo-American Popular Culture in Peace and War

Mass Media

One of the less obvious effects of World War I was that it acted as a stimulus for the growth of the mass media.

Cinema

In the aftermath of World War I, cinema expanded rapidly in Britain. Large cinemas were built throughout the country, even in impoverished areas. In the early 1920s it was estimated that over 40% of the population of Liverpool attended the cinema at least once a week.

While the British film industry was ruined by the war, the American industry thrived. Films produced in Hollywood dominated the British market throughout the 1920s.

Hollywood

The Nestor Company opened the First Hollywood studio in 1911 in a converted grocery store. Within a year, 15 other studios had opened nearby. Throughout the 1920s, American film producers sent agents to Europe to bring back the cream of European actors to Hollywood. As the popularity of individual actors grew, so too did their earnings. By 1917 the Canadian-born actress Mary Pickford was earning $350,000 per movie (considered a huge sum in 1917).

In 1927 an act was passed in Britain to ensure that a quota of films shown in British cinemas be produced in Britain. Despite their best efforts, British film companies were unable to compete with their American rivals, and the products of Hollywood dominated the market.

Charlie Chaplin was one of cinema's most popular stars. He was born in South London in 1889. His first public appearance was on the music hall stage when he was only five years old. However, it was his screen persona – a pathetic little tramp with a smudge moustache and bowler hat – which made him one of Hollywood's greatest stars. He played this classic role in over 70 films during his career.

In 1913 Chaplin moved to Los Angeles, where he joined Mack Sennett's Keystone Company. He produced and starred in a number of silent movies including *The Rink* (1916), *The Kid* (1920) and the *Gold Rush* (1925). In 1919 a number of leading stars, including Mary Pickford, Douglas Fairbanks and Charlie Chaplin, joined forces with film director DW Griffith to form their own independent production company, United Artists. His other films include *City Lights* (1931), *Modern Times* (1936), *The Great Dictator* (1940), *Monsieur Verdoux* (1947) and *Limelight* (1952).

Charlie Chaplin (1889–1977) in his most successful role as 'Adenoid Hynkel' in **The Great Dictator** in 1940.

Charlie Chaplin was fiercely anti-Nazi. *The Great Dictator* (1940), in which a rebellious Jewish ghetto resident barber lives under the regime of Adenoid Hynkel (Hitler), was perhaps his greatest success. Chaplin played both characters in this, his first full talkie. He invested two million dollars of his own money in the film. The film became a great box-office success, grossing over five million dollars. However, some members of the public were disappointed by the fact that their beloved silent clown spoke on screen for the first time.

Chaplin's popularity in America received a blow when he was accused of having communist sympathies. As a result, he left the USA in 1952 and moved to Switzerland. Charlie Chaplin received two special Oscars, one in 1928 and the other in 1972.

On 25 December, 1977, Chaplin passed away of natural causes in his home in Corsier-Sur-Vevey, Switzerland. He was 88 years old. He was married to Oona Chaplin at the time, who had been his wife for 36 years.

Hollywood Exiles

Following Hitler's rise to power in 1933, many German film producers, cameramen and actors emigrated to America. The vast majority went to Hollywood, where they contributed greatly to the American cinema industry throughout the 1930s and 1940s. Among the leading German actors who emigrated were Conrad Veidt, Peter Lorre, Elisabeth Bergner and Marlene Dietrich.

Cinema During the War

British cinema flourished during the war years (1939–45). When war was declared, the British Government ordered the closure of places of entertainment for fear of an immediate bombing onslaught. However, within a few weeks cinemas began to open once more and the Government were quick to realise the propaganda value of the British film industry. In Britain, between 25 and 30 million cinema seats were sold each week; this would suggest that many people attended more than once a week.

The increase in ticket sales provided a welcome boost for the British film industry. Weekly newsreels were shown before each feature film. Documentary films such as *The Next of Kin* (1942), *Target for Tonight* (1941) and *Fires were Started* (1943) were made to warn the public against 'careless talk'. Other films, such as *The Foreman went to France* (1942), about Dunkirk, and *In which We Serve* (1942), about life in the British Army, acted as morale boosters at a crucial time when Britain was standing alone in the war. George Formby, Will Hay and the **'Crazy Gang',** who appeared in popular wartime comedies, provided some light entertainment to the harassed British nation.

The greatest British wartime movie was Laurence Olivier's production of Shakespeare's *Henry V.* It was released to coincide with the Allied landings on the Normandy beaches in 1944. The film was produced in Ireland using expensive technicolor. A young RAF pilot, Peter Nichols, described its effect on the morale of the armed forces in 1944:

We thrilled at the shared victory, the king's nocturnal (night-time) *conversations with his soldiers, the Robin Hoodness of it all... The four of us aesthetes* (artists) *went, on one of the few nights we were allowed out, to see the film for the third or fourth time in the nearby steeltown of Corby. Running through the wet streets for the last bus back to camp, we swore to be brothers forever, our boy-faces lit by flashes from blazing foundries* (metal workshops).   As quoted in **The Experience of World War II** by John Campbell, 1989.

American War Films

As the war progressed and shortages became severe, British film companies were forced to cut back on output. The gap was filled by an increasing number of feature films from Hollywood. Comedy films featuring the trio of Bing Crosby*, Bob Hope and Dorothy Lamour, produced by Cecil B. De Mille's Paramount Studios, flooded the British cinema market. Anti-Fascism was explored in Paramount's version of Ernest Hemingway's *For Whom the Bell Tolls* (1943), about Republican forces in the Spanish Civil War, which stared Gary Cooper and Ingrid Bergman. The latter also starred along with Humphrey Bogart in Hollywood's most popular war film, *Casablanca* (1943). This film won an Oscar for best picture in 1943. The film appealed to many because of its contrasting characters, with Bogart playing the role of a cynical American living abroad, while Bergman portrayed European idealism.

Errol Flynn was one of Hollywood's most popular wartime movie stars. He stared in Warner's film *Desperate Journey* (1942), about an RAF pilot trapped in Germany, alongside Ronald Reagan, who later went on to become the US President. Flynn also starred as a pilot in *Dive-Bomber* (1944); as a member of the Canadian Mounties chasing a Nazi in *Northern Pursuit* (1944); and as a Norwegian resistance fighter in *Edge of Darkness* (1945).

▲ Film poster for Hollywood's most popular war film, **Casablanca** (1943), which starred Ingrid Bergman and Humphrey Bogart.

 # Key Personality: Bing Crosby

Bing Crosby was born Harry Lillis Crosby in Tacoma, Washington in May 1903. He was the first American popular singer to make a successful transition from dance hall performer to motion picture actor.

He achieved success in the early 1930s as a nightclub performer, with his distinctive style of crooning. He was constantly in demand on record and radio as a solo artist and as a member of the band, the Rhythm Boys.

In 1932 Crosby signed a contract with Paramount Pictures. In the same year his first feature film, *The Big Broadcast,* was released and was well received by film critics. He went on to star in a series of musicals such as *Mississippi* (1935), *Anything Goes* (1936) and *Waikiki Wedding* (1937).

▲ Bing Crosby (1903–77) with Dorothy Lamour in **Road to Singapore** (1940).

His most successful spell as an actor was in the 1940s, when he stared in a series of 'Road' films *(The Road to Singapore* etc.) alongside Hollywood actress Dorothy Lamour and comedian Bob Hope. The mixture of song and comedy provided some light relief to millions during the darkest days of the war. However, it was for his role in *Going My Way* (1944), at the height of his wartime fame, that he won an Oscar. In this film Crosby plays a hip young Catholic priest, Father O'Malley, who arrives to help a troubled parish struggle back to its feet.

▲ **Road to Singapore** was the first of the popular 'Road' movies that paired Bing Crosby with Bob Hope.

Crosby's portrayal of an alcoholic actor down on his luck in the film *Country Girl* (1954) is seen by many film critics as the finest performance of his career. Although he continued to star in films throughout the 1960s, his earlier work remains his most popular.

Crosby's radio and recording career was also extremely successful. His Kraft Music Hall radio show, broadcasted throughout the 1940s, was one of the top-rated radio shows of its time. He had over 300 chart hits in America, including 36 number ones. His recording of American composer Irving Berlin's *White Christmas* in 1942 became one of the best-selling records of all time. Crosby also recorded with other well-known stars, including Louis Armstrong, Fred Astaire, Judy Garland and Frank Sinatra.

Crosby's career as an actor and singer spanned from the 1920s until his death in 1977, making him one of the most famous and best-loved entertainers of the twentieth century.

Radio

The development of wireless broadcasting during the inter-war period provided cheap entertainment for the masses.

Radio broadcasting to the general public did not begin on a large scale until after World War I. America led the way. In 1920 the Westinghouse Electric Company of Pittsburgh, Pennsylvania, established the first commercially-owned radio station. Operating under the title KDKA, it broadcast musical programmes by placing a type of record player next to a microphone. Listeners were not required to pay a licence fee for the service. The Westinghouse Electric Company used the station as a means of advertising the sale of radio sets to the public, and therefore financed its operation. Other US manufacturers were quick to realise the commercial value of radio broadcasting. By 1934 almost 600 radio stations were broadcasting throughout America. Between 1922 and 1929 the number of American households with radio sets rose from 60,000 to 10 million. As the home market became saturated with radio sets, broadcasting companies began to sell advertising time as a means of making a profit.

British Broadcasting

Radio broadcasting in Britain remained independent from commercial interests. In 1904 the Post Office secured control over radio broadcasting. A sponsored company, the British Broadcasting Company (BBC), was established in 1922 to take control and regulate public broadcasting. Unlike America, the service was not free, but instead was financed by charging an annual licence fee on the ownership of a radio set. Over 36,000 licences were granted in its first year of broadcasting.

The BBC's Director General, Sir John Reith, insisted that the service not only entertain, but also inform and educate its listeners. Reith maintained that radio broadcasting should preserve a high moral tone. He insisted that radio announcers wear evening dress when presenting programmes. The BBC broadcasted a mixture of news bulletins, discussion programmes, dramas and music, which contrasted sharply with the 'lighter programmes' produced by American commercial channels.

▲
BBC's Director General, Sir John Reith, who insisted that the service educate as well as entertain.

That a voice could be heard in innumerable (countless) *homes, as speaking there, was wonderful; and as soon as that marvel was achieved, the question arose: Whose was to be that voice and what was it to say? In other countries, the voice might be monopolised by a party or put up for sale, precious moments purchased to praise a pill, explain a soap's excellence, but in England, in Sir John Reith's words, what was aimed at was an expression of 'British mentality at its best'. This ideal was assiduously* (tirelessly) *pursued, he the man to pursue it – a tall Scotsman, Calvinist in origins, a very incarnation of British mentality at its best. Debates were arranged between persons holding different opinions, rehearsed and broadcast so that all points of view might be known and impartially considered. A policeman on his beat, a lighthouse keeper on his solitary vigil, a ship's captain on his bridge, all might be listened to, as well as politicians, authors, scientists, clergymen, peers and peeresses.* From **The Thirties**, by Malcolm Muggeridge, 1940.

The creation of the BBC weakened the political power of the print media. Leading politicians became regular contributors to political discussion programmes. Some politicians, such as Stanley Baldwin and Philip Snowden, adapted quickly to the new medium, while others, such as Lloyd George and Anthony MacDonald, who were used to addressing live audiences, were less comfortable with radio broadcasting.

Radio During the War Years (1939–45)

On the outbreak of war in 1939, the BBC was reduced to providing an emergency news service. However, after its evacuation to the countryside in early 1940, the BBC became the main news communicator and entertainer of the nation.

During the war, radio broadcasts carried news directly from the battlefield to the homes of millions throughout the world. Edward R Murrow, an American radio presenter, delivered nightly live broadcasts from the rooftop of the CBS news bureau in London, describing German bombing raids during the Battle of Britain (p. 104).

US President Franklin D. Roosevelt frequently used the radio as a means of addressing the nation. During The Great Depression, he sought to calm American fears with his so-called 'fireside chats'. He promised the American people a 'New Deal', telling them that they had 'nothing to fear, but fear itself'. Roosevelt continued to address the American public in this way throughout the war.

As well as news programmes, the BBC also broadcast 'Forces Shows' like *Navy Mixture, Ack Ack Beer Beer* and *Much Binding in the Marsh*, which were light-hearted features about the war. Daily broadcasts aimed at factory workers included *Workforce Playtime* and *Music While You Work*.

▲ Vera Lynn, 'the force's sweetheart' entertained the forces with popular songs such as 'We'll Meet Again'.

▲ American jazz bandleader Glenn Miller with his 42 piece Air Force band.

The 'Force's Favourites'

Music from British singer Vera Lynn and American jazz bandleader Glenn Miller received much radio airtime on both sides of the Atlantic. Known as 'the force's sweetheart', Vera Lynn became famous with such songs as 'We'll Meet Again' and 'White Cliffs of Dover'. These songs were optimistic in content and tone, and were important for the morale of those at home as well as for soldiers on front-line duty.

In 1942 trombonist Glenn Miller shocked the music world when he disbanded his orchestra and enlisted in the US Air Force. Miller formed a 42-piece Air Force band, which entertained Allied forces by means of regular radio broadcasts throughout the war. He achieved huge success with such hits as 'Moonlight Serenade' and 'In the Mood'. Many hearts were broken when Glenn Miller disappeared without trace in 1944 during a flight across the English Channel in bad weather.

Ordinary Level

Look at the photograph on page 197 and read the newspaper report on the right, then answer these questions.

1. Give three possible reasons, as outlined in the newspaper report, why the film *Modern Times* (1936) was banned in Germany.

2. How had Chaplin's films been received in Germany prior to 1936?

3. What characters did Chaplin play in the film *The Great Dictator* (1940)? Looking at the picture (p. 197), can you see any similarities between Chaplin and Adolf Hitler?

Write an account on one of the following:

1. Charlie Chaplin's contribution to the popularity of cinema.

2. Bing Crosby.

3. Radio and cinema during the war years, 1939–45.

Higher Level

1. Trace developments in radio broadcasting in Britain and America during the years 1920–45.

2. 'The British film industry faced stiff competition from its American counterpart during the years 1920–45.' Discuss.

3. Describe how Anglo-American popular culture in radio and cinema was used to great effect to boost the morale of the general public during the war years 1939–45.

Nazis Prohibit Chaplin Film

Charlie Chaplin's new film *Modern Times* has been prohibited in Germany. Reuter was informed at the Propaganda Ministry this afternoon that there was at present no prospect that the picture would be shown in this country. Another Nazi spokesman said that reports from abroad had indicated that the picture had a 'Communist tendency' and that this was no doubt the reason why the picture was unacceptable.

This is the latest move in the Nazi drive to purge Germany of Chaplin. In recent months Charlie Chaplin's films, which used frequently to be viewed in Germany, have vanished from the screen on account, it has been presumed, of doubts existing here as to the Aryan purity of the comedian's ancestry. Picture postcards of Chaplin, which used to be displayed in shop-windows all over Berlin, have now vanished, and it is understood that by official order no more are now being issued.

When the famous Rivels clowns recently came to a leading Berlin music-hall with their act, which used to include a parody of Charlie Chaplin, the clown who played the mock Charlie abandoned his little moustache and bowler and appeared in another disguise.

[It was suggested by Mr AE Newbould, publicity director of the Gaumont British Film Company, last night that, though it might sound absurd, 'Chaplin's moustache is so like Hitler's that I am of the opinion it may have played some part in the Prohibition of the film.']

'Nazis Prohibit Chaplin Film' from **The Manchester Guardian**, 18 February, 1936.

16 The Technology of Warfare

The Arms Race

Throughout the war, scientists and engineers were hard at work trying to develop more sophisticated methods of waging war. A technological arms race developed as both sides sought to tilt the balance of favour. The technological development of weapons was more evident in the air and at sea than it was on land.

Key Concept: Blitzkrieg

The Nazis used the term *Blitzkrieg* to describe their tactic of rapid offensive using armoured tank divisions in conjunction with air support. *Blitzkrieg* was first launched against Poland in September 1939. With its elements of speed and shock, it was a new approach to war. Never before had a nation's military defence collapsed so quickly. The British shortened the word to *Blitz* in referring to the intense bombing campaign from the air of Britain by Germany between 1940 and 1941. Much of the success of *Blitzkrieg* was due to the development of aircraft and tanks prior to the outbreak of World War II.

Aircraft

A new breed of fighter aircraft, such as the British Spitfire, the American Mustang and the Japanese Zero, which were capable of far greater speeds than their predecessors, were developed during the war. Wind-driven sirens were fitted to the undercarriage of the German dive-bombing plane, the *Stuka*. As if the sight and sound of an enemy bomber diving right at you was not frightening enough, Adolf Hitler ordered to equip the *Stuka* with a screaming siren that made the sound of its dive far more frightening, which terrorized enemy civilians and soldiers, including anti-aircraft gunners.

By 1943 the Allies had gained the upper hand in the design of aircraft. A new generation of American bomber planes, such as the Flying Fortress and the Liberator, coupled with long-range fighter planes, such as the Thunderbolt and Mustang, ensured that the Allies maintained aerial supremacy. On the Eastern Front, although Soviet and German aircraft were of equal quality, the Soviet Union was able to beat the Germans in aircraft production. By the winter of 1944–5, Germany was losing a quarter of its fighter planes every month. German industry struggled to replace these planes as its factories were constantly being attacked during Allied daytime strategic bombing raids.

Spitfires of an Australian fighter squadron pictured at a fighter command airfield in England during World War II.

The air offensive could not deliver victory by itself, as early advocates (supporters) had argued, but it was a powerful weapon in weakening war production and German resistance on all fronts.

From **The Changing Nature of Warfare 1700–1945** by Neil Stewart, 2001.

Tanks

The tank played a major role in the early stages of World War II. German Panzer divisions came to importance during Hitler's *Blitzkrieg* tactics of 1939–41. As the war progressed, larger and more armoured tanks, like the American Sherman, the Soviet T-34 and the German Panther, replaced more lightly-armed tanks, such as those in the Panzer divisions. The greatest tank battle in history took place at Kursk in the Soviet Union in July 1943 (p. 111).

The tank never achieved total dominance on the battlefield, and could be easily attacked from the air by tank-busting aircraft, such as the American Swordfish plane.

The Soviet T-34 Tank was a large armoured tank that played a major role in the early stages of World War II.

Weapons

Rockets

The Germans were more successful than the British or the Americans at developing jet-propelled rockets known as V-1s (vengeance weapons). These fast pilotless rockets were capable of carrying a one-ton missile. They could be fired from over 300 kilometres from their target. The engines would cut out over the target and the bomb would drop with a buzzing sound.

In the summer of 1944, over 8,000 of these so-called **'buzz-bombs'** exploded in London. Many more were shot down over the sea, or were actually returned by RAF fighters tipping them with their wings to redirect them over the English Channel.

Hitler poured vast sums of money into rocket production in the hope that the Germans could regain some ground in the technological battle. However, the rockets proved to be unreliable, and their development came too late during the war to have any real effect on the outcome.

The Atomic Bomb

The main military innovation of World War II was the development of the atomic bomb.

Refugee scientists living in the US warned that Germany was advanced in work on nuclear fission. In October 1939 two of them, Winger and Szilard, persuaded Albert Einstein, a Jewish refugee and the greatest physicist of his time, to sign a letter to President Roosevelt warning him of the probability that Germany might produce a uranium bomb.

Very little happened until 1941 when Vannevar Bush, the president's scientific adviser, reported that the construction of an atomic bomb seemed possible.

The Manhattan Project

After the bombing of Pearl Harbour (December 1941), the Americans accelerated their secret atomic research. A programme codenamed 'The Manhattan Project' costing two billion dollars was created. Dr Robert Oppenheimer, a leading US physicist, was put in charge of the project. Twenty of America's top physicists worked on the project, as did top mathematicians, chemists, metallurgists and engineers. British and Canadian scientists also joined the project.

At 5.30 a.m. on 16 July, 1945, the first atomic bomb was successfully detonated at Los Alamos in the New Mexico desert. The tower from which the bomb was exploded was vaporised (turned into gas) and the surrounding desert sand was turned to glass.

President Truman learned of the explosion while attending the Potsdam Conference (p. 118). He received a coded message stating:

Doctor has just returned. Most enthusiastic and confident that the little boy (codename for bomb intended for Japan) is as strong as his big brother.

On 25 July Truman recorded in his diary:

We have discovered the most terrible bomb in the history of the world.

On 17 July, Truman informed Churchill of the explosion. A few days later he told Stalin:

We have a new weapon of unusual destructive power.

Stalin only learned the true nature of the atomic bomb when, on the morning of 06 August, 1945, a B29 Bomber called the **'Enola Gay'** dropped one on Hiroshima in Japan. The bomb exploded 2,000 feet above the centre of the city, incinerating 60% of the city. More than 70,000 people died instantly. Thousands more died later from burns and radiation sickness. The commander of the mission, Colonel Tibbets, described the scene:

The day was clear when we dropped the bomb, it was a clear sunshiny day and the visibility was unrestricted. As we came back around again, we saw this cloud coming up. The cloud by this time, now two minutes old, was up at our altitude. We were 33,000 feet at this time and the cloud was up there and continuing to go right on up in a boiling fashion, as if it was rolling and boiling. The surface was nothing but a black boiling... barrel of tar. Where before there had been a city with distinctive houses, buildings and everything that you could see from our altitude, now you couldn't see anything except black boiling debris down below.
From **The World at War** by Mark Arnold, 1981.

While the dropping of the Atomic Bomb was the last act of World War II, it can also be seen as the first act of the Cold War. It could be argued that Truman may have decided to drop the bomb as a warning to Stalin not to extend his power beyond Eastern Europe.

Specialist Equipment

Many new weapons were developed in Britain and America to facilitate a successful landing on the Normandy beaches during the D-Day invasion (06 June, 1944, p. 114):

- American factories produced thousands of landing craft. At least 12 different types of landing craft, with hulls that could open and close, were used to ferry thousands of soldiers to the beaches.

- Major-General Percy Hobart designed a range of specialist vehicles known as **'funnies'**. The Sherman Amphibious (existing on land and water) Tank, which was fitted with inflatable tubes, was one such vehicle.

- On the night of 05 June, some 74 out of a total of 92 German radar stations were electronically jammed by the Allies. The other stations were deliberately left operational so that they could receive false information. This electronic jamming caused the Germans to expect an attack across the Pas de Calais, the narrowest crossing in the English Channel. Fake Army camps were built in Sussex and Kent and railways in the southeast were kept busy, suggesting a massive movement of troops. The RAF used an important deceptive practice known as **'window'** or 'chaff'. It involved the dropping of strips of tinfoil from aircraft, which simulated an invasion fleet on the German radar. These diversionary tactics convinced Rommel, who was in charge of the Atlantic defences, that Calais was the most likely target for an invasion. Accordingly, Normandy was more lightly defended.

▲
Windows, known as 'chaff' in the US, consisted of small strips of aluminium foil dropped by aircraft. This foil could be detected by radar, and so confuse those pinpointing the position of the aircraft.

- In 1942, when the Allies began to plan their return to mainland Europe, they accepted that they could not rely on capturing a harbour in working order. Prefabricated harbours, codenamed **'Mulberry Harbours',** were towed across the Channel. These artificial ports had loading platforms and jetties, which were almost three quarters of a mile long. Once the harbour had been put in place, engineering crews began to build roads over the beaches. Metal or coconut mats were laid over the sand and stones.

- To ensure that vital oil supplies reached the Allied vehicles in Europe during 1944–5, **'pluto',** a pipeline under the ocean, was laid from England across the Channel. Not only did the lines deliver 172,000,000 gallons by Victory in Europe (VE) Day (08 May, 1945), but they also became the start of the offshore oil industry.

Detection Devices

Radar

'Radar' (**ra**dio **d**etection **a**nd **r**anging) was invented in 1932. Robert Watson-Watt discovered that moving objects could be detected by picking up the waves they reflected when a radio transmitter was trained on them. Developed by

Watt and Sir Henry Tizard, radar contributed significantly to the defence of their country in the Battle of Britain (p. 104). The effectiveness of radar was increased with the introduction of IFF equipment **(Identification Friend or Foe).** By using this system, radar operators were able to identify friendly aircraft or ships on the radar screen.

Radio beams were also used to guide bombers to their target. The most sophisticated device was the H^{2}S, a radar transmitter and receiver that was fitted to the bomber.

The use of radar equipment proved of vital importance to Britain during the Battle of Britain, by detecting incoming planes, and in the Battle of the Atlantic (p. 106), by pin-pointing enemy U-boats from the air. Although Germany also had radar equipment, it was not as advanced as the British system. The Germans failed to appreciate the importance of radar during the early stages of the war, as they were confident that the tactic of *Blitzkrieg* would bring the conflict to an early end.

Sonar

During World War I, Paul Langevin developed sonar (**so**und **na**vigation **r**anging). 'Sonar' is a system that uses transmitted and reflected underwater sound waves to detect and locate submerged objects or measure their distances underwater. The device was improved considerably by the British Navy before 1939, and by the US Navy during the war. In combination with radar, it contributed significantly to the Allied victory at sea, notably during the Battle of the Atlantic, by increasing the Allies' ability to detect German and Japanese submarines.

Ultra

'Ultra' was the codename of a special interception device used by the British. With Polish help, the British foreign intelligence service, MI6, obtained a copy of Germany's most secret code machine – **Enigma.** By breaking the codes used on the machine, the Allies were able to read many of Hitler's personal instructions on highly-secretive matters as soon as they were issued.

The British Government poured huge resources into the 'signals intelligence effort' or the art of breaking codes. Universities were combed to find the most intelligent people. Classical scholars, especially those who were good at bridge or chess, were recruited to work at the British Intelligence Headquarters at Bletchley Park in Buckinghamshire.

Casualties

World War II resulted in five times the number of deaths as had been inflicted by World War I. There is little doubt that the development of more destructive tactics and weapons of war contributed significantly to the increase in casualties, especially amongst the civilian population. In bombing raids alone, Britain lost some 60,000 civilian lives and Germany and Japan nearly 400,000 each. In World War I, civilians accounted for one-twentieth of the war dead, whilst in World War II, over half of the war dead were civilians.

Outcome

As soon as the Soviet Union and the US entered the war in 1941, the technological advantage tilted in favour of the Allies. The Axis powers failed to match the sheer quantity of weapons produced in the USA and the Soviet Union.

The decision by Stalin to move factories eastwards, beyond the reach of the Germans, proved to be vital. The emergence of outstanding engineers and designers from the Soviet education system (p. 69), also meant that the quality of weapons produced there was superior to that of the Germans. The Soviet T-34 tank and the *Katyusha* rocket launcher were amongst the best produced military weapons during World War II.

The long-established American car industry, with its efficient production-line methods, was used to the same effect to produce tanks, planes and ships during the war. From as early as 1942, the US was producing more weapons than the combined output of all the Axis powers.

? **Questions**

Ordinary Level

Describe how two of the following contributed to the outcome of World War II:

1. Radar.

2. Aircraft.

3. Tanks.

Higher Level

1. In what way did the technology of war contribute to the outcome of World War II?

2. Describe the main technological advances that took place during World War II.

European History: Dictatorship and Democracy, 1920–45

Index

Bibliography

The following books are recommended for additional reading:

Campbell, John: *The Experience of World War II*, Equinox Limited, 1989.

Cobban, Alfred: *A History of Modern France, Volume 3: 1871–1962*, Penguin Books, 1974.

Deutscher, Isaac: *Stalin*, Pelican Books, 1988.

Evans, David and Jenkins, Jane: *Years of Russia and the USSR*, 1851–1991, Hodder Arnold, 2001.

Foster, Arnold: *The World at War*, William Collins and Sons, 1981.

Joll, James: *Europe Since 1870*, Penguin Books, 1990.

Knopp, Guido: *Hitler's Holocaust*, Sutton Publishing, 2000.

Mack Smith, Denis: *Mussolini*, Weidenfeld and Nicolson Ltd, 1970.

Neville, Peter: France 1914–69: *The Three Republics*, Hodder & Stoughton, 1995.

Shirer, William L: *The Rise and Fall of the Third Reich*, Arrow Books, 1998.

Speer, Albert: *Inside the Third Reich*, Weidenfeld and Nicolson, 1970.

Stewart, Neil: *The Changing Nature of Warfare 1700–1945*, Hodder & Stoughton, 2001.